Between Deleuze and Derrida

Between Deleuze and Derrida

Edited by

PAUL PATTON

and

JOHN PROTEVI

continuum
LONDON • NEW YORK

Continuum

The Tower Building, 11 York Road, London SE1 7NX

370 Lexington Avenue, New York, NY 10017–6503

www.continuumbooks.com

First published 2003 by Continuum

British Library Cataloguing-in-Publication Data
A catalogue record for this book is available from The British Library

ISBN 0-8264-5972-2 (hardback)
ISBN 0-8264-5973-0 (paperback)

Typeset by SetSystems, Saffron Walden, Essex
Printed and bound in Great Britain by
Biddles Ltd, Guildford and King's Lynn

Contents

Contributors

ERIC ALLIEZ holds the Chair in Aesthetics at the Akademie der Bildenden Künste (Vienna), where he is co-directing the TransArt research program (four volumes published by Turia+Kant, Vienna). Among other works, he is the author of the series *Les Temps capitaux* (Paris: Cerf, 1991/1999), the first book of which was translated into English in 1996 by the University of Minnesota Press as *Capital Times: Tales from the Conquest of Time*. He is also author of *La Signature du monde, ou Qu'est-ce que la philosophie de Deleuze et Guattari?* (Paris: Cerf, 1993), which will be translated into English by Continuum in 2003. In addition, he is directing the edition of the *Œuvres de Gabriel Tarde* (Paris: Les Empêcheurs de penser en rond/Seuil), and is a member of the editorial board of the journal *Multitudes*.

BRANKA ARSIĆ is Assistant Professor of English at SUNY Albany (New York, USA), where she teaches critical theory. Her book *The Passive Eye*, on Bishop Berkeley's theory of vision and Samuel Beckett's *Film*, is forthcoming from Stanford. She is currently working on a new project on Deleuze and Melville's Bartleby.

GREGG LAMBERT is Associate Professor of English and Textual Studies at Syracuse University (New York, USA). He is author of *The Non-Philosophy of Gilles Deleuze* (Continuum, 2002) and *Report to the Academy* (Davies, 2001). His forthcoming book is entitled *The Return of the Baroque: Art, Culture and Theory in the Modern Age*, also from Continuum.

LEONARD LAWLOR is Dunavant Distinguished Professor of Philosophy at The University of Memphis (Tennessee, USA). He is the author of *Derrida and Husserl: The Basic Problem of Phenomenology* (Indiana, 2002), *Imagination and Chance: The Difference between the Thought of Ricoeur and Derrida* (SUNY, 1992) and *Thinking Through French Philosophy: The Being of the Question*

(Indiana, 2003). He is also the co-editor and co-founder of *Chiasmi International: Trilingual Studies Concerning the Thought of Merleau-Ponty*.

ALPHONSO LINGIS is Professor Emeritus of Philosophy at the Pennsylvania State University (USA). His most recent books include *Dangerous Emotions* (California, 2000), *The Imperative* (Indiana, 1998), *Phenomenological Explanations* (Kluwer, 1997) and *Abuses* (California, 1995).

TAMSIN LORRAINE is an Associate Professor of Philosophy at Swarthmore College (Pennsylvania, USA). She has published various articles in the area of feminist theory and recent continental philosophy. Her latest book is *Irigaray and Deleuze: Experiments in Visceral Philosophy* (Cornell, 1999), and she is currently working on a book tentatively titled *Feminism and Deleuzian Subjectivity*.

JEFFREY T. NEALON is Professor of English at the Pennsylvania State University (USA). He is author of *Alterity Politics: Ethics and Performative Subjectivity* (Duke, 1998) and *Double Reading: Postmodernism after Deconstruction* (Cornell, 1993), as well as co-editor of *Rethinking the Frankfurt School* (SUNY, 2002).

PAUL PATTON is Professor of Philosophy at The University of New South Wales (Australia). He has published widely on aspects of French poststructuralist philosophy and political theory. He is the author of *Deleuze and the Political* (Routledge, 2000), translator of Deleuze's *Difference and Repetition* (Athlone/Columbia, 1994), and editor of *Deleuze: A Critical Reader* (Blackwell, 1996) and (with Terry Smith) *Jacques Derrida Deconstruction Engaged: The Sydney Seminars* (Sydney: Power Publications, 2001).

ARKADY PLOTNITSKY is Professor of English and Director of the Theory and Cultural Studies Program at Purdue University (Indiana, USA). He is the author of *The Knowable and the Unknowable: Modern Science, Nonclassical Thought, and 'The Two Cultures'* (Michigan, 2001); *Complementarity: Anti-Epistemology After Bohr and Derrida* (Duke, 1994); *In the Shadow of Hegel: Complementarity, History and the Unconscious* (University Press of Florida, 1993); and *Reconfigurations: Critical Theory and General Economy* (University Press of Florida, 1993); and editor (with Barbara Herrnstein Smith) of *Mathematics, Science and Postclassical Theory* (Duke, 1997).

JOHN PROTEVI is Assistant Professor of French Studies at Louisiana State University (USA). He is author of *Time and Exteriority: Aristotle, Heidegger, Derrida* (Bucknell, 1994); *Political Physics: Deleuze, Derrida, and the Body Politic*

(Athlone/Continuum, 2001); and co-author (with Mark Bonta) of *Deleuze and Complexity: A Guide and Glossary of Geophilosophy* (Edinburgh, forthcoming). He is also editor of the *Edinburgh Dictionary of Continental Philosophy* (forthcoming).

DANIEL W. SMITH is Assistant Professor of Philosophy at Purdue University (Indiana, USA). He has translated Deleuze's *Francis Bacon: The Logic of Sensation* (Continuum, 2003) and *Essays Critical and Clinical*, with Michael A. Greco (Minnesota, 1997) as well as Pierre Klossowski's *Nietzsche and the Vicious Circle* (Chicago, 1997) and Isabelle Stenger's *The Invention of Modern Science* (Minnesota, 2000). He is currently working on a book-length study of Deleuze's philosophy.

Acknowledgement

The chapter by Eric Alliez originally appeared as 'Ontologie et logographie: La pharmacie, Platon et le simulacre', in *Nos grecs et leurs modernes*, textes réunis par Barbara Cassin, Seuil 1992, pp. 211–31. The editors gratefully acknowledge the permission of the author and Editions du Seuil to publish this text in translation.

Introduction

Paul Patton and John Protevi

Gilles Deleuze and Jacques Derrida have long been acknowledged to be among the outstanding French philosophers of the postwar period. Literary theorists, philosophers and others have devoted considerable effort to the critical examination of the work of each of these thinkers, but very little has been done to explore relations between them. *Between Deleuze and Derrida* is the first collection which aims to address this critical deficit by providing rigorous comparative discussions of the work of these two philosophers.

AFFINITIES

Deleuze was born in 1925, Derrida in 1930. Both completed their studies in Paris, Deleuze at the Sorbonne during the late 1940s and Derrida at the École Normale Supérieure in the early 1950s. In Derrida's words, they belong to 'what we call with that terrible and somewhat misleading word, a "generation"' (Derrida 2001a, 193). In Deleuze's words, this was a generation of philosophers, formed in the aftermath of the Second World War and the Liberation of France, who were nevertheless 'plunged into Hegel, Husserl and Heidegger' (Deleuze and Parnet 1987, 12). This generation, which included Foucault, Althusser, Lyotard, Serres, Faye and Châtelet, among others, was in Deleuze's view 'strong' (Deleuze 1995b, 27). We can add that, since it came of age in the 1960s, this generation had the good fortune to reach intellectual maturity during one of the most extraordinarily creative decades in twentieth-century French thought.

It was in the 1960s that both Deleuze and Derrida made their first important contributions to the French philosophical scene. Deleuze's *Nietzsche and Philosophy* (1962) is credited with reviving philosophical interest in Nietzsche in France, while the significance of his three books in 1968–9: *Spinoza: Expressionism in Philosophy*, *Difference and Repetition* and *The Logic of Sense* has yet to be fully appreciated. For his part, Derrida published three landmark books in 1967: *Writing and Difference, Of Grammatology* and *Speech and Phenomena*. After their translation into English in the 1970s, deconstructive thought became one of the most significant intellectual movements in literary theory and throughout much of the humanities and social sciences.

Although the 1960s in France was associated above all with the predominance of structuralist thought in philosophy and the social sciences, Deleuze and Derrida remained on the margins of this movement, and in fact both contributed to the emergence of what has come to be called 'post-structuralism', by writing important critical essays on key aspects of the structuralist programme. Derrida's 'Structure, Sign and Play in the Discourse of the Human Sciences' was first presented at the famous 1966 Johns Hopkins conference on structuralism before it appeared in *Writing and Difference* (1967c; 1978). In this talk, after analysing the structuralist rupture that eliminated the dependence of thought on a centre that governs meaning from outside a system, Derrida juxtaposed two responses to the 'loss' of that centre: a Rousseauist nostalgia for a lost naturality which puts up with interpretation as an exile, and a Nietzschean affirmation of interpretation and innocent play with no relation to loss. Deleuze's 'How Do We Recognize Structuralism?' was also written in 1967, although not published until 1973 (Deleuze 2002; English translation in Stivale 1998). In this essay, Deleuze offers seven or eight criteria by which to recognise the structuralism associated with linguistics, anthropology and psychoanalysis. However, as is generally the case with his reconstructions of a particular philosophy, Deleuze's criteria serve to transform the key concepts associated with structuralism. In effect, he redefines the nature of structures along the lines of the open-ended and virtual assemblages which appear as 'transcendental Ideas' in *Difference and Repetition* or as 'sense' in *The Logic of Sense*.

These critical responses to structuralism are indicative of some of the most important thematic concerns or philosophemes common to the work of Deleuze and Derrida. In the eulogy that he wrote immediately after Deleuze's death in 1995, 'I'm Going to Have to Wander All Alone', Derrida said that he felt a 'nearly total affinity' between his work and that of Deleuze, at least on the level of 'theses' (the word appears in scare quotes in Derrida's text, and he adds 'but the word doesn't fit' at one point), even while acknowledging the 'very obvious distances in what I would call – lacking any better term – the "gesture", the "strategy", the "manner": of writing, of speaking, of reading perhaps' (Derrida 2001a, 192). The contrast between Derrida's cautious and heavily qualified writing and the legendary 'dryness' of Deleuze's prose[1] is apparent to the reader at first glance. Yet over and above the differences in the manner of writing, there are parallels between the manner in which each of them forged a path out from under the repressive apparatus of the history of philosophy by inhabiting canonical texts in their own way in order to transform or deform the thought in question.

Deleuze commented in an interview: 'I belong to a generation, one of the last generations, that was more or less bludgeoned to death with the history of philosophy. The history of philosophy plays a patently repressive role in philosophy, it's philosophy's own version of the Oedipus complex: "You can't seriously consider saying what you yourself think until you've read this and that, and that on this, and this on that"' (Deleuze 1995b, 5). He explains how he freed himself from this repression and 'found his own voice' through a kind of depersonalisation, learned from reading Nietzsche: 'It was Nietzsche, who I read only later, who extricated me from all this. . . . He gives you a perverse taste . . . for saying simple things in your own way, in affects, intensities, experiences, experiments'. Deleuze explained that it was in this manner that he began to write in his own name:

> It's a strange business, speaking for yourself, in your own name, because it doesn't at all come with seeing yourself as an ego or a person or a subject. Individuals find a name for themselves, rather, only through the harshest exercise in depersonalization, by opening themselves up to the multiplicities everywhere within them, to the intensities running through them. A name as the direct awareness of such intensive multiplicities is the opposite of the depersonalization effected by the history of philosophy; it's depersonalization through love rather than subjection. (1995b, 6–7)

Derrida's own vexed relation to the standard teaching of the history of philosophy is of course one of the most remarkable aspects of his work. Although he began his career by positing the deconstructive intervention into the great texts of the Western tradition as aiming at the difference between the author's intention and the performance of the text, he quickly moved to pinpointing the location of the deconstructive lever between readings of the text devoted to presence and those devoted to ferreting out the often occluded ways in which a productive difference had always already constituted the longed-for presence. In this insistence on examining reading strategies, and on the institutional powers that reinforce presence-oriented readings as they teach the history of philosophy, we see one of the clearest affinities between Deleuze and Derrida.

In his eulogy for Deleuze, Derrida listed among their exemplary points of agreement 'the [thesis] concerning an irreducible difference that is in opposition to dialectical opposition, a difference "more profound" than a contradiction (*Difference and Repetition*), a difference in the joyously repeated affirmation ("yes, yes"), a taking into account of the simulacrum' (Derrida 2001a, 192–3). Both wrote significant essays on Plato and Platonism in which a number of these overlapping themes appear, most notably the revaluation of simulacra in the course of a reading of a number of Platonic texts against the grain of what subsequently became accepted as Platonic doctrine. Eric Alliez's essay in this volume, which is a translation of one of the few explicit comparisons to have appeared in French, identifies a number of similarities between their proto-deconstructive readings of Plato, including their common debt to Nietzsche. In his reply to Alliez's essay and another which appeared in the same collection, by Francis Wolff, Derrida endorses the project of attempting to outline the resemblances, analogies and underlying configuration common to these responses to Greek thought from within a certain French philosophical milieu, even while he cautions against an assimilation of disparate projects which would overlook significant differences between them.[2]

While the necessity of developing a non-Hegelian 'philosophy of difference' was deeply felt by both Deleuze and Derrida, such a project was by no means confined to these two philosophers. Indeed, it was an influential means by which a number of French thinkers sought to reconcile and move beyond two strands of their German heritage: the phenomenology of Hegel-Husserl-Heidegger and the historical-libidinal materialism of Marx-Nietzsche-Freud. In a chapter entitled 'Difference', Vincent Descombes presents the philosophy of difference as the culmination of an entire tradition of Franco-German philosophy, describing it as 'that remarkable point of modern metaphysics which all preceding discourse had indicated like a flickering compass', namely the attempt to elaborate 'a non-contradictory, non-dialectical consideration of difference, which would not envisage it as the simple contrary of identity, nor be obliged to see itself as "dialectically" identical with identity' (Descombes 1980, 136). The agreement between Deleuze and Derrida on the idea of such a non-dialectical difference, although developed in different contexts and philosophical idioms, carried over into a number of ways in which, in their subsequent work, concepts of differential repetition, iteration and continuous variation served to counteract philosophical prejudice in favour of unity, closure and homogeneity over diversity, openness and heterogeneity.

DIVERGENCES

In view of the many points of contact and resonance between their work, and the fact that they belonged to the same generation and to some extent the same intellectual milieu, it is all the more surprising that there has been so little serious comparative discussion of these two philosophers. A variety of explanations for this have been advanced. First and foremost, critics point to their different philosophical allegiances. For Jean-Luc Nancy, for example, Deleuze's thought remains 'far removed from the sources, schemata and codes of conduct which, for me, are those of philosophical work . . . he never turned to Hegel, was never tied to a dialectical continuity woven at once from the logic of a process . . . and from the structure of a subject' (Nancy 1996, 107–8). It is true that Hegel, Husserl and Heidegger are significant for Derrida in a way that they are not for Deleuze. The first 15 years of Derrida's career were devoted to the study of Husserl, from his 1953 mémoire *Le Problème de la genèse dans la philosophie de Husserl* (Derrida 1990c) to *La Voix et le phénomène* (1967b). For a long time, Derrida pursued the 'deconstruction' of metaphysics, in a sense quite close to Heideggerian *Destruktion*. The centrality of Heidegger to Derrida's concerns is evident throughout his writing, beginning with 'Ousia et Grammē' in 1968 (in Derrida 1972b; 1982) and continuing through to *Of Spirit* (1987a; 1989b), *Aporias* (1993a), *Politics of Friendship* (1994a; 1997a), and other works of the 1990s.

While it would be too simple to say that Derrida's notion of difference is essentially post-phenomenological and ethical and Deleuze's notion of difference is material and forceful, this characterisation does reflect real differences in their sources and philosophical orientations. It is nevertheless true that Derrida cites Deleuze's discussion of differential forces in *Nietzsche and Philosophy* in his 'Différance' essay (Derrida 1972b, 18–19; 1982, 17; cf. Deleuze 1962, 49; 1983, 43), while Deleuze has always emphasised the ethical import of his own reconceptualisation of difference. Nor are phenomenological and Heideggerian themes entirely absent from Deleuze's work. Indeed, both *Nietzsche and Philosophy* (1962) and *Difference and Repetition* (1968) contain responses to Heideggerian theses about being, time and difference, while *The Logic of Sense* engages quite closely with some theses of Husserl (e.g., Deleuze 1969, 117–21; 1990, 96–9). On the other hand, there is something to these distinctions. It is true, for instance, that Heidegger's thought of the history of metaphysics is much more important to Derrida than to Deleuze, who once said, 'I've never worried about going beyond metaphysics or the death of philosophy, and I never made a big thing about giving up Totality, Unity, the Subject' (Deleuze 1995b, 88). It is also true that, while Derrida always takes phenomenology as his point of departure, even as he relentlessly shows its limitations, Deleuze never really takes it that seriously, certainly not after his meeting with Guattari. While he mentions Sartre's 'Transcendence of the Ego' on more than one occasion, even in his last published work ('Immanence: A Life' [1995c, 4n2; 2001, 32n2]), this is only as an independent attestation of the need for a thought of immanence rather than a bona fide departure from a phenomenological starting point.

We noted above that Deleuze and Derrida share a strong reaction against the standard teaching of the history of philosophy. We must also note however that this reaction took different forms: for Deleuze, a sort of innocent glee in doing philosophy afresh, versus a sort of anxiety of influence on the part of Derrida, leading to the redoubtable caution and reflexive awareness of his writing. Responding to a question about Foucault's remark that 'one day, perhaps, this century will be seen as Deleuzian', Deleuze says: 'He may perhaps have meant that I was the most naive philosopher of our generation. In all of us you find themes like multiplicity, difference, repetition. But I put forward almost raw concepts of these, while others work with more mediation . . . Maybe that's what Foucault meant: I wasn't better than the others, but more naive, producing a kind of *art brut*, so to speak, not the most profound but the most innocent (the one who felt the least guilt about "doing philosophy")' (Deleuze 1995b, 88–9). Derrida affirms the notion of Deleuzean 'innocence' in philosophy in his eulogy: 'Yes, we will have all loved philosophy, who can deny it? But, it is true – he said it – Deleuze was the one among all of this "generation" who did/made [*faisait*] it the most gaily, the most innocently' (Derrida 2001a, 193, trans. modified.)

Deleuze and Derrida differ in the manner in which each confronts the standard approaches to the history of philosophy. Even when they write about the same thinkers, such as Kant or Nietzsche, the accents are not the same.[3] But in addition, they differ in their selection of preferred thinkers from within the tradition. Deleuze found the philosophical resources for his own creation of concepts in a lineage which included Lucretius, Spinoza, Hume, Nietzsche and Bergson. In all of these thinkers, he discerned 'a secret link' formed by 'their critique of negativity, their cultivation of joy, the hatred of interiority, the externality of forces and relations, the denunciation of power' (Deleuze 1995b, 6). The joyful affirmation common to these thinkers is echoed in his own innocent love of philosophy, on which we remarked above. But these figures are largely absent from Heideggerian accounts of the *Seinsgeschichte* ('history of being') and, with the exception of Nietzsche, they are rarely discussed by Derrida.

In his chapter of this book, Daniel Smith invokes Giorgio Agamben's suggestion that two trajectories may be distinguished in recent French philosophy, both of which involve a relationship to Heidegger. The first relies upon a figure of transcendence, and passes from Kant and Husserl through Levinas and Derrida, while the second relies upon figures of immanence and passes from Spinoza and Nietzsche through Deleuze and Foucault. But there is reason to suppose that things are not so simple, for it can equally be argued that Deleuze seeks an immanence that is not immanent 'to' anything else, and is therefore equivalent to a pure outside. And while Deleuze seeks to begin with the pure outside or plane of immanence and show the construction of the inside or transcendent plane by restriction or folding of the outside, Derrida seeks to show that the outside or plane of transcendence is prior or interior to the supposed inside or plane of immanence.

It is true that there were political differences, or perhaps different political trajectories followed by these two philosophers. One of the significant differences between Deleuze and Derrida is surely that a major part of Deleuze's work was carried out in collaboration with the radical psychoanalyst Félix Guattari, whom he met in the aftermath of 'the events of May'. May '68 was a turning point in the lives of many who belonged to this postwar generation; Deleuze, for one, never renounced its importance or its impact on his own thinking. He insisted that his work with Guattari sought to give theoretical expression to the reality of the movement which erupted in '68: '*Anti-Oedipus* was about the univocity of the real, a sort of Spinozism of the unconscious. And I think '68 was this discovery itself. The people who hate '68, or say it was a mistake, see it as something symbolic or imaginary. But that's precisely what it wasn't, it was pure reality breaking through' (Deleuze 1995b, 144–5). Even more than the tumultous events themselves, what mattered for the subsequent careers of both men were the institutional paths followed in the aftermath. For Deleuze, the creation of Paris VIII (Vincennes) where he taught alongside Badiou, Châtelet, Lyotard, Rancière and others, and under the extraordinary conditions described in his 'Abecedaire' interview with Claire Parnet, had a lasting impact on his conception and practice of philosophy.

Derrida's reaction to '68 was more muted. Although 'the events' are mentioned in 'The Ends of Man' (in Derrida 1972b; 1982), he never felt himself to be a *soixante-huitard*, as he comments in a 1991 interview: 'Even though I participated at that time in demonstrations and organized the first general meeting at the École Normale, I was on my guard, even worried in the face of a certain cult of spontaneity, a fusionist, anti-unionist euphoria, in the face of the enthusiasm of a finally "freed" speech, of restored "transparence", and so forth. I never believed in those things' (Derrida 1995d, 347–8). Nonetheless, he continues, 'something else happened' in May 1968, 'a seismic jolt that came from far away and carried very far. In the culture and in the University, these shock waves are not yet stabilized'. Derrida pursues the theme in the following manner:

> Through the cult of spontaneity and a certain naturalist utopianism, people doubtless became aware of the artificial, artifactual character of institutions. One didn't need May '68 to realize this, to be sure, but perhaps one was able to realize it more practically, more effectively, because these non-natural, founded, historical things were clearly no longer functioning. As

usual, it is the breakdown that lays bare the functioning of the machine as such. And with that, because these non-natural, historical, founded institutions were no longer working, they were found to be altogether unfounded, unfounded in law, illegitimate. (1995d, 348)

Indeed, one of the most interesting divergences of Deleuze and Derrida lies in their responses to this institutional crisis, as two noteworthy institutional efforts mark Derrida's career, for which there are no Deleuzean counterparts. In 1974, as part of a movement to counteract threats by certain conservative politicians to restrict the teaching of philosophy in the French national education system, Derrida helped found GREPH (Groupe de Recherches sur l'Enseignement Philosophique) (see Derrida 2002b). In 1983, in the rather different political climate of the early Mitterand years, he helped found the Collège International de Philosophie (see Derrida 1990d), which is dedicated to giving a new form to the institutional framework of advanced philosophical research. While he himself never complained about the heavy demands these commitments entailed, Derrida notes in his eulogy that Deleuze once told him, 'with a concern like that of an older brother: "It pains me to see you put so much time into this institution [the Collège International de Philosophie], I would prefer that you write"' (Derrida 2001a, 193).

In addition to these stylistic, intellectual and political forces which have kept apart the work of Deleuze and Derrida and mitigated against any rigorous comparison or confrontation between them, we can also point to the differential reception of their work in the Anglophone world. Neither Derrida nor Deleuze first became known through the discipline of philosophy. Instead, both entered the English-speaking academic world via other areas of the 'humanities', including departments of literary studies, art history and theory, film and architecture. Only secondarily has their work begun to have an impact upon branches of the social sciences, such as political theory, speech communication, and human geography, or indeed upon philosophy itself. While they both took the same sort of 'detour' as it were before their – albeit still marginalised – reception in the Anglophone philosophical world, the rhythms of translation of their work have been quite different. Of the three works Derrida published in 1967, *Speech and Phenomena* appeared in English in 1973, *Of Grammatology* in 1974, and *Writing and Difference* in 1978. Two works published in 1972, *La Dissémination* and *Margins*, appeared in 1981 and 1982 respectively, while the monumental *Glas* (1974), perhaps understandably, had to wait until 1987 for translation. Since the mid-80s however, the gap between publication and translation of works by Derrida has shrunk considerably, from 7 to 10 years to virtual simultaneity for some works.

While Deleuze's collaborative works with Guattari were quite rapidly translated – *Anti-Oedipus* (1972) appeared in 1977 and *A Thousand Plateaus* (1980) in 1987 – the major works of the 1960s, *The Logic of Sense* (1969) and *Difference and Repetition* (1968) had to wait 21 and 26 years respectively for their English translations in 1990 and 1994. The historical works of the 1960s on Nietzsche, Spinoza and Bergson endured similar gaps of at least 20 years for translation. Thus it was not until the mid 1990s that a reasonably complete corpus of Deleuze's works existed in English translation, a good 15 to 20 years after Derrida had become a staple of Anglophone Continental philosophy. Perhaps the differences in the timing of their English-language translation can be explained in part by the fact that Derrida was a traveller in a way Deleuze never was. As early as 1956–7, Derrida was at Harvard doing archival research. Thereafter, he held visiting professorships at Yale, California-Irvine and New York, and was a regular speaker at conferences in Britain as well as North America. By contrast, Deleuze never taught abroad and attended only one memorable conference in New York.[4]

Whatever the reason for this differential rate of reception, a similar pattern appears with regard to secondary works. Attention to Derrida's work reached a peak in the mid-80s, while Deleuze began to be an object of critical study in the mid- to late 90s. In 1986, secondary literature on Derrida's philosophical significance entered a new phase with the publication of three English language monographs: Rodolphe Gasché's *The Tain of the Mirror*, Irene Harvey's *Derrida and the Economy of Différance*, and John Llewelyn's *Derrida on the Threshold of Sense*. Since then there have been an increasing number of other books and essay collections on Derrida's work. By contrast, it was not until the mid-1990s that major work on Deleuze's thought began to appear in English, notably in the form of three major essay collections: Boundas and Olkowski (1994); Patton (1996); and Ansell-Pearson (1997). The Anglophone book-length studies on Deleuze have also followed the translation pattern, with interest at first primarily directed to Deleuze's collaboration with Guattari, notably Massumi (1992); Goodchild (1996); Stivale (1998); and Holland (1999). To date there is no full-length treatment of Deleuze's philosophical work in English, although there are specialised works which treat particular aspects of his work, such as Hardt (1993); Ansell-Pearson (1999); Buchanan (2000); Patton (2000); and Protevi (2001b).

CHAPTERS

While the extraneous factors referred to above may go some way towards explaining the relative lack of comparative study of the similarities and differences between Deleuze and Derrida, there is no justification for a continued failure to do so. The essays assembled here compare aspects of the work of Deleuze and Derrida via a number of key themes, including the philosophy of difference, language, memory, time, event, and love, as well as relating these themes to their respective approaches to Philosophy, Literature, Politics and Mathematics. This book seeks to effect a number of 'transverse communications' between the work of these two important thinkers and also establish basic lines of research for further work in this field.

PAUL PATTON argues that, over and above the differences between their respective practices of philosophy, Deleuze and Derrida share an ethico-political orientation towards the future, where the future is understood as open and as implying the possibility of the deconstruction or deterritorialisation of existing forms of thought and action. He compares the type of conceptual analysis undertaken by deconstruction in its so-called affirmative phase with certain features of the conceptual creation undertaken by Deleuze and Guattari, in order to identify a number of similarities between them. In both cases, there is a particular use of the idea of the absolute or the unconditioned which ensures that philosophy is also a political activity. Thus, just as the deconstructive 'invention' of the future is not invention in the ordinary sense because it concerns the advent of the absolute or entirely other, so Deleuze and Guattari's political ethic of deterritorialisation relies on a distinction between relative and absolute 'deterritorialisation'. In this manner, and through the discussion of other examples, Patton argues for a degree of convergence between the respective philosophical vocabularies of Deleuze and Derrida, especially in relation to their respective conceptions of the political function of philosophy and its relationship to the future.

TAMSIN LORRAINE compares writings by Deleuze (*The Logic of Sense, Difference and Repetition*) and Derrida (*Given Time: 1 Counterfeit Money, Specters of Marx*) with regard to the manner in which they present our relationship to time. Pursuing a line of flight between them, she argues that both philosophers provide reason to think that the reconceptualisation of time is a crucial component of a 'postmodern' ethics. Deleuze's comments on the adventures of Lewis Carroll's Alice provide the occasion to investigate his concept of the event and the syntheses of time articulated in *Difference and Repetition*. Lorraine articulates Deleuze's concept of time with that implied by Derrida's remarks on the gift, justice and 'time out of joint', and suggests that both lead us towards a non-representational image of time and a different kind of subjectivity.

DANIEL W. SMITH argues that, despite the apparent parallels between Deleuze and Derrida as philosophers of difference, there are significant differences between them. In particular, he identifies the crucial difference in terms of the answers they each give to the question 'what is it that "causes" the differential movement of concepts and things?': is it the transcendence of the absolute as wholly Other (the tendency of Derrida's thought) or the immanent movement of difference-in-itself (the tendency of Deleuze's thought)? Smith develops his differential analysis of Deleuze and Derrida via a discussion of three privileged scenes in which the difference between their immanentist and transcendentist allegiances are played out: subjectivity and the theory of desire; ontology and the divine-names tradition; and epistemology and Kantian transcendental ideas. For Smith, however, it is the ethical realm that provides the arena in which the differences between the immanentist and transcendentist allegiances in philosophy displayed in these other areas are sharpest and most consequential.

LEONARD LAWLOR finds the 'point of diffraction' between the thought of Deleuze and Derrida in the different principles of their thought, immediate duality and mediate unity, respectively. Lawlor examines the notions of simulacrum, language, time, voice and death in *Difference and Repetition*, *The Logic of Sense*, *Voice and Phenomenon* and *Dissemination*, proposing four oppositions as means of preventing the diffraction from collapsing into the 'nearly total affinity' Derrida notes between his thought and that of Deleuze. These oppositions are expressed in terms of duality and unity; positivity and negativity; the 'non-lieu' and the 'mi-lieu'; self-interrogation and interrogation by the other.

ERIC ALLIEZ'S contribution is a translation of his article 'Ontologie et logographie: la pharmacie, Platon et le simulacre', previously published in Cassin 1992. Under the sign of Nietzsche's goal of 'overturning Platonism', Alliez undertakes a comparison of the 'deconstructive' readings of Plato by Derrida in 'Plato's Pharmacy', and by Deleuze in 'Plato and the Simulacrum'. Identifying their convergence on the themes of force and the outside and their divergence on the question of question of textuality and the sign enables Alliez to articulate the relationship between Derrida and Deleuze as a crucial point in the development of metaphysics after Nietzsche and Heidegger.

ARKADY PLOTNITSKY identifies a specifically mathematical stratum in both Deleuze's and Derrida's work and argues for a degree of similarity and qualified difference between them in this regard. He suggests that there is a relationship to Leibniz and to Mallarmé in each case, although not to the same dimensions of their approach to mathematics and the fold. Deleuze's approach is primarily geometrical/topological, while Derrida's is primarily algebraic. Plotnitsky argues for this *différance* by aligning Deleuze's work with Riemannian mathematics and the spatiality of Leibniz's baroque, while linking Derrida's philosophical undecidability with Mallarmé's demonstration of the textual character of mathematics and Gödel's demonstration of the undecidability of formal logical systems. In this way, he seeks to offer a new perspective on the epistemology of modern mathematics and science, and on the relationship of Deleuze and Derrida's philosophical conceptuality to these novel epistemological conditions.

GREGG LAMBERT argues that in the work of Deleuze and Derrida we find an intensive dialogue between philosophy and literature operating on a number of levels: specific encounters with literary figures as well as reflections on philosophical writing, style and the historical relations between the institutions of philosophy and literature. Lambert pursues the comparison of Deleuze and Derrida with respect to this dialogue via a discussion of several common thematic concerns including: the critique of representation and the phenomenon of the double, the phantasm and the simulacrum; repetition and 'weak memory' or 'improper anamnesis'; the relation to the outside; and the question of style. He argues that, for both Deleuze and Derrida, the renewal of philosophy in the modern period is linked to the question of writing.

BRANKA ARSIĆ takes the readings of Melville's 'Bartleby the Scrivener' by Deleuze and Derrida as the occasion to compare their respective concepts of passivity, and to pursue an original philosophical investigation of activity and passivity. Weaving together Melville's text and the work of Deleuze and Derrida, along with elements of Leibniz and Blanchot, Arsic explores the themes of 'static ontological genesis', passive synthesis, addiction, habit, differential repetition, death, trembling, passion, sleep and insomnia. Her examination of the impersonal and sub-individual phenomena that constitute while eviscerating our selves, our subjectivities and our activities throws new light on life as refracted by Derrida's *différance* and Deleuze's plane of immanence.

JEFFREY T. NEALON approaches the differences between Derrida and Deleuze by way of their reception in North American Cultural Studies, where recent enthusiasm for Deleuze has largely been based on the belief that his work (with Guattari) abandons the literary paradigm of signification and interpretation in favour of pragmatics. In contrast to this widespread opinion, and in response to Derrida's own perception of 'affinity' with Deleuze at the level of theses, Nealon argues that Deleuze and Derrida agree on the irreducible role of illocutionary force in language. Contrary to some of the ways in which it has been practised and defended, Derridean deconstruction is not a demonstration of lack, negativity or a practice of neutralisation, but the affirmation of the possibility of context breaking and the necessity of emergence of the event. Derrida and Deleuze (DG) are in agreement that the meaning effects of language are beholden to a field of forces that is 'asyntactic, agrammatical . . . language is no longer defined by what it says, even less by what makes it a signifying thing, but by what causes it to move, to flow, and to explode' (DG 1984, 33). Nealon asks what follows from an appreciation of this common concern with illocutionary force for the future of Cultural Studies.

In 'Language and Persecution' ALPHONSO LINGIS develops a meditation on language, expression and subjectivation. He begins by invoking the Derridean claim that textuality entails a continual deferment of presence, a deferment that precisely persecutes us by provoking 'unending explications of every word'. Seeking escapes from interpretation, Lingis first explores the way 'expressions intervene . . . in the course and rhythm of our movements and interactions with our environment'. After this analysis of 'direct expression', Lingis examines the endless circles of interpretation the question 'what does it mean'? traps us in, the question asked by the face. He then moves to examine two forms of subjectivation explicated in the work of Deleuze and Guattari: (1) as the constitution of a subject as 'self-conscious consciousness', which 'generates energies outside the semiotic circle'; (2) as the subject of a passionate love. For Lingis, both of these subjectivations enable us to bypass or break out of interpretation in different, albeit finite ways.

For JOHN PROTEVI, the ambiguity of the French word *expérience* (which can mean both 'experience' and 'experiment') expresses the profound difference between Derrida the post-phenomenologist and Deleuze the historical-libidinal materialist. Focusing on the fundamental philosophical concept of 'love', Protevi contrasts love as experience of aporia for Derrida and love as exercise in depersonalisation for Deleuze. Using *Memoires: for Paul De Man* and 'Aphorism Countertime', Protevi shows that for Derrida, love is the relation to alterity, the other, which pulls apart the supposedly self-identical metaphysical subject by forcing it to undergo the tragic experience of aporia. In other words, for Derrida, love destroys the identity of the subject by taking on the risk of living on, that is, the necessary possibility of mourning the death of the other. On the other hand, using *A Thousand Plateaus*, Protevi shows that for Deleuze and Guattari, love is deterritorialisation, that is, the changing of the material flows and affects of the body in order to produce new bodies, to do new things. In other words, for Deleuze and Guattari, the *expérience* of love is experimentation, contra the Oedipal organism, leading to adventures of new bodies on a 'new earth'.

Notes

We are especially grateful to Keith Ansell-Pearson for his encouragement and advice regarding this project; to Tristan Palmer for his constant support; and to David Wills for his advice and assistance.
1. Clément Rosset recounts the story of a reader of *Différence et répétition* who

commented that reading this book was like eating a biscuit made without butter: excellent but dry (Rosset 1972).

2. In response to the fact that 'at this moment, in a given country, a certain number of philosophers, who belong to more or less the same generation and to institutions which are very close neighbours if not the same, and who publish at more or less the same time, say similar things', Derrida admits that it is one of the tasks of the 'Enlightened' of our time to determine 'in what these resemblances consist and what explains their appearance with or without the knowledge of the "authors"' (Derrida 1992d, 225).

3. In 'Nous Autres Grecs', Derrida comments that his own reading of Nietzsche, and indeed his own debt to Nietzsche, 'remains very different from that of Deleuze: in its style, its translations, in the treatment of text and language, by virtue of its insistent passage through Heidegger and through "critical" questions posed to Heidegger and to Heidegger's "Nietzsche"' (Derrida 1992d, 258).

4. This was the Schizo-Culture Conference, organised by *Semiotext(e)*, which took place at Columbia University in November 1975.

CHAPTER I

Future Politics

Paul Patton

> The future can only be anticipated in the form of an absolute danger. It is that which breaks absolutely with constituted normality and can only be proclaimed, *presented*, as a sort of monstrosity. (Jacques Derrida)

> As for the third time in which the future appears, this signifies that the event and the act possess a secret coherence which excludes that of the self; that they turn back against the self which has become their equal and smash it to pieces, as though the bearer of the new world were carried away and dispersed by the shock of the multiplicity to which it gives birth. (Gilles Deleuze)

INTRODUCTION

For Deleuze and Guattari, philosophy is the invention or creation of concepts, the purpose of which is not accurate representation of how things are but to call for 'a new earth and people that do not yet exist' (DG 1994b, 108). The creation of concepts is inseparable from the elaboration of new vocabularies such as those put forward in *A Thousand Plateaus*: a theory of assemblages defined by their lines of flight or deterritorialisation, their particular combinations of content and expression, their forms of stratification and the abstract machines which they express; the battery of terms employed in the elaboration of a micropolitics of desire, including body without organs, intensities, molar and molecular segmentarities; an account of capitalism as a non-territorially based axiomatic of flows; a concept of abstract machines of metamorphosis (nomadic war-machines) which are the agents of social and political transformation; a vocabulary in which to describe various processes of becoming: becoming woman, becoming animal, becoming imperceptible, and so on.

These schizoanalytic or pragmatic vocabularies provide us with philosophical concepts rather than social science. Nevertheless, they enable a form of description which is immediately practical, to the extent that, for example, it makes a difference whether we are dealing with the effective deterritorialisation of a given apparatus of capture rather than simply a modification of its mechanism. Deleuze and Guattari's account of the different kinds of line which define individual or collective bodies enables questions such as the following: 'What are your lines? What map are you in the process of making or rearranging? What abstract line will you draw, and at what price, for yourself and for others? What is your line of flight?' (DG 1987, 203). Even though the aim of philosophy is change rather than truth, these descriptive vocabularies serve that aim by providing new means of orientation in relation to everyday events and processes. They provide new means of description and therefore new ways of understanding and acting upon the world.

For Derrida too, the aim of philosophy is not truth but the destabilisation or deconstruction of established institutions so as to open up 'the passage toward the other' (Derrida 1992a, 341). In common with Deleuze and Guattari's practice of philosophy as invention of concepts, deconstruction aspires to be inventive and consequential. In 'Psyché: Invention of the Other', Derrida asserts that deconstruction 'is inventive or it is nothing at all' (1992a, 337). In 'Force of Law', he affirms that deconstruction seeks to intervene in order to change things, or at least to engage with events and transformations already underway in a manner that contributes to making the future different from and in some sense 'better' than the past (Derrida 1992b, 8–9). In *Specters of Marx*, he endorses a form of Marxism that is heir to the spirit of the Enlightenment and that in turn justifies a 'radical and interminable' critique of the present. This critique, he continues, 'belongs to the movement of an experience open to the absolute future of what is coming . . .' (Derrida 1994b, 90). Contrary to the suggestion that he is an anti-Enlightenment thinker, Derrida affirms his belief in perfectibility and progress.[1] However, just as Deleuze and Guattari remain silent about the character of the new earths and peoples which philosophy helps to bring into being, so we must understand 'progress' here to be defined negatively, perhaps in the manner of Foucault's characterisation of the ethos of enlightenment as freedom from past constraints or passage beyond 'the contemporary limits of the necessary' (Foucault 1997, 313).

While there are undeniable differences of style and method between Deleuze and Derrida, these should not be allowed to mask the similarities between them. Derrida acknowledges their 'affinity' with regard to some 'theses' even as he 'grumbles' about others such as the idea that philosophy consists in creating concepts (Derrida 2001a, 193). It is not clear that he is entitled to grumble.[2] It all depends on what is mean by 'creating' and what is meant by 'concepts'. Deleuze and Guattari's characterisation of the creator of concepts as a 'friend' in the sense that a craftsman is a friend of his chosen material shows that they do not envisage the creation of concepts ex nihilo. Rather, concepts are produced by means of the transformation and combination of certain conceptual or pre-conceptual raw materials. In this sense, Derrida's practice of deconstruction has involved the production of a whole series of novel 'concepts' such as writing-in-general, the trace, the supplement, *différance*, generalised metaphoricity and so on. Moreover, there are a number of formal parallels between these 'aconceptual' concepts or non-concepts, as Derrida calls them, and the concepts that Deleuze and Guattari define as the objects of specifically philosophical invention.[3] These parallels are sufficient to rule out any simplistic contrast between deconstructive analysis on the one hand and philosophy as the invention of concepts on the other.

Nonetheless, it will be objected that deconstruction does not invent new concepts much less provide new means of description. On the contrary, and above all in its affirmative phase, deconstruction is applied exclusively to existing concepts such as invention, justice, democracy, friendship, the gift, hospitality, forgiveness. Surely this indicates a fundamental difference from Deleuze and Guattari's constructivism? Without wishing to deny their differences, I will argue that Deleuze and Derrida share an ethico-political conception of philosophy as oriented towards the possibility of change. For both, philosophy is a political activity oriented towards the future, where the future is understood only in terms of its potential difference from the present. For both, the future must be understood as open, rather than determined by the past, and for both the task of philosophy in relation to this future relies on a certain usage of the absolute or the unconditioned. In this manner, over and above the differences between their respective philosophical vocabularies, we can perceive a zone of convergence or undecidability with respect to their concepts or 'theses' relating to the political function of philosophy.

AFFIRMATIVE DECONSTRUCTION

The practice of 'affirmative' deconstruction relies upon at least two distinct strategies with regard to the analysis of concepts. Firstly, a genealogical study of the history and interpretations of a given concept, along with the interconnections it has to other concepts or philosophemes. Thus, the discussion of the concept of invention in 'Psyché: Invention of the Other' included a discussion of the ways in which invention has been recognised in legal, literary, intellectual and technological domains. Similarly, the examination of law and justice in 'Force of Law' alluded to the need for an historical genealogy of different concepts of law, right, justice and the manner in which these are bound up with responsibility and the network of concepts related to this, such as property, intentionality, will, freedom, conscience, consciousness, etc. (Derrida 1992b, 20).

A second form of deconstructive analysis, and the one on which I propose to focus, offers a redescription of existing concepts which reproduces in each case a distinction between a contingent or conditioned form of the concept and an absolute or unconditioned form, where in each case the absolute or unconditioned form of the concept is always paradoxical or impossible. Thus, the aporetic analysis of invention in 'Psyché: Invention of the Other' leads to a distinction between two kinds of invention, namely ordinary invention which is always the invention of the possible and an extraordinary or pure invention which would involve the appearance of something truly or radically other. This other is literally impossible, in the sense that it implies the appearance of something beyond or outside the order of the possible. In this form of deconstructive analysis, everything is organised around the invention of the other, which John Caputo takes to mean the 'in-coming of the other, the promise of an event to come, the event of the promise of something coming' (Caputo 1997, 42). In a series of parallel analyses of the gift, justice, responsible decision, democracy, the cosmopolitan right of hospitality and a number of other concepts, affirmative deconstruction invents or reinvents a distinction between two poles of the concept in question in order to argue two things: first, that the difference between these two poles is irreducible; and second, that the ever-present possibility of invention, reconfiguration or transformation in our existing, historically conditioned and contingent ways of understanding the phenomenon in question is guaranteed by the existence of the absolute or unconditioned form of the concept.

In each case, too, this aporetic analysis also leads to a phenomenology of the 'experience' of this impossible act. In 'Force of Law' it is the distinction between law and justice which corresponds to the difference between a conditioned and an unconditioned form of the concept. The law, which is subject to historical conditions and is therefore open to modification or change, is contrasted with justice, which is that in the name of which the law is modified and which therefore remains essentially undeconstructible. Justice is manifest both in particular applications of the law, and in particular improvements or modifications of the law, but neither of these implies an experience of justice as such. Justice as such, supposing there is such a thing, is an impossible object of experience. In so far as deconstruction is concerned with justice, it is concerned with the experience of that which we are not able to experience or the experience of the impossible (Derrida 1992b, 16).[4] This experience of the impossible should not be understood as as a barrier or limit but as 'an ordeal, a test, a crucial moment through which we have to go' (Derrida 2001c, 63). 'Possible' here should not be understood simply in the negative sense of something not actual but also as 'something through which a possibility is given' (Derrida 2001c, 64). In effect, any decision involves an experience of this kind. On the one hand, if it is to be properly a decision and not simply a mechanical procedure it must involve more than simply acting in accordance with a given rule. On the other hand, a decision must have some relation to a rule and not be simply capricious or unmotivated. In these terms, we might say that this form of aporetic analysis provides new means of describing the decision which is always implicit in occasions or situations of this kind.

To give a more concrete ethical and political sense to this form of analysis, consider Derrida's recent discussion of the concept and the politics of forgiveness. 'On Forgiveness' takes its point of departure from the proliferation of 'scenes of repentance, confession, forgiveness or apology' entered into by Governments, Heads of State, Churches and other corporate bodies in recent years (Derrida 2001b, 28). Examples of such 'geopolitical' scenes in which the concept of forgiveness plays a central role include the South African Truth and Reconciliation Commission and the Australian Reconciliation process. In this essay, Derrida argues that the Christian or Abrahamic tradition from which our use of the term derives is fundamentally divided between a concept of unconditional, infinite, forgiveness and a forgiveness which is possible only upon certain conditions, such as the repentance of the perpetrator. Under this condition, the guilty party recognises the crime and in so doing becomes transformed so that it is no longer the guilty as such who seeks forgiveness.[5]

In addition, Derrida argues that, strictly speaking, forgiveness only applies in relation to the unforgivable. It follows that true forgiveness is strictly speaking impossible and therefore paradoxical: how can one forgive the unforgivable? Yet it is only the existence of the unforgivable that gives force, or meaning, to the idea of forgiveness. 'Must one not maintain that an act of forgiveness worthy of its name, if ever there is such a thing, must forgive the unforgivable and without condition?' (Derrida 2001b, 39). The reason is that if one forgave only that which is forgivable the concept of forgiveness would lose its force, just as the concept of a gift would lose its force if one gave only that which one was able to give, or the concept of justice would lose its force if it were reduced to the idea of procedural justice in accordance with law, or the concept of hospitality would lose its force if it did not imply a relation to an unconditional hospitality.

For Derrida, to say that the logic of forgiveness relies upon this paradox is not to disqualify it. On the contrary, it is to draw a line between the logic of forgiveness as such, forgiveness proper if there is such a thing, and all forms of conditional forgiveness. Accordingly, the first consequence which he draws from this analysis is that forgiveness proper remains heterogeneous to the order of political or juridical thought. On the one hand, he argues that, in all these geopolitical scenes of forgiveness or reconciliation, there is an implicit appeal to 'a certain idea of pure and unconditional forgiveness, without which this discourse would not have the least meaning' (Derrida 2001b, 45). On the other hand, he points out that we could never 'in the ordinary sense of the words', found a politics or law on forgiveness in this unconditional sense (Derrida 2001b, 39). In practice, it is never a question of pure forgiveness since there is always some kind of 'transaction' or exchange involved.[6]

Nonetheless, and this is the second consequence Derrida draws from this analysis, the fact that these two heterogeneous poles of the concept of forgiveness are indissociable from one another, as in the intimate relationship between law and justice, guarantees that the question of the conditions under which forgiveness can occur remains open.[7] On the one hand, forgiveness is irreducible to the order of conditions, on the other hand, it is only manifest insofar as it engages with the conditions which obtain in particular historical scenes of forgiveness. The resolution or non-resolution of particular processes of reconciliation necessarily takes place in the interval between these two poles. In effect, the indissociability of these two poles amounts to a call for the invention of new protocols of forgiveness capable of meeting the demands of a particular situation: 'it is between these two poles, *irreconcilable but indissociable*, that decisions and responsibilities are to be taken' (Derrida 2001b, 45; emphasis in the original). Far from paralysing the desire for resolution or improvement in a given situation, Derrida suggests that this distinction requires us to invent new intermediate *schemas* in the Kantian sense of protocols that serve to actualise concepts in the field of the sensible (Derrida 2000b, 147). In the specific case of the law of hospitality, it is 'a question of knowing how to transform and improve the law, and of knowing if this improvement is possible within an historical space which takes place *between* the Law of an unconditional hospitality . . . and *the* conditional laws of a right to hospitality, without which *The* unconditional Law of hospitality would be in danger of remaining a pious and irresponsible desire . . .' (Derrida 2001b, 22–3).

Finally – and this is the third consequence which Derrida draws in this case as in other versions of this distinction between the unconditioned and conditioned form of the concept – he argues that the unconditioned is necessary in order to inflect politics or to bring about change. It is by appealing to justice or to 'a certain beyond of the law' that the law is modified or improved. It is only by reference to the paradoxical idea of the unforgivable that we can 'orient' an evolution of the law or 'inspire' new forms of responsibility. Thus, for example, when in 1964 the French Government decided that there should be no statute of limitations for crimes against humanity, they did so on the basis of an appeal to a certain idea of the unforgivable and an implicit reference to the transcendent order of the unconditional (Derrida 2001b, 53). The case for the establishment of an international criminal court might also be supposed to involve an appeal to the idea of unforgivable crimes which justify a recourse to law over and above that of sovereign states.

In all cases, the distinction between these two indissociable but heterogeneous orders is a reason to think that 'we are not defined through and through by the political . . . Must we not accept that, in heart or in reason, above all when it is a question of forgiveness, something arrives which exceeds all institution, all power, all juridico-political authority?' (Derrida 2001b, 54). This 'beyond' is what interests Derrida throughout his analyses of ethico-political concepts. It appears under a variety of names: the Other, justice, unconditional or absolute hospitality and so on. In all cases, it provides the aporetic assurance of an open future: at once both the condition of possibility and the condition of impossibility of change. Since Deleuze and Guattari's constructivism involves a similarly ambivalent opening towards the future and the possibility of change, it is possible to establish a number of connections between their disparate philosophical vocabularies around this point.

THE ETHICS OF DETERRITORIALISATION

Deleuze and Guattari rely upon their own version of the distinction between conditioned and unconditioned forms of the concept. Consider the concept of deterritorialisation which lies at the heart of the political ethic elaborated in their mature work. In the concluding statement of rules governing certain key concepts in *A Thousand Plateaus*, deterritorialisation is defined as the complex movement or process by which something escapes or departs from a given territory (DG 1987, 508), where a territory can be a system of any kind, conceptual, linguistic, social or affective. On their account, such systems are always inhabited by 'vectors of deterritorialization' and deterritorialisation is always 'inseparable from correlative reterritorializations' (DG 1987, 509). Reterritorialisation does not mean returning to the original territory, but rather refers to the ways in which deterritorialised elements recombine and enter into new relations in the constitution of a new assemblage or the modification of the old. Absolute and relative deterritorialisation are distinguished on the basis that relative deterritorialisation concerns only movements within the actual – as opposed to the virtual – order of things. By contrast, absolute deterritorialisation takes place in the virtual – as opposed to the actual – order of things. In itself, absolute deterritorialisation remains an unrealisable or impossible figure, manifest only in and through relative deterritorialisation. Conversely, relative deterritorialisation only occurs because there is 'a perpetual immanence of absolute deterritorialization within relative deterritorialization' (DG 1987, 56). In this sense, absolute deterritorialisation is the underlying condition of all forms of actual or relative deterritorialisation. At one point, they describe it as 'the deeper movement . . . identical to the earth itself' (DG 1987, 143). In effect, in the relationship between these two heterogeneous but indissociable movements of deterritorialisation, Deleuze and Guattari present in ontological form a version of the relationship which Derrida discerns between the conditioned and unconditioned poles of the concept.

Deleuze and Guattari's concept of becoming, which in its pure form amounts to something very similar to what Derrida calls iteration, also involves a distinction between conditioned forms of becoming and an absolute or pure form. In *What is Philosophy?* they define becoming as 'the action by which something or someone continues to become other (while continuing to be what it is)' (DG 1994b, 177 trans. modified). In *A Thousand Plateaus* they describe a whole series of more specific and conditioned processes by which something or someone becomes other in relation to the real or imagined capacities of something else: becoming-animal, becoming-child, becoming-woman and the like. These different becomings may be ordered in various ways. For example, in relation to the masculine standard of European cultural and political normality, they argue that 'all becomings begin with and pass through becoming-woman' (DG 1987, 277). But in another series, defined in relation to the unconditioned form or 'immanent end' of all becomings, what they call 'becoming-imperceptible' or 'becoming-world' stands apart. This is a becoming in which an individual is reduced to an abstract line that can connect or conjugate with other lines thereby making 'a world that can overlay the first one, like a transparency' (DG 1987, 280). This is an absolute becoming in which the movement is infinite and therefore imperceptible. In effect, it is a paradoxical form of becoming in which everything changes while appearing to remain the same.

The authors do not dwell on the aporetic character of the extreme or unconditioned form of the concepts outlined in *A Thousand Plateaus*. However, it is not difficult to find the elements of paradox in each case. For example, relative deterritorialisation can be either positive or negative. It is negative when the deterritorialised element is immediately subjected to forms of reterritorialisation which enclose or obstruct its line of flight. It is positive when the line of flight prevails over secondary reterritorialisations, even though it may still fail to connect with other deterritorialised elements or enter into a new assemblage. Relative deterritorialisation therefore can lead either to effective change or transformation within a given territory or system or to defeat and immediate reterritorialisation. Since absolute deterritorialisation is the underlying condition of relative deterritorialisation in all its forms, it follows that it is both the condition of possibility of change and the condition of its impossibility.

Alternatively, consider the ambiguous status of the lines of flight along which individual or collective assemblages break down or become transformed. At one point, they refer to the 'paradox' of fascism understood in terms of the ambiguity of the line of flight (DG 1987, 230). Lines of flight or deterritorialisation are at once both the source of the highest creativity and the affect associated with this state, namely joy, and the source of 'a strange despair, like an odor of death and immolation, a state of war from which one returns broken' (DG 1987, 229). The molecular as opposed to the molar line already constitutes a mortal threat to the integrity of a subject with a given set of desires, aspirations or notions of the good. It is along this line that the subject undergoes 'molecular changes, redistributions of desire such that when something occurs, the self that awaited it is already dead, or the one that would await it has not yet arrived' (DG 1987, 199). The freedom expressed in this kind of becoming other is incompatible with the continued existence of the stable subject of liberal political philosophy.[8] However, the freedom expressed in Deleuze and Guattari's third line, the line of flight or absolute deterritorialisation, is positively monstrous, an even more profound form of 'absolute danger'. Once embarked on this line, 'One has become imperceptible and clandestine in motionless voyage. Nothing can happen, or can have happened, any longer . . . Now one is no more than an abstract line, like an arrow crossing the void. Absolute deterritorialization' (DG 1987, 199–200).

CONVERGENCE: PURE EVENTS AND THE EVENT TO COME

In *What is Philosophy?*, Deleuze and Guattari provide another vocabulary in which to express the distinction between conditioned and unconditioned forms of a given concept when they define the objects of philosophical concepts as pure events. Philosophical concepts, they say, express pure events. While pure events are expressed or incarnated in bodies and states of affairs in the course of everyday or historical events, the pure event in itself exists independently of these impure incarnations: 'what History grasps of the event is its effectuation in states of affairs or in lived experience, but the event in its becoming, in its specific consistency, in its self-positing concept, escapes History' (DG 1994b, 110). So, for example, the political philosophical concept of a social contract might be supposed to express the pure event of incorporation of a political and legal system with certain features – guaranteed personal freedoms, rights to property, to equal treatment before the law and so on. This pure event is expressed in different concepts of the nature of the social contract, and more or less imperfectly actualised in societies founded upon a rule of law, but it remains irreducible to this series of expressions and actualisations. Understood in this manner, the concepts set out in *A Thousand Plateaus* are in the first instance the expression of pure events of deterritorialisation, becoming, incorporeal transformation, capture, metamorphosis and the like. In themselves, and in accordance with the paradoxical character of the unconditioned described above, such pure events are unrealisable or 'unlivable' forms (1994b, 156).[9] They are actualised only secondarily, through their incarnation in particular historical phenomena as contingent and conditioned versions of such events: *this* form of capture, *this* process of deterritorialization, becoming-animal as opposed to becoming-child or becoming-non-European and so on.

The concept of the pure event does not feature prominently in Derrida's work, although in 'Signature, Event, Context' he does explain the 'enigmatic originality' of every signature by reference to 'the pure reproducibility of the pure event' (Derrida 1982, 20). In his later work, however, the concept of the event 'to come' plays a parallel role. Just as Deleuze and Guattari distinguish the idea of revolution from the bloody historical events associated with this concept (DG 1994b, 100–1), so Derrida distinguishes the idea of democracy from its more or less inadequate historical determinations (Derrida 2002, 179). However, whereas Deleuze might have referred to the pure event of democracy irreducible to its incarnation in any existing political system, Derrida prefers to speak of a perpetually inaccessible 'democracy to come' where what is important is not so much 'democracy' as the 'to come' (Derrida 2002, 182). In the same way that justice is not a determinate ideal, 'democracy to come' is not the name of any future democracy but the paradoxical combination of a promise, which implies deferred presence, with the effectivity of the event of that promise in the singular now that is irreducible to any present (Derrida 2002, 180). This is a concept of democracy understood in terms of the logic of *différance* or iterability which, according to Derrida, characterises any event. The pure event of democracy.

The shorthand description of the absolute form of the concept as an unconditioned suggests a correspondence with Kant's transcendental Ideas which Derrida is careful to disavow. Democracy to come or justice in itself have the structure of a promise rather than that of a determinate ideal against which particular acts may be measured or towards which our present social arrangements might be said to progress. The deconstructive concept of justice 'has no horizon of expectation (regulative or messianic)'. But for this very

reason it may have an *avenir*, an *à venir* or 'to-come' which Derrida characterises as 'the very dimension of events irreducibly to come' (Derrida 1992b, 27).
The phrase 'to-come' here functions as a name for the future understood in
such a way that it is not to be identified with any modality or modification of
the present, but rather with a structural future that will never be actualised in
any present. In other words, it stands for a perpetually open, yet to be
determined future, a 'to come' understood as 'the space opened in order for
there to be an event, the to-come, so that the coming be that of the other'
(Derrida 2002a, 182).

It is this constant orientation towards the other, or towards the open future
which is named by the phrase 'to-come', which underwrites the political
function of this form of deconstruction analysis. It is precisely because justice
remains to come that 'justice, insofar as it is not only a juridical or political
concept, opens up for *l'avenir* the transformation, the recasting or refounding
of law and politics' (Derrida 1992b, 27). I suggested earlier that what motivates
deconstruction in its aporetic analysis of concepts is the relation which emerges
in each case to something beyond. Another way of describing the achievement
of this form of conceptual analysis is to say that it invents, in a variety of
specific vocabularies tailored to fit the needs of a particular occasion, a series
of descriptions of this 'beyond'. As noted above, this beyond is invariably
associated with an experience of the impossible in the sense that an invention
properly so called would involve the coming about of something which does
not belong to the existing order of possibilities. The beyond is an impossible
object of experience to the same degree and in the same sense that the truly
other or the pure event are impossible.[10] It comes not from the future present
but from the absolute future which is necessarily monstrous: 'A future that
would not be monstrous would not be a future' (Derrida 1995d, 387).

At this point, the common political orientation which informs both Derrida's and Deleuze and Guattari's practice of philosophy manifests itself in a
partial convergence of their respective vocabularies with regard to the future
and the pure event. As we saw above, there is an internal connection between
Deleuze and Guattari's ethic of deterritorialisation and the orientation towards
a perpetually open future or 'to-come'. This is apparent in the role played by
the concept of absolute deterritorialisation in the ontology of assemblages
outlined in *A Thousand Plateaus*: even though in itself it is an impossible or
'unlivable' state, absolute deterritorialisation is like a reserve of freedom or
movement in reality which is activated whenever relative deterritorialisation
takes place. Absolute deterritorialisation is the underlying principle which
ensures that the future will be different from the past, or that the future must
be understood as inhabited by the permanent possibility of otherness or
monstrosity. In political terms, absolute deterritorialisation is manifest as

revolution or the minor forms of becoming-revolutionary which are not to be confused with the past, present or future of actual revolutions, but which nonetheless call for new earths and new peoples (DG 1994b, 101, 112).

In *What is Philosophy?*, this orientation towards an open future is transposed onto philosophy itself. Deleuze and Guattari call the process of inventing concepts which extract events from existing states of affairs the 'counter-effectuation' of those events: 'the event is actualized or effectuated whenever it is inserted, willy-nilly, into a state of affairs; but it is *counter-effectuated* whenever it is abstracted from states of affairs so as to isolate its concept' (DG 1994b, 159). In counter-effectuating events, we attain and express the sense of what is happening around us. To think philosophically about the present is therefore to counter-effectuate the pure events which animate everyday events and processes. Conversely, to describe current events in terms of such philo-sophical concepts is to relate them back to the pure events of which they appear only as one particular determination, thereby dissociating the pure event from the particular form in which it has been actualised and pointing to the possibility of other determinate actualisations. But philosophy as the creation of untimely concepts does not extract just any event from things but 'new' events, meaning events which are forever new, like justice, unconditional forgiveness, absolute hospitality or democracy to come.[11] Herein lies the utopian vocation of philosophy, which Deleuze and Guattari redefine as the manner in which philosophy engages with the present. Even as they admit that perhaps utopia is not the best word for what they mean, they assert its etymological connection with the now-here, the singular moment at which absolute deterritorialization meets the present relative milieu of bodies and states of affairs (DG 1994b, 100). This is the same singular and paradoxical moment at which, for Derrida, the event of the promise implied in the 'to-come' takes place in the present (Derrida 2002, 180).[12] It therefore comes as no surprise that Deleuze and Guattari should describe the object of philosoph-ical creation, the concept, as 'the contour, the configuration, the constellation of an event to come' (DG 1994b, 32–3).

Philosophy, they argue, is a vector of deterritorialisation to the extent that it creates concepts which break with established or self-evident forms of understanding and description. Philosophy does not create just any concepts but untimely concepts that serve the overriding aim of opening up the possibility of transforming existing forms of thought and practice. The con-cepts that they themselves invent, such as becoming, capture, lines of flight and deterritorialisation, are not meant as substitutes for existing concepts of justice, rights, democracy or freedom. Nevertheless, they only serve the political task of philosophy to the extent that they assist in bringing about another justice, new rights or novel forms of democracy and freedom. For

Derrida, the irreducible gap between the conditioned and unconditioned forms of the concept, combined with the inevitable reference to the unconditioned, remind us of both the possibility and the importance of departing from existing forms of thought or practice. Whenever the question of the purpose or the politics of deconstruction is raised, he points to the undesirability of having a 'good conscience' about established ways of acting and thinking. In other words, he points to the desirability of being willing to question and challenge what is currently accepted as self-evident in our ways of thinking and acting. In this sense, he shares with Deleuze and Guattari a commitment to the permanent possibility of movement beyond present limits to our individual and collective capacities, in other words a commitment to what Foucault referred to as the 'undefined work of freedom' (Foucault 1997, 316).

Notes

1. In response to questions about the possibility of improving existing law in relation to hospitality, put to him by Penelope Deutscher in Sydney in 1999, Derrida asserted 'I am for the Enlightenment, I'm for progress, I'm a "progressist". I think the law is perfectible and we can improve the law' (Derrida 2001c, 100).
2. In 'Derrida and the question of the creation of concepts', a paper delivered at 'Derrida/Deleuze: Politics, Psychoanalysis, Territoriality', Critical Theory Institute, University of California at Irvine, 12–13 April 2002, Jesper Lohmann provided an excellent analysis of the possible grounds for Derrida's concern about the creation of concepts.
3. Derrida calls these 'aconceptual concepts' to signal that they are not concepts in the commonly accepted sense of the term, but rather successive versions of his attempt to think 'beyond the concept' or to think the process of concept formation in terms other than the classical logic of disjunction and inclusion. As such, they are open multiplicities in a sense not unlike the mobile concepts which Deleuze and Guattari outline in *A Thousand Plateaus*. I comment on these formal similarities between Deleuzian and Derridean concepts in Patton 1997 and 2000. John Rajchman also comments on the affinities between the 'other logic' which Derrida counterposes to the classical logic of disjunction and inclusion and the logic of qualitative multiplicities which informs Deleuze and Guattari's practice of conceptual creation, in Rajchman 2000, 50–76.
4. Derrida often invokes the idea that deconstruction, in its affirmative phase, is especially interested in this 'experience of the impossible'. In 'Psyché: Invention of the Other', for example, he writes that 'the interest of deconstruction . . . is a certain experience of the impossible' (Derrida 1992a, 328). Caputo points out that this experience of the impossible is not experience in the 'traditional, dusty phenomenological sense' where this means to perceive what appears or presents itself, but rather experience in a deconstructive sense in which

'experience' means running up against the limits of the unpresentable and unrepresentable (Caputo 1997, 33).

5. Derrida also argues, in accordance with Deleuze and Guattari's account of the nature of concepts and his own logic of iterability, that forgiveness is a complex and open-ended concept. It is uncertain whether it applies first to acts or to persons. It is unclear whether is it only the wronged party who can offer forgiveness or whether it can or must involve some third party who intervenes between victim and perpetrator. On the one hand, there is reason to accept that forgiveness 'in the strict sense' must be a direct and unmediated matter between the parties involved. On the other hand, there is reason to say that forgiveness can only be realised by virtue of the mediation of some universalising instance such as the State, the law or language. There can be no scene of forgiveness without a common language in which to understand the nature of the wrong, the identity of the guilty party, etc.: 'when the victim and the guilty share no language, when nothing common and universal permits them to understand one another, forgiveness seems deprived of meaning' (Derrida 2001b, 48).

6. In the Australian case, the exchange involved is that of the legitimacy of a nation-state which aspires to be post-colonial in return for land and perhaps some special rights on the part of the indigenous inhabitants. 'It is always the same concern: to see to it that the nation survives its discords, that the traumatisms give way to the work or mourning, and that the nation-State not be overcome by paralysis' (Derrida 2001b, 41).

7. With regard to law and justice in general, Derrida argues that the deconstruction of existing law 'takes place in the interval that separates the undeconstructibility of justice from the deconstructibility of *droit* (authority, legitimacy and so on)' (Derrida 1992b, 15).

8. In *Deleuze and the Political*, I call this 'critical freedom' in order to distinguish it from liberal concepts of positive and negative freedom (Patton 2000, 83–7).

9. In his earlier work, Deleuze did point to the paradoxical character of the objects of specifically philosophical thought. For example, in *The Logic of Sense*, he introduces the concept of pure events via a discussion of the Stoics and the paradoxes which they identified in relation to the temporal identity of events (Deleuze 1990, 1, 8). In *Difference and Repetition*, he drew on Kant's suggestion that the transcendental ideas which are the objects of reason are like problems which have no solution in order to describe the objects of philosophical thought as transcendental ideas or problems. Just as pure events are supposed to be independent of their actualisations so transcendental problems were considered to be irreducible to the particular solutions in which they are incarnated. The clearest cases of irresolvable problems are of course paradoxes and, at one point, Deleuze refers to the transcendental object of the faculty of sociability as 'the paradox of society' (Deleuze 1994, 208).

10. 'The event only happens under the aegis of the impossible. When an event, efficiency, or anything is deemed possible, it means that we have already mastered, anticipated, pre-understood and reduced the eventhood of the event' (Derrida 2002a, 194).

11. See Deleuze's comments on the sense in which Nietzsche called for the creation of new values where the new 'with its power of beginning and beginning again, remains forever new . . .' (Deleuze 1994, 136).

12. See the comments on Deleuze and Derrida and the time of the event in Lorraine, Chapter 2, pp. 36–9, 41–3, and also the comments by Lawlor, Chapter 4, pp. 75–7. Simon Critchley comments, with regard to the role of the concept of the here-now (*l'ici-maintenant*) in *Specters of Marx*, 'that the entire plausibility of *Specters of Marx* rests upon the difficult thought of the *here and maintaining-now without presence as an impossible experience of justice*. If this thought proves absolutely unintelligible, then one can perhaps follow Derrida no further' (Critchley 1999, 153–4).

CHAPTER 2

Living a Time Out of Joint

Tamsin Lorraine

INTRODUCTION

Gilles Deleuze's critique of representational thought and Jacques Derrida's critique of the metaphysics of presence have radical consequences for the way we view ourselves and our relationship to time. Each attempts a philosophy true to the differentiating movement of life rather than the reified fixations of a world construed in terms of the category of substance. Both go beyond Heidegger's notion of human being-in-the-world as ecstatic temporality and gesture towards the dispersed self of a time out of joint. This self and this time defy representation and can appear only through what would be paradoxical to common-sense thought. And yet it is in the attempt to think beyond the confines of common sense that Deleuze and Derrida believe the ethics of a new millennium is to be found. For both, to confine ourselves to the stable identities and chronological time of conventional meaning is to stifle our creative capacity to respond to life's novelty. We can never do justice to the singularity of this experience here-right-now with representations drawn from our past. To think that we can is to do violence to what always exceeds such representations: the dynamic force of life in its singular unfolding. A dynamic conception of life demands confrontation with the paradoxes that challenge our positioning in the temporal whole. Deleuze and Derrida take on this task in various ways throughout their work. Here I explore the ramifications of their respective notions of time through the exemplary struggles of characters like Alice and Hamlet as they are pushed against the limits of ordinary temporality.

Alice is the little girl who experiences the strange becomings (of her own body, of babies to pigs, of chess pieces to people) and bizarre time (the white rabbit's incessant tardiness, the tea party where it is always 6 o'clock, the backward-running time of the looking-glass world) of a humorous world beyond ordinary sense. Her adventures with seismic body-becomings and monstrous word-play entail exploring the limit between words and things where chronology breaks down and identity fractures. And yet, despite an occasional twinge of anxiety, Alice participates in her new surroundings with delightful ease and resourcefulness. If Lewis Carroll is fascinated with little girls, it is likely because they can handle the becomings of his invented worlds with such aplomb. By the end of *Through the Looking Glass*, when Alice has managed to make the chess moves needed to become queen, one imagines that she will have grown up enough to play by the 'right' rules and will thus no longer be able to tolerate the ambiguities of Wonderland. At the same time as one has to applaud her for satisfying her most fervent wish, one must also mourn her departure from a realm where becoming reigns supreme and meaning extends beyond its usual limits.

While Carroll's work could be read as a childish fantasy, Hamlet's darker experience of another time may seem all too real: acts beyond Hamlet's control command him to respond, but since those acts monstrously violate the sense of his world, time itself is out of joint, leaving him paralysed. To honour his father, he must set things right. But to set things right, he must be other than he is. Hamlet, like Alice, is forced to deal with unsettling becomings and a time out of time that puts his reality as well as his identity at risk. Exploring these two figures (as well as one or two others along the way) in light of Deleuze's notions of the time of Aion and the empty form of time, and Derrida's notions of the impossible time of the gift and the mad moment when justice is done, reveals the possibility of a subject able to do life justice by affirming the fractured effects of an unrepresentable time.

Derrida and Deleuze have very different styles and projects, and yet, what I have chosen to do here is to pursue a line of flight between the two. While Derrida shies away from any ontologising definition of a new time and self, Deleuze is less reticent. Rather than focus on how one or the other falls short in terms of the standards set by the other, I have linked their work into a Deleuzean trajectory that aligns the intensities of particular texts. Derrida's deconstructive strategy loosens our grip on traditional points of reference in deference to the singularity of the here-right-now. The practice of an incessant deconstruction refuses the lures sense can provide in the stabilised meanings of propositional thought and thus performatively confronts us with a time out of time. Deleuze, by giving us concepts to track what insists in our lives without being fully present, gives us another kind of strategy for leaving the reference points of equilibrium states behind and conceiving of time as a fractured chaosmos of incompossible perspectives. Together they suggest that the reconception of time is a crucial component of a 'post-modern' ethics.

SENSE, THE EVENT AND THE TIME OF AION

In *The Logic of Sense*, Deleuze claims that Carroll's play with the paradoxes of sense in his books recounting Alice's adventures involve a category of 'very special things': pure events (Deleuze 1990, 1). Deleuze takes the notion of the incorporeal realm of the event from the Stoics whom he claims were the first to distinguish it from the realm of mixed bodies and states of affairs. The time of this realm of becomings is the time of Aion – an achronological time where everything always has already happened and is yet to come. In this section, I explore Deleuze's conception of the 'pure event' and the logic of sense it comprises by considering Alice's adventures in another time. I elaborate a conception of a subject able to live in a time out of time by taking into account Deleuze's description of three syntheses of time in *Difference and Repetition*. In the first synthesis of habit (inspired by Hume) chronological before and after emerge in the habitual patterns of organic stimulus and response. The second synthesis of active memory (inspired by Bergson) is dependent upon a pure past never actually lived. It is the third synthesis (inspired by Nietzsche) – where habits and memories are lost and only the empty form of time remains – that is the closest to the time of Aion. These syntheses can be correlated with three subjects: an organism ruled by instinctual response, a human subject who can learn from her mistakes by reflecting upon the past, and Nietzsche's overman – a subject beyond the human who affirms life by evolving with (rather than within) an unrepresentable time. Although Alice's marginality as a little girl may give her an advantage in the humorous realm of the event, it will take Hamlet and Nietzsche's notion of the overman to suggest some answers to the question of how one can live an impossible time that ruptures all chronology as a subject of the realm of actual states of affairs as well as the realm of incorporeal becoming.

In Wonderland the temporality of good sense and the personal identity of common sense are broken, but rather than schizophrenia or psychosis, the humorous result reveals the surface effects of a sense upon which both good sense and common sense are predicated. Carroll's play with the paradoxes of sense exploits relations of meaning that violate our sense of physical possibility. In *The Logic of Sense*, Deleuze elaborates how Carroll's 'nonsense' pertains to the realm of a 'very special' kind of incorporeal entity that 'frolics' above physical things. We ascribe propositions ('Alice eats cake') to mixtures of bodies and states of affairs (Alice eats a piece of cake while sitting under a table or growing out of a house). 'The event is not what occurs (an accident), it is rather inside what occurs, the purely expressed' (Deleuze 1990, 149). I can ascribe the proposition 'Alice becomes larger' to a little girl with a cat named Dinah, but the sense of this proposition also expresses an event or pure becoming where becoming goes in both directions at once; 'one becomes larger than one was and smaller than one becomes' (Deleuze 1990, 1). There is no good sense by which to establish the 'appropriate' direction of a pure becoming; it 'divides itself infinitely in past and future and always eludes the present' (Deleuze 1990, 5). An event is not a living present, but an infinitive. Events are actualised in individuals and states of affairs, but subsist in those actualisations rather than being completely manifest in them; any number of states of affairs can actualise the same events. Furthermore, events have relationships that are independent of the instantiations of those events in specific states of affairs. I can extrapolate various connections among propositions like 'Alice knows a Cheshire cat' and 'cats can grin' that may or may not be related to physical states of affairs. Such connections are indicative of relations among incorporeal events (being Alice, knowing a Cheshire cat, being able to grin) distinct from those of material things. The relations of events taken independently from the mixtures of bodies and states of affairs of the material world act as a kind of quasi-cause. On the one hand, this realm is impassive when it comes to states of affairs – the relations of the three events of being Alice, eating cake, and shrinking will never produce the state of affairs in which Alice eats cake and shrinks (except in Wonderland!). On the other hand, sense is productive – little girls may act in what may seem to be peculiar ways because they believe they will shrink upon eating a piece of cake.

When I have the good sense to adhere to the laws of logic that suggest that things have a time and a place (and so can not be in two places at one time), then other people are able to understand what I say. But when I enter the realm of the pure event, I may begin to speak 'nonsense'. Good sense entails a socially sanctioned chronology according to a shared time-line by which what happens is unambiguously marked as before or after other occurrences. Common sense tells Alice that her faculties of sensation, imagination, memory and thought are all those of one 'I' and that the different sensations, imaginings, memories and thoughts she has can be grouped according to their objects.

The nonsensical world of Wonderland is the realm of the event or pure becoming – a time of the meanwhile in which the distinction between 'before' and 'after' is lost, cats vanish into thin air, and Alice is no longer sure of who she is. At the Mad Hatter's tea party the event of having tea at six always has already started and is yet to start (it is always simultaneously closer to six o'clock than it was and further from six than it will be). In this time of the meanwhile, habitual reaction and chronological time are suspended. At the Mad Hatter's tea party there is always room for more bread and butter and time does not pass as it should. According to Deleuze's description of the second synthesis of time, the memory of a specific past moment depends upon the passive synthesis of a virtual past that is irreducible to past moments; it is only with respect to the past in general that a memory can stand out as a memory. The expansion of the meanwhile in the time of Wonderland evokes this Bergsonian notion of a virtual past: in the achronological time of Aion all events can relate in a pure becoming freed from the restrictions of physical causation. From the perspective of the third synthesis inspired by Nietzsche's notion of the eternal return, the virtual past is a generative force of becoming that manifests in the present actualisations of an incoherent and incompossible totality of refracting viewpoints towards an inconceivable future. It is the overman who is able to break free from representations of a chronological past in order to draw upon the virtual past as a durational whole in resolving the problems of living. A brief recap of Deleuze's three syntheses of time – habit, memory and the empty form of time – indicates how sense can insist in the virtual past in the form of a problem and how Alice, although able to live beyond conventional chronology, has not quite attained the life-affirming capacity of the Nietzschean subject able to act in a time out of time.

Deleuze derives a notion of the living present as a contraction or synthesis of time from Hume: two moments (for example the tick-tock of a clock) are impressed upon the imagination which acts as a kind of sensitive plate that retains one moment (or one case of two moments) as the next appears. This results in a living present that is a synthesis of the past (the retention of preceding moments or cases, say two tick-tocks) and the future (anticipation that the next moment or case will be like the past, the expectation that yet another tick-tock will follow). In *Difference and Repetition*, Deleuze suggests that the passive perceptual syntheses of imagination are preceded by thousands of passive syntheses at the organic level of the organism which are 'the primary habits we are' (Deleuze 1994, 74). Habit is thus a contraction of habitual contractions that occur on multiple levels. The synthesis of habit is prior to the memory and recollection of conscious thought. It provides a rule for the future lived by the body in the form of sensory-motor responses to present stimuli that anticipate that the future will be like the past. The past is retained in the depth of bodies through habitual patterns of instinctual response from which it is difficult to detach. In *Creative Evolution*, Bergson claims that what distinguishes instinctual response from the free response of a thinking organism that can make choices is that there is a gap between the stimulus and response of the latter. The instinctual organism responds with the one response the stimulus calls for. The thinking organism can make a choice between more than one kind of response through a comparative analysis of situations that may be similar although they are never exactly the same. This allows the organism to learn from situations and adapt its responses to changing circumstances.

Bergson's conception of memory in *Matter and Memory* suggests that through the creation of recollection-images drawn from the virtual totality of the past, human beings are able to respond creatively to problems posed by the present. Deleuze elaborates Bergson's notion of a virtual or 'pure' past, claiming that this past that has never actually been lived 'insists' (as opposed to overtly manifesting or actualising) in the present in the form of a problem. The second synthesis of time involves both a passive and active synthesis of memory. Memory passively synthesises the pure past in relation to which the present now and a former present moment can stand out as particular moments with a specific place ('now' and 'before') in a temporal chronology. It is due to the active syntheses of memory and understanding (founded upon the passive syntheses of the living present of habit and grounded in the passive synthesis of the 'pure past' of memory) that the past can become a series of representations upon which the subject can reflect (Deleuze 1994, 71). The passive syntheses of habit and memory are sub-representative. It is the active syntheses of memory and understanding that turn life into repeatable representations that have a specific place in a chronology. The relations of the active syntheses of memory include 'relations of virtual coexistence between the levels of a pure past, each present being no more than the actualisation or representation of one of these levels' (Deleuze 1994, 83).

Deleuze appeals to Proust to show that there is a way in which we could 'live the being in itself of the past in the same way that we live the passive synthesis of habit' (Deleuze 1994, 84). Proustian reminiscence refers to an involuntary memory (as opposed to an active searching into the past for a specific memory-image) that concerns the past not as it has been, but as it never was – for example, the splendour of Combray (evoked by the eating of the madeleine). It is our experience of a pure past never actually lived that provides hints of the transcendental field of the virtual and a conception of time as a durational whole. Involuntary memories link together two moments – a present moment and a past moment never actually lived drawn from the virtual relations of the pure past – in keeping with an unrepresentable problem. A specific state of affairs may actualise an event, but only with respect to a problem that can never be manifest in a given state of affairs or fully presented in a proposition. It is to this problem that life responds without being able to articulate it as such. Like the generative force of time or sense, this problem pushes us towards a future that cannot be constrained within representations drawn from the past. Just as the relations of events in the meanwhile of pure becoming defy the constraints of physical causality and the instinctual response of habit, so do the relations of the various levels of the pure past defy chronology. Active memory becomes creative when it moves beyond chronological representations and actualises the relations of the virtual past in response to a present problem.

According to Deleuze's conceptions of the time syntheses of habit and memory, chronological time is constructed not simply through the mental representations of our minds, but the needs of our bodies. The play of nonsense locates us in the realm of the pure event or the incorporeal entities of sense where sense is related through a quasi-cause independent of the causal relations of physical things. This allows us to move beyond the merely reactive responses of habitual response and creatively access the virtual totality of time. Mechanical repetition is superceded by creative evolution. Time as a virtual chaosmos is replete with the force of novel becomings that defy the represent-able forms of the past. The direct time-image of the third synthesis emphasises a virtual past that never existed in the moment-to-moment experience of any given individual and yet subsists in the present with implicit force. Events like 'to eat cake' and 'to grow' constitute the force of time or temporal becoming. They inhere in the determinate series that actualise them (Alice eats cake and grows smaller, Alice eats cake and grows larger) without ever becoming completely present. Happenings like Alice's fall down the rabbit hole are implicit in the sense of events like 'being Alice' and 'to fall' and yet can never exhaust all the forms the actualisations of those events might take.

Because Carroll emphasises the paradoxical realm of the event, Alice may not be the best example of a subject grappling with a problem organically experienced through the habitual responses of the body as well as the more active responses of reflective consciousness. The Alice books mark the transi-tion a little girl makes from the infant plunged into the depths of bodily concerns to the realm of the surface prior to developing the sexuality of an adolescent or adult. She is thus able to inhabit a world where she is not predominated by bodily need. A language that speaks only to things descends to the depths and loses the world of the pure event. A language that speaks only of events ascends to the heights and loses the world of bodies that affect and are affected by other bodies. It is in living at the limits of both words and things where sense operates in tension between the two, that Alice could become the Nietzschean subject able to increase her power to affect and be affected by creatively actualising forces subsisting in the virtual past in response to problems posed by a specific confluence of forces in the present.

Alice accepts the fluctuations of her body and the bodies around her and is able to create new sense by making connections drawn from the virtual relations of events, but it is to Hamlet we may need to look for an example of someone fully alive to the tension between words and things. Hamlet is Deleuze's example of someone forced by circumstances to experience the third synthesis of time. Prior to his father's murder, the time of Hamlet's world was subordinated to 'those properly cardinal points through which pass the periodic movements which it measures' (Deleuze 1994, 88); time was measured with respect to the orderly movements of his world. A 'time out of joint means demented time or time outside the curve which gave it a god . . . freed from the events which made up its content, its relation to movement overturned' (ibid.). Chronological time is measured against events that repeat at regular intervals: the sun rises and sets, the king takes a queen, they have a son, the king dies, the prince becomes king. The time of life unfolds against the rhythm of a specific set of events against which the rest can be measured. With the murder of the king by his own brother and the unnatural marriage of the murderer to Hamlet's mother, the movements by which time had been measured are disrupted, leaving only the empty form of time. Time itself unfolds rather than being measured against the movement of things unfolding within it. If a king's throne and bed can be usurped by his own brother, then there is no set of events that come in a chronological order with respect to which other events can be ordered. Chronology is ruptured and the time of Aion – the time of the meanwhile in which all events are related to all other events – comes to the fore.

Shakespeare's play recounts a temporal as well as ethical dilemma. The time out of joint looms for Hamlet as the totality of time in the act required to set things right, 'a unique and tremendous event, an act which is adequate to time as a whole' (Deleuze 1994, 89). Hamlet must reestablish the meaning of his world by establishing a new chronology despite his glimpse of a time without the repetition of events that happen at regular intervals. The symbolic act of murdering his uncle is the act by which he will attempt to reorder chronology. The temporal series of past, present and future that Hamlet undergoes in the madness of a time that has lost its bearings are distributed with respect to this symbolic event. The first part of the symbolic act is lived in the past when Hamlet imagines the required act as too big for him and can only obsess about the monstrous murder of his father and heinous marriage of his mother. The act of murdering his uncle will establish the new before and after against which time can be measured. It will establish the self he is as a past self, one that belongs to the old order, the ruptured order put right by the self of the new order. The second part of the symbol is lived in the present of metamorphosis – the sea voyage upon which Hamlet experiences 'a becoming-equal to the act and a doubling of the self, and the projection of an ideal self in the image of the act'. Hamlet moves into the present of the symbolic act as he draws upon the virtual past, the meanwhile in which all events are related, to become-equal to the event of murdering his uncle. The future of the symbolic event is where 'the event and the act possess a secret coherence which excludes that of the self' (Deleuze 1994, 89). Hamlet becomes equal to the event in a becoming-other in which his self is smashed to pieces: 'what the self has become equal to is the unequal in itself' (Deleuze 1994, 90). To murder his uncle, Hamlet must become a self that would have made no sense to the self of the old order – the self who regulated his meaning and his movement against the regularities of kinship and the king. To become the Hamlet that can set things right, he must measure himself against an order that is yet to be created. He becomes equal to the empty form of time (and loses himself in the process) by becoming with time itself rather than measuring time by the movements contained within it.

In *The Logic of Sense*, Deleuze alludes to an ethics derived from Stoicism: to be ethical is 'not to be unworthy of what happens to us' (Deleuze 1990, 149). This entails becoming the quasi-cause of what is produced within us. That is, one wills 'not exactly what occurs, but something *in* that which occurs, something yet to come which would be consistent with what occurs, in accordance with the laws of an obscure, humorous conformity: the Event' (ibid.). The meaning of what happens to us may be expressible in propositions, but we will never be able to express fully the sense of what happens to us, no matter how long we talk. Events are caused by states of affairs and the passions and actions of bodies, but their quasi-causality expresses 'an aggregate of noncausal correspondences which form a system of echoes, of resumptions and resonances, a system of signs' (Deleuze 1990, 170). The relations of events express alogical compatibilities or incompatibilities. An event can generate propositions that defy conventional notions of identity and time.

It was Leibniz, according to Deleuze, who was the important theoretician of the event. His concepts of compossibility and incompossibility refer to the convergence of series informed by the conjunctive 'and' and the divergence of series informed by the disjunctive 'or'. The series of states of affairs that actualise the event of being Hamlet can be expressed in the predicates that converge in the world of Shakespeare's play (Hamlet sees his father's ghost, murders Polonius, is poisoned, dies). It was Nietzsche who posited a point of view which is opened onto a divergence of series it affirms. Nietzsche's discovery was that of a world of nomadic singularities, no longer imprisoned in God or the finite subject. Prior to the death of his father, Hamlet could be a good son *and* a good nephew *and* a good prince, but how could he affirm the diverging series 'good son to his father' *or* 'good son to his mother' *or* 'good nephew' *or* 'good prince' upon the rupture of the old order in which his self made sense? In Nietzsche's notion of the eternal return, all events communicate and no predicate is excluded in the event of events. This is a synthetic, affirmative disjunction which spells death to the self, the world, and God 'to the advantage of divergent series as such, overflowing now every exclusion, every conjunction, and every connection' (Deleuze 1990, 176). Instead of excluding predicates from a thing in virtue of the identity of its concept, Nietzsche opened each 'thing' up to the infinity of predicates through which it passes, 'as it loses its center, that is, its identity as concept or as self' (1990, 174). Hamlet is faced with a similar opening of meaning with the rupture of the old order. Even Zarathustra, Nietzsche's teacher of the eternal return, could only hint at the overman as the possible subject of such a synthesis of time: a nomadic subject actualised in a divergent series of states rather than a coherent subject actualised in a series converging upon a recognisable identity or biography. To be worthy of an event is to respond to the generating force of sense as a dynamic and always unpredictable force of becoming. It is to respond to the insistence of a problem actualising the potential subsisting in a virtual past that defies capture in a representable chronology. Hamlet was forced to respond to a time out of joint and was able to overcome his paralysis by committing himself to a temporal order that constituted a break with a representable past. But he was destroyed in the process. The Nietzschean subject, instead of succumbing to confusion or paralysis in the presence of an incoherent convergence of forces, will further develop and differentiate the extent to which it can affect and be affected. It will actualise (and counter-actualise, cf. Deleuze 1990, 150) events in ways that increase the power of the body, even if one form of its body is left behind in its unfolding process of becoming-other. It will affirm this process of becoming-other and the disjunctions that spell death to particular formations of the self (and God) and unfold with (rather than within) an unmeasurable time.

Alice is a fascinating example of a little girl able to depart from good sense in order to experience the strange time of the surface and abandon common sense in order to experience the vicissitudes of a fluctuating self. This allows her to depart from the problems posed by common sense and respond to problems that defy a conventional understanding of selves and time. Neither Alice nor Hamlet, however, is fully able to complete the transition to the time of the Nietzschean subject of the eternal return – the overman able to make the shift to a new image of thought. While most of us live by the time of good sense, the Nietzschean subject is able to defy such sense and experience the creative evolution of self in exploration of a deeper memory – the virtual memory of the pure past as the event of events of the eternal return. Rather than a self-identical self, the self of the third synthesis of time is a creatively evolving self who is able to genuinely affirm life as metamorphosis.

THE GIFT, JUSTICE AND THE TIME OUT OF JOINT

Derrida, like Carroll, often evokes paradox by playing with the precise meaning of words. It is by pursuing meaning to its limits that he goes beyond common sense to the mad sense that encompasses it. It is the 'proper' self who remains the same from chronological instant to instant who assimilates her understanding of herself and others to a symbolic economy in which all subjects and outcomes can be calculated. Such assimilation refuses difference and the truly novel. It reduces the other to the status quo and innovation to the repetition of the same. Madame de Maintenon (the non-wife of the king), like Alice, is enough of a non-subject to have a different relationship to time than that of a more 'proper' subject. In this section, I consider Derrida's treatment of Maintenon's relationship to time and the gift in *Given Time*, and then turn to his discussion in *Specters of Marx* of Hamlet's attempt to 'learn to live' in a time out of joint. Derrida's notions of the impossible time of the gift as well as of that mad moment when justice is done, like Deleuze's notions of Aion and the third synthesis of time, point towards an unrepresentable time beyond time.

Derrida begins *Given Time* with a letter from Madame de Maintenon in which she talks about giving time she doesn't have to give: 'The King takes all my time; I give the rest to Saint-Cyr, to whom I would like to give all' (Derrida 1992c, 1). Derrida points out that when Maintenon says that 'she would like to give all [*elle voudrait* le tout *donner*]' the meaning of this phrase is equivocal between 'all my time' and 'all of the rest of my time' (left by the King), and further equivocal between the time left by the King and the time left after giving to Saint-Cyr ('the rest of the rest of time'). In any case, Derrida claims, one hears 'the infinite sigh of unsatisfied desire': Madame de Maintenon desires to give what she cannot give, 'everything leaves her something to be desired' (Derrida 1992c, 4). She cannot give all her time to Saint-Cyr since the King takes (all) her time. She cannot give the rest of her time to Saint-Cyr since there is no left-over time to give. For a similar reason, she cannot give the rest of the time left over after giving the rest of her time to Saint-Cyr.

Furthermore, since time does not belong to anyone as such – 'one can no more *take* it, itself, than *give* it' – neither can the King take her time, nor can she give her time to Saint-Cyr. '[O]ne can only exchange, one can only take or give, by way of metonymy, what is *in* time' (Derrida 1992c, 3). The whole of her desire is 'this rest of the rest of time, of a time that moreover is nothing and that belongs properly to no one' (Derrida 1992c, 4). Maintenon would like to make a 'present' of this time, but it is both impossible to make 'a present' of activities that extend over time as well as to 'give herself this power of giving' that would refuse delimitation into one who gives, something that is given, and one who takes (ibid.).

The gift Maintenon wants to give is doubly impossible since it is the gift of time. If there is a gift, it – like time itself – must concern what occurs before 'any conscious or unconscious relation to self or the subject' (Derrida 1992c, 24). The excessive sense of a gift event is cancelled out by the very words ('donor', 'gift', 'receiver') with which we attempt to acknowledge it. If the gift is to do more than cancel or incur a debt, it must somehow break out of an economy of exchange and the symbolic economy of language. To do this would require a 'paradoxical instant . . . [that] tears time apart' (Derrida 1992c, 9). That Maintenon attempts to express an impossible desire, Derrida implies, is because she is able to tolerate the ambiguity of an incalculable subject position (in her case, being the non-wife of the king) and a time that refuses the traditional divisions of chronology.

In *Specters*, Derrida considers the case of Hamlet, a young man who is confronted with the daunting task of 'learning to live' (Derrida 1994b, xviii) in a 'time out of joint'. In 'The Time Out of Joint', Derrida writes that Hamlet survives 'what one does not survive' (Derrida 1995f, 36–7): he witnesses the disorder and injustice caused by a man who with his murder of Hamlet's father and marriage to Hamlet's mother not only violates the bonds of blood (by murdering his own brother), but also usurps the father's place in bed and upon the throne. Derrida quotes Nietzsche to suggest that Hamlet is like the Dionysian man in that the knowledge he has gained looking 'truly into the essence of things' inspires nausea rather than action. Both 'feel it to be ridiculous or humiliating that they should be asked to set right a world that is out of joint. Knowledge kills action; action requires the veils of illusion: that is the doctrine of Hamlet' (Derrida 1995f, 36). If Hamlet's dilemma was simply to respond as one should given his unambiguous location in a world ordered into one seamless whole (as son to his father, the King of Denmark, for example), setting things right would have meant simply to restore the rightful order. But what Hamlet knows is that life has no one order; there is no definitive meaning that can be given to Hamlet's situation. The order of his father has been overturned. The present order profanes his father's spirit. How is Hamlet to deal with the disjuncture of the two orders? What action could set things right?

In *Specters*, Derrida emphasises the ambiguous status of Hamlet's ghost. He is wearing full armour and so is visored in a way that allows him to see without being seen, putting his identity into doubt. Hamlet must take the word of a spectre between being and non-being about the crime of another, a crime that he has not himself witnessed, but can only fantasise. Hamlet curses the destiny that makes him the one 'to do justice, to put things back in order, to put history, the world, the age, the time *upright*, on the right path, so that, in conformity with the rule of its correct functioning, it advances straight ahead [*tout droit*] – and following the law [*le droit*]' (Derrida 1995f, 20). To do justice to Hamlet's inheritance, he must struggle to align the sense of the present with his sense of an order that no longer exists. To act justly, Hamlet must come to terms with all the spectres that haunt his current situation. This includes not simply the spectral hovering of his father, but also the spectral nature of a crime committed by another, a crime 'whose event and reality, whose truth can never *present themselves* in flesh and blood, but can only allow themselves to be presumed, reconstructed, fantasized' (Derrida 1995f, 21). Derrida points out that the disjuncture of Hamlet's dilemma is not simply that caused by an unjust act, but the perennial disjuncture that is the 'place for justice'. That is, the disjuncture 'that opens up the infinite asymmetry of the relation to the other' (Derrida 1995f, 22). When he declares that 'the time is out of joint', '[w]hether he knows it or not, Hamlet is speaking in the space opened up by this question – the appeal of the gift, singularity, the coming of the event, the excessive or exceeded relation to the other' (Derrida 1995f, 23). Justice, like the gift and time itself, is no-thing. It can never be fully present; it can only insist in laws like the spectre of our father haunting us to do right without being able to show us how.

Reading 'Force of Law', one could say that deconstruction – as a kind of justice that is not law, a movement at work in law that demands gift 'without exchange, without circulation, without recognition or gratitude, without economic circularity, without calculation and without rules, without reason and without rationality' – responds to the spectres that haunt us by refusing the lures of stabilised meaning that would let us off the hook (Derrida 1992b, 25). The place for the gift, the place for justice, is opened in a time out of joint. The murder of a king is but one form the silencing of another can take. To act justly requires letting the other come to presence even when that presencing challenges ourselves and our place in a temporal order. It requires a giving that exceeds subject/object distinctions as well as the distinctions of chronology. It requires doing justice not merely to the spectre of the father, but to the spectral other whose 'crime' against paternal order can never be fully presented. The instant of the just decision 'must rend time' because the decision is a 'finite moment of urgency and precipitation' (Derrida 1992b, 26). It is in the moment of pragmatic action that interpretation of the law gets ahead of itself, leaving in its wake any regulative or messianic horizon of expectation. Because of 'this always excessive haste of interpretation getting ahead of itself,' Derrida asserts, it may have a 'to-come' which 'I rigorously distinguish from the future that can always reproduce the present' (Derrida 1992b, 27).

According to Derrida, justice is incalculably geared towards the singular, and therefore fails insofar as it is calculated according to a rule of law or assimilated to a symbolic economy. And yet, like the excess of the gift, it is the excess of justice – that which we can never make present, that sense which is forever beyond the reach of the present meaning of our words – that provides the force that makes the symbolic economy run. Derrida suggests that deconstruction may consist in 'putting "out of joint" the authority of the "is"' (Derrida 1995f, 25). His problem is to do this without succumbing to either madness or nonsense. To be just, Hamlet must consider the spectres that put his time out of joint and yet make a decision and take action. To be a just queen, Alice, from a Derridean perspective, must do better than the Queen of Hearts with her arbitrary rules (be it for croquet or the trial of the Knave of Hearts); she must do justice to the spectres that insist in the laws we inherit.

Derrida shows us how to read texts and situations in a way that honours their polyvocal resonances rather than assimilating them to any easy application of a rule. The words we use enter into relations of their own independently of the actual situation in which we use them. They can be impervious to our intended meanings, alluding to meanings we never consciously had in mind. And yet it is the singularity of the here-right-now to which we want our words to do justice. To do justice to the here-right-now means precisely not to assume that the meanings of our words are fully present. Instead it means to pursue the differentiating force of sense in light of a living present that is never a plenitude, but always bears traces of another time.

Deconstruction walks the tension between words and things by forever refusing to finalise an interpretation. Instead, it exploits the relations of sense at work in a text, rendering them explicit in order to show how all meaning draws upon and returns to a paradoxical set of relations. Some of these relations are more 'just' to a given situation. They may exert a force upon it that shows us something new about what we can do, how we can act. But all form the background to any given interpretation. The more we attend to unravelling the meaning of our words, the more we realise how difficult it is to do justice to life. The more we try to take responsibility for the trails of sense that lie in the wake of our speech, the more we find ourselves connected to a larger context that forever eludes us. The ultimate context is the world as a whole, a world with no beginning or end that provides the background to all our experiences. This world is not the rational, totalisable whole of absolute time and space where everything has its 'proper' location. Instead it is the non-totalisable whole of différance out of which emerge paradoxical times and impossible subjects. Deconstruction asks us to challenge our comfortable positioning in the contemporary order (if, indeed, our positions are comfort-able) to become another kind of subject. One who attempts to take responsi-bility for the proliferating trails of sense she leaves behind in her meaning-making. One who attends very carefully both to pragmatic context and the use of language in order to do justice to the here-right-now of singular situations. One who refuses the comfort of a designated place in a temporal whole in order to embrace a fractured time open to the 'infinite asymmetry of the relation to the other'.

TIME OUT OF JOINT: THE TIME OF A
DELEUZEAN/DERRIDEAN ETHICS

Chronological time suggests that each moment in our existence is securely established and that our deeds and accomplishments are somehow enshrined in a past that remains stable – even as it recedes from us. As each moment slides from the present into the past, we can reassure ourselves that we are adding recognisable blocks to a building of our future we collectively share. A time out of joint suggests that there is no way to calibrate the pasts of our lived experience into a unified chronology. Chronological time is constructed out of the habitual reactions of bodies, the memories and expectations of conscious reflection, and collective forms of interpreting the past insisting in our present. We erase incongruities and smooth out paradox in order to create the delusion of time as a seamless whole.

The time of the gift and justice is the time of the meanwhile where the 'proper' boundaries between subject and object, before and after, dissolve and all becomings are ultimately related in the event of events of the eternal return. Such a time breaks with representation and traditional forms of narrative. The dissolved self of the meanwhile forgets habitual responses and represents no former present to herself. Instead she extends her actions in a movement of creative evolution. Virtual events are actualised in the unfolding series of states constituting her individuation. The events of 'to give' and 'to be just' thus actualised communicate with other events in the chaosmos of the transcendental field of virtualities. Individuals unfold in rhythm with problems incommensurate with the problems of others. The time out of time hinted at by the temporal paradoxes of living suggest not an infinite container encompassing the finite times of individuals, but a temporal chaosmos or virtual totality actualised in incompossible perspectives. Each expression of this impossible time is a shard refracting a durational whole, attempting to manifest the full power to affect and be affected of a singularity in its unfolding among the other processes of individuation that enhance and impede its actualisation. Time is the unrepresentable totality of these refracted lives that can never be gathered into the rationalised unity of one temporal order.

Language (and art forms like cinema) allows us to access time as a virtual totality. Just as sense insists in the meaning of our propositions, unfolding in the strange adventures of Alice in Wonderland or the multiple deaths of Hamlet's tragedy, so does the past insist in our present. If an event like 'to live' is a virtual singularity inhering in all its actualisations and counteractualisations, then each of us actualises that event in our own way, doing our best to become worthy of living by willing the meanings we think are expressed in that event. Even as we confront the barriers created by incommensurate problems and perspectives we are connected by converging series of actualisations and the virtual chaosmos that is their condition.

Both Derrida and Deleuze advocate a shift to a way of thinking that refuses the comfortable illusions of captured sense and instead pursues the force of time in the becoming of meaning. Derrida prefers staging encounters with this impossible time to naming it, demanding that we do justice to the abyssal dissonance created in each encounter. Responsibility to the other demands disjointing our time in order to allow the presencing of others even when such presencing violates our own sense of the 'proper'. Congealing our meaning in metaphysical language is a continual threat to the temporality in which this responsibility can unfold. Deleuze creates a series of concepts meant to track a sense that can never be completely present at the same time that it insists in the fractured perspectives of a durational whole. The concepts of the event, the time of Aion, and the event of events of the eternal return are virtual singularities through which we can actualise a thinking that approaches an unrepresentable time. The shift to a non-representational image of time – one that could reveal the intensive processes of becoming rather than reifying the equilibrium states of its continual unfolding – could reveal a different kind of subjectivity, one able to do justice to the other, to the tension between words and things, and to life, despite the fractured time of its evolutions in learning to live.

CHAPTER 3

Deleuze and Derrida, Immanence and Transcendence: Two Directions in Recent French Thought

Daniel W. Smith

In a recent essay, Giorgio Agamben has identified two different trajectories in contemporary French philosophy, both of which pass through Heidegger: a trajectory of *transcendence*, which includes Levinas and Derrida, and goes back through Husserl to Kant; and a trajectory of *immanence*, which includes Foucault and Deleuze, and goes back through Nietzsche to Spinoza.[1] Deleuze and Levinas are no doubt the most obvious representatives of these two trajectories: Deleuze explicitly describes himself as a philosopher of immanence, while Levinas explicitly claims the mantle of transcendence (the 'Other' being the paradigmatic concept of transcendence). But Derrida clearly belongs to the trajectory of transcendence as well, and Agamben's typology thus provides us with a valuable grid for assessing the relation between Derrida and Deleuze, at least in a preliminary manner. Agamben does not himself develop his insight in detail, and perhaps for good reason. Immanence and transcendence are both highly overdetermined terms in the history of philosophy, and it is not immediately clear what it would mean to be a philosopher of either one. The very term 'transcendence' has theological and spiritual overtones that tend to obscure the wider history and varied philosophical uses of the concept. Moreover, one might be tempted to question the use of such a 'binary opposition' to characterise philosophers like Derrida and Deleuze, given their shared critique of the use of oppositional strategies in philosophy. But such a dismissal would be both hasty and superficial. Immanence and transcendence are relative terms, not opposites, which means that in each case one must ask: Immanent to what? Or transcendent to what? As such, immanence and transcendence can be helpful terms not so much in determining the differing 'positions' of Derrida and Deleuze, but rather as means of charting out their differing philosophical 'trajectories', at least relative to each other. There are three traditional areas of philosophy, in particular, in which these terms have found a specific use – namely, the fields of subjectivity, ontology and epistemology. Derrida and Deleuze have written on each of these topics, and although these fields certainly do not exhaust the themes of immanence and transcendence, they nonetheless provide points of reference from which we can evaluate the work of Derrida and Deleuze using Agamben's typology. In what follows, then, I would like to consider each of these domains in turn, showing how, in each case, Derrida explicitly aligns himself with the trajectory of transcendence, while Deleuze consistently follows the trajectory of immanence. At best, this is a propadeutic study, a kind of 'vectorial' analysis that seeks to diagram, in a general manner, the divergent directions Derrida and Deleuze have followed in their philosophical careers, despite (or perhaps even because of) their initial interest in a number of shared problematics.

The tradition of subjectivity provides us with a first and obvious model of transcendence. For any philosophy that begins with the subject – that is, much of post-Cartesian philosophy – the concept of immanence refers to the sphere of the subject, while transcendence refers to what lies outside the subject, such as the 'external world' or the 'other'. In this tradition, the term 'transcendence' refers to that which transcends the field of consciousness immanent to the subject. On this score, one has only to think of the problems posed in Husserl's fifth *Cartesian Meditation*, the theme of 'Being-with-Others' in Sartre, or Levinas' own philosophy of alterity. But one also finds, in the subjectivist tradition, a second, and perhaps more profound, problem of transcendence, which is what Sartre called, in his article of the same name, 'The Transcendence of the Ego'. In Kant, the ego or the 'I think' accompanies all (or most of) my representations – it is precisely what makes them *mine*. Against Kant, Sartre pushed for a conception of an impersonal transcendental field that was without an ego, much like William James' notion of a 'pure flux of consciousness'.[2] In other words, when one says that the field of consciousness is immanent *to* a transcendental subject, one is already erecting the subject as an element of transcendence that goes beyond the flux of experience.[3] Already, then, we find two models of transcendence at work in the subjectivist tradition: the other (or the 'world', in Heidegger) is what transcends the self, but the subject itself is already transcendent in relation to 'experience' (passive syntheses). Consequently, one might say that there are two general means by which one can call into question the status of the transcendental subject (the well-known theme of the 'death of the subject'): by appealing either to *the transcendence of the other* or to *the immanent flux of experience* itself. It would be simplistic to suggest that Derrida simply followed the first path and Deleuze the second, but the 'elective affinities' of the two thinkers seem evident.

Derrida and Deleuze, however, are both critical of the subjectivist tradition, and the more telling differences between them lie elsewhere.

A second model for thinking about the immanence/transcendence distinction is related, not to the question of subjectivity (the field of consciousness) but rather to the question of ontology (the field of Being). Put simply, an immanent or pure ontology would be an ontology in which there is nothing 'beyond' or 'higher than' or 'superior to' Being. By contrast, the fundamental ontological categories of transcendence would include the 'God' of the Christian tradition, the 'Good' in Plato, the 'One' in Plotinus[4] – all of which are said to be 'beyond' Being, 'otherwise' than Being ('transcendent' to Being), and are thereby used to 'judge' Being, or at least to account for Being.[5] On the question of Being, Derrida and Deleuze – like all contemporary thinkers – are clearly indebted to Heidegger, who inaugurated the renaissance of ontology in twentieth-century thought (which is why Heidegger rightly functions as the lynchpin in Agamben's classification). Yet it is equally clear that Deleuze and Derrida take Heidegger's ontological project in two very different directions: Deleuze attempts to develop an immanent ontology, while Derrida's deconstruction necessarily operates on the basis of a formal structure of transcendence.[6] On this score, we can make use of several rubrics to help map the divergent ontological trajectories of Derrida and Deleuze: their respective relation to metaphysics, their different concepts (or 'quasi-concepts') of 'difference', and their contrasting uses of the history of philosophy (using the 'divine names' tradition as an example).

Early in his career, Derrida took over, in his own manner, the Heideggerian task of 'overcoming metaphysics', while Deleuze, for his part, would later say that 'going beyond metaphysics or the death of philosophy' had never been an issue for him (Deleuze 1995b, 88). It would not be an exaggeration to say that it was their respective adoption and rejection of this Heideggerian problematic which initially set Derrida and Deleuze on their divergent trajectories of transcendence and immanence. In Derrida, metaphysics is determined by its structural 'closure', and deconstruction is a means of disturbing this closure, creating an opening or an interruption. The notion of metaphysical closure itself depends on a movement of transcendence, that is, an 'excess over the totality, without which no totality would appear'.[7] Since one cannot transcend metaphysics as such – there is no 'outside' to the metaphysical tradition – one can only destructure or deconstruct metaphysics from within. The project of 'overcoming metaphysics', in other words, is an impossibility, but it is this very impossibility that conditions the possibility of deconstructing the philosophical tradition from within. Rather than trying to get outside metaphysics, one can submit 'the regulated play of philosophemes' in the history of philosophy to a certain slippage or sliding that would allow them to be read as 'symptoms of something that *could not be presented* in the history of philosophy' (Derrida 1981b, 6–7).[8] Immanent within metaphysics, there lies a formal structure of transcendence that can never be made present as such, but that nonetheless functions as the condition (the 'quasi-transcendental' condition) of metaphysics itself. Derrida thus situates his work, he says, at 'the *limit* of philosophical discourse', at its margins, its borders or boundary lines (Derrida 1981b, 6). The border he straddles is the border between the closed and immanent totality of metaphysics, with its exhausted concepts and philosophemes, and that which exceeds that totality, that is, a formal structure of transcendence that is, as it were, everywhere at work in metaphysics, though it can never be made present as such.

Derrida attempts to *think* this formal structure of transcendence through concepts such as *différance* (which is, then, at best a 'quasi-concept', since the notion of a concept is itself metaphysical). If metaphysics is defined in terms of presence, then *différance* is that which marks 'the disappearance of any originary presence',[9] that which thereby exceeds or transcends metaphysics, and thereby, at the same time, constantly disrupts and 'destabilises' metaphysics. Commenting on Heidegger's notion of the 'ontological difference', Derrida writes that 'there may be a difference still more unthought than the difference between Being and beings. . . . Beyond Being and beings, this difference, ceaselessly differing from and deferring (itself), would trace (itself) (by itself) – this *différance* would be the first or last trace if one still could speak, here, of origin and end' (Derrida 1982, 67). The long series of notions developed in Derrida's work – not only *différance* and the trace, but also text, writing, the hymen, the supplement, the *pharmakon*, the *parergon*, justice, messianicity, and so on – are all traces of this formal structure of transcendence, marked by their aporetic or antinomial status, their possibility conditioned by their impossibility, and so on. Deconstruction thus operates in *the interval* between the closed totality of metaphysics and the formal transcendence of *différance* (or as Derrida says in 'Force of Law', in the interval between the deconstructibility of law [*droit*] and the undeconstructibility of justice (1992b, 243).

Deleuze, by contrast, has a very different and non-Heideggerian relation to metaphysics. He described himself candidly as a 'pure metaphysician' in the mould of Bergson and Whitehead. 'I feel myself to be a pure metaphysician', he said in a late interview, 'Bergson says that modern science hasn't found its metaphysics, the metaphysics it would need. It is this metaphysics that interests me' (Villani 1999, 130). He consequently saw himself as 'the most naïve philosopher of our generation. . . . the one who felt the least guilt about "doing philosophy"' (Deleuze 1995b, 88–9). If one is critical of traditional metaphysics, or metaphysical concepts such as identity or essence, he suggests, then the philosophical task is not to attempt to 'overcome' metaphysics, but rather to

actively construct *a different metaphysics*. This is why one does not find, in
Deleuze, any general pronouncements concerning the 'nature' of 'Western
metaphysics' (as 'logocentric', or as a 'metaphysics of presence'), since, as
Derrida notes, the only position from which one could make such a pronouncement is a position of transcendence, which Deleuze rejects. Consequently,
there is no concept of closure in Deleuze either (since closure likewise depends
on transcendence). From the start, Deleuze defined structures as such –
whether mathematical, philosophical, or otherwise – as fundamentally 'open',
and he saw metaphysics itself as an open structure, which is far from having
exhausted its 'possibilities'. This not only means that the 'creation of the new'
is possible within metaphysics, but also that one can retrieve or repeat – to use
Heidegger's term – avenues of thought in the history of metaphysics that were
once opened, only to be quickly closed off again (for instance, the concept of
univocity). Deleuze sees his work as being strictly *immanent* to metaphysics:
creation and transformation are possible within metaphysics, and there are
virtualities in past metaphysics that are capable of being reactivated, as it were,
and inserted into new contexts, and new problematics. Metaphysics itself, in
other words, is dynamic and in constant becoming.

Put crudely, then, if Derrida sets out to undo metaphysics, Deleuze sets out
simply to *do* metaphysics. The results can appear to be very similar – after
Deleuze died, Derrida wrote, in a short memorial text, of the 'near total
affinity' he saw between Deleuze's work and his own – but in fact the context
of their work is very different: a horizon of transcendence in Derrida (*overcoming* or going beyond metaphysics), and a function of immanence in Deleuze
(*doing* metaphysics).[10] This difference may appear to be slight, but its very
slightness acts like a butterfly effect that propels Derrida and Deleuze along
two divergent trajectories that become increasingly remote from each other, to
the point of perhaps being incompatible. Nowhere is this more evident than in
Deleuze's own theory of difference. Deleuze and Derrida are both seen –
rightly – as philosophers of difference. Derrida's essay 'Différance' and
Deleuze's book *Difference and Repetition* both appeared in 1968, and Heidegger's notion of the 'ontological difference' between Being and beings was one
of the primary (though not the only) impetuses in their development of a
theory of difference. But Derrida moves immediately in the direction of
transcendence: what he was seeking, he tells us, is a difference 'beyond Being
and beings', and this is precisely how he characterises *différance*: 'a difference
still more unthought than the [ontological] difference between Being and
beings' (Derrida 1982, 67).

In *Difference and Repetition*, by contrast, Deleuze proposes an interpretation
of the ontological difference that radicalises it in the direction of immanence.
'In accordance with Heidegger's ontological intuition', he writes, 'difference

must be articulation and connection in itself; it must relate different to different without any mediation whatsoever by the identical, the similar, the analogous or the opposed. There must be a differenciation of difference, an in-itself which is like a *differenciator* [a *Sich-unterscheidende*] by virtue of which difference is gathered all at once rather than represented on condition of a prior resemblance, identity, analogy, or opposition' (Deleuze 1994, 117). The project of *Difference and Repetition*, in other words, is to provide an immanent analysis of the ontological difference in which *the different is related to the different through difference itself*: Being must not only be able to account for the external difference between beings, but also the fact that beings themselves are marked by an 'internal difference'; and the ontological difference must not only refer to the difference between Being and beings, but also the difference of Being from itself, 'an alliance of Being and itself in difference' (Deleuze 1994, 231). The concepts of difference that Deleuze develops in *Difference and Repetition* – 'difference in intensity, disparity in the phantasm, dissemblance in the form of time, the differential in thought' (Deleuze 1994, 145) – have a very different status than the notion of difference Derrida develops in his essay 'Différance'. For Derrida, *différance* is a relation that transcends ontology, that differs from ontology, that goes beyond or is more 'originary' than the ontological difference between Being and beings. Deleuze's aim, by contrast, is to show that ontology itself is constituted immanently by a principle of difference (and is thus a 'concept', in the Deleuzian sense of the term, and not merely a 'quasi-concept'). Deleuze is not often thought of as a Heideggerian, but *Difference and Repetition* can be read as a direct response to *Being and Time* from the standpoint of immanence: for Deleuze, Being is difference, and time is repetition.

Deleuze has himself provided a way of assessing the status of Derrida's quasi-concept of *différance*. In *What is Philosophy?*, Deleuze and Guattari present a rather summary typology of three general strategies by which transcendence has been introduced into philosophy. The first, and no doubt paradigmatic, type is the one found in Platonism and its variants: the field of immanence is a simple field of phenomena or appearances, which only possesses secondarily what is attributed first of all to the anterior unity of the Idea (or in later variants, to the 'One beyond Being' in Plotinus, or to the transcendence of the Christian 'God').[11] Modern philosophy effected a second type of transcendence: beginning with Descartes, and then with Kant, the cogito made it possible to treat the plane of immanence as a field of consciousness, which was attributed, as we have seen, no longer to the transcendence of the Idea, but rather to the transcendence of the Subject or the Ego. Finally, the third (and contemporary) form of transcendence – which is the one that concerns us – was introduced by phenomenology and its successors. When immanence becomes immanent to a transcendental subjectivity, it is from *within its own field* that the mark of transcendence must appear. 'Husserl conceived of immanence as the flux of lived experience within subjectivity', write Deleuze and Guattari, 'but since this lived experience, pure and even primordial, does not belong completely to the self that represents it to itself, it is in the regions of *non-belonging* that the horizon of something transcendent is reestablished' (DG 1994b, 46). Deleuze and Guattari do not name names here, but one can easily imagine examples. Levinas, for example, founds ethics on the infinite transcendence of the 'Other' which challenges the status of the reflective subject and undoes the primacy of the Same.[12] In a different manner, Habermas attempts to ground ethics on the privileged transcendence of an intersubjective world populated by other selves, and regulated by a 'communicative consensus'. Whatever form it takes, in this contemporary moment of transcendence one no longer thinks of immanence as immanent *to* something (the Idea, the Subject), but on the contrary 'one seeks to rediscover a transcendence *within* the heart of immanence itself, as a breach or interruption of its field' (DG 1994b, 46). One seeks, in other words, a transcendence *within* immanence.

Derrida, in his own manner, clearly belongs to this contemporary (and post-phenomenological) tradition of transcendence. This is evidenced, moreover, in his many readings of texts in the history of philosophy, which attempt to uncover, within the immanent and manifest movement of traditional philosophical concepts and their 'binary oppositions', a latent and transcendent movement of *différance* that is never present as such in the text but constantly serves to disrupt and destabilise it. This way of treating the history of philosophy raises a question that is intrinsically linked to the ontological theme of transcendence and immanence. What Heidegger bequeathed to contemporary philosophy was not only a rejuvenation of ontology, but concomitant with that, a certain treatment of the history of philosophy under the double theme of the 'destruction' of the history of ontology as well as the 'retrieval' or 'repetition' of that history. Indeed, for the generation to which Deleuze and Derrida belonged, the philosophical training one received in the French university was oriented almost exclusively towards the history of philosophy. Deleuze and Derrida's contrasting relation to metaphysics is thus reflected in their contrasting relation to the history of philosophy. In this regard, we can consider, as a precise historical example, an aspect of the medieval philosophical tradition in which Heidegger took a strong interest – the theological tradition of the 'divine names'. Heidegger himself first formulated his ontological question in the context of these medieval debates, and in taking up these debates for their own account, Derrida and Deleuze have each moved in clearly differentiated directions: Derrida in the direction of 'negative theology' (transcendence) and Deleuze in the direction of 'univocity' (immanence).[13]

Heidegger wrote his doctoral thesis on Duns Scotus, who was engaged in a rather lively thirteenth-century debate concerning the nature of Being. Being is said of beings, *but in what sense*? The Scholastics used three precise terms to designate the various ways of resolving the problem: equivocity, univocity and analogy. To say that Being is *equivocal* means that the term 'Being' is said of beings in several senses, and that these senses have no common measure: 'God is' does not have the same sense as 'man is', for instance, because God does not have the same type of being as man. By contrast, to say that Being is *univocal*, as Duns Scotus affirmed, means that Being has only one sense, and is said in one and the same sense of everything of which it is said, whether it be God or man, animal or plant. Since these positions seemed to lead to scandalous conclusions – equivocity denied order in the cosmos, univocity implied pantheism – a third choice was developed between these two extremes: Being is neither equivocal nor univocal but *analogical*: there is indeed a common measure to the forms of Being, but this measure is analogical, and not univocal. This was the position of Aristotle, which Heidegger discusses in the opening pages of *Being and Time*: Being is said in several senses, and these senses are the categories, which are related to Being, and to each other, by means of analogy. Christianity famously transposed this ontological problem into a theological problem, which was concerned less with the relation of Being to being than the relation of God to his creatures (hence the Heideggerian thematic of 'onto-theology').

Medieval theology had developed a syncretic solution to the immanence/transcendence problem: it insisted on the requirement of *immanence*, that is, the ontological requirement that the first principle (God) be a *being*; but it also insisted on the more powerful requirement of *transcendence*, that is, the requirement that the transcendence of God be maintained as the One *beyond* Being. What came to be known as the 'divine names' tradition was situated at the nexus of these two requirements. The problem was: How can the traditional divine attributes – such as goodness, love, wisdom, power and so on – which are finite and immanent, be predicated of God, who is infinite and transcendent? It was Thomas Aquinas who, following Aristotle, developed the Christian interpretation of analogy. Positive qualities can indeed belong to God substantially, but only insofar as they are treated 'analogically': *either* in terms of an ordered relationship between two proportions (for example, the divine goodness is to God as human goodness is to man – the 'analogy of proportionality'); *or* by reference to a focal meaning or 'prime analogate' (for example, 'Goodness', which God is said to possess eminently and creatures only derivatively – the 'analogy of proportion').[14] In France, Neo-Thomists such as Etienne Gilson were the great defenders of analogy, which attempted to straddle the immanence/transcendence tension in theology.

It is not difficult to ascertain how Derrida and Deleuze position themselves rather definitively on either side of this orthodox divide. Derrida was early on seen to have a kind of 'elective affinity' with what was known as 'negative theology', which insisted that God in his absolute substance or essence can only be defined negatively, according to strict rules of transcendence. Meister Eckhart, for instance, preferred to say 'God is not' rather than 'God is', because 'x is' is a statement that is said of beings like you and me, whereas God is eminently superior to Being, beyond Being.[15] This allows God to appear in his 'supra-substantial' or 'hyper-essential' eminence, as far from all negation as he is from any affirmation. In negative theology, one goes beyond affirmations (God is good) via negations (God is not good in the human sense of the term), and beyond both affirmations and negations to attain God's *eminence* (God is good with an 'incomparable' or 'ineffable' Goodness, a goodness that transcends all goodness, that is beyond goodness). Or, as Derrida says, what is 'proper' to God is to have no properties as such, or to 'be' 'nothing'. The logical formula of transcendence is to say that something 'is' neither *x* nor *not-x*, because it is beyond them both.[16] Derrida, by his own admission, adopts this formula of transcendence in his analyses of *différance*. *Différance*, he says,

> 'is' neither this nor that, neither sensible nor intelligible, neither positive nor negative, neither superior nor inferior, neither active nor passive, neither present nor absent, not even neutral, not even subject to a dialectic with a third moment, without any possible sublation (*Aufhebung*). Despite appearances, then, it [*différance*] is neither a concept nor even a name; it does *lend itself* to a series of names, but calls for another syntax, and exceeds even the order and the structure of predicative discourse. It 'is' not and does not say what 'is'. It is written completely otherwise. (Derrida 1992e, 74)

It is true that Derrida is not 'doing' a negative theology, in so far as the latter seems to reserve, 'beyond all positive predication, beyond all negation, even beyond Being, some hyperessentiality, a being beyond Being' which would perhaps be given in some sort of 'intuition or vision' (Derrida 1992e, 77, 79). But although Derrida refuses to assign any *content* to this transcendence, what he retains from the tradition is its *formal* structure: *différance* is that which is never present as such, is absolutely other, discernible only through its trace, whose movement is infinitely deferred, infinitely differing from itself, definable, at best, in terms of what it is *not*. This is why Derrida can write: 'I trust no text that is not in some way contaminated with negative theology, and even among those texts that apparently do not have, want, or believe they have any relation with theology in general' (Derrida 1995c, 69). There is no text of the metaphysical tradition that is not 'contaminated' with this formal structure of transcendence, or this movement of *différance*.

When Deleuze, for his part, injects himself into the divine-names tradition, he is equally critical of both analogy *and* negative theology, and explicitly aligns himself with the tradition of univocity (first formulated by Duns Scotus, and which Deleuze sees extended in Spinoza and Nietzsche). The reason is clear: the sole raison d'être of negative theology is to *preserve* transcendence (we have to negate all predicates or properties of God, because God transcends them all), whereas univocity is the position of immanence pushed to its most extreme point. As formulated by Duns Scotus, it says that the term 'Being' is always used univocally, in other words, when I say that 'God is' or 'Man is' or 'a cat is' or 'a flea is', the word 'is' is being used *in one and the same sense* in all these sentences. In other words, God does not have a different mode of being from other creatures – that is, a transcendent mode of being that could be accessed (or not) only through negation or analogy. The univocity of Being entails the radical denial of any ontological transcendence, and for this reason was a highly heterodox – and often heretical – position because it hinted at pantheism or even atheism. (The English word 'dunce' is derived from the term of disapprobation used to describe the followers of Duns Scotus.) Deleuze suggests that the tradition of univocity was continued in Spinoza, for whom God and Nature are one and the same thing, and then in Nietzsche. In this sense, univocity can be read as the medieval ontological version of the 'death of God'. *Difference and Repetition* is, among other things, an attempt to follow through on the ontological – and not merely theological – implications of univocity. Tellingly, to my knowledge, Derrida never mentions the tradition of univocity in his writings. This example from the history of philosophy exemplifies the broad differences between the ontologies of Deleuze and Derrida: in Deleuze one finds an ontology that seeks to expunge from Being all remnants of transcendence, whereas in Derrida one finds an ontology that seeks to trace the eruptions and movements of transcendence *within* Being.

We turn now to the third context in which the immanence-transcendence distinction has played a historically important role, which is found in Kant and is oriented primarily towards epistemology. At one point, Kant describes the entire project of the first critique in terms of the immanence/transcendence distinction: 'We shall entitle the principles whose application is confined entirely within the limits of possible experience, *immanent*, and those, on the other hand, which profess to pass beyond these limits, *transcendent*' (Kant 1929, A295–6/B352). In a famous image, Kant portrays the domain of the understanding as a demarcated 'territory' or island (immanence) surrounded by a vast ocean of metaphysical illusion (transcendence).[17] When I use a concept such as 'table' or 'chair' to synthesise my intuition or perceptions, I am operating immanently within the bounds of possible experience. But when I use a concept like the 'soul' or the 'world' or 'God', I am going beyond the bounds of possible experience, transcending them. Following Plato, Kant will call these concepts that transcend experience 'Ideas'. The Idea of the world, for example, as the totality of what is, has no intuition or perception that could ever correspond to it. To use the famous Kantian distinction, we can *think* the World, but we can never *know* it; strictly speaking, it is not an object of our experience. Hence, we are led into inevitable *illusions* when we ask questions about the World *as if* it were an object of experience. For instance: Did it have a beginning in time, or is it eternal? Does it have boundaries in space, or does it go on forever? The same holds for our Ideas of the Soul and God: Soul, World and God are all transcendent Ideas, and in the 'Transcendental Dialectic', the longest section of the *Critique of Pure Reason*, Kant analyses the nature of the paradoxes or aporias reason is led into because of these illusions: the paralogisms of the Soul, the antinomies of the World, the ideal of God. Kant called his project a *transcendental* philosophy because it sought *immanent* criteria that would allow us to distinguish between these legitimate and illegitimate uses of the syntheses of consciousness. In this sense, the 'transcendental' is opposed to the 'transcendent': the aim of Kant's transcendental philosophy is the critique of transcendence, and hence the search for immanent criteria of critique – that is, immanent to reason itself. A transcendental critique is a purely immanent critique.

The Kantian formulation of the distinction between immanence and transcendence is useful to our purposes for two reasons. On the one hand, Kant defines his project in immanent terms as a critique of transcendence, and thus functions as a precursor to Deleuze. On the other hand, Kant nonetheless resurrects the transcendent Ideas, in the second critique, as the necessary postulates of *practical* reason, thereby assigning to Ideas an important regulative role, and in this respect functioning as a precursor to Derrida. Indeed, the notion of an 'Idea' is an explicit touchstone for both Deleuze and Derrida. Deleuze devotes an entire chapter of his magnum opus *Difference and Repetition*, as one might expect, to developing a purely *immanent* theory of Idea (as a multiplicity). Derrida, for his part, repeatedly flags the fact that many of his notions – such as the gift, opening, democracy, etc. – have a status that is 'analogous' to transcendent Ideas 'in the Kantian sense'.[18] For instance, in his analyses of the gift, Derrida says that a pure gift, a pure giving, is an impossibility, because when I say 'Thank you', or even accept the gift, I start cancelling the gift, since, in a movement of reappropriation, I am proposing a kind of equivalence between the giving and my gratitude. The transcendent logic of the pure gift is thereby incorporated into an immanent economy of exchange and debt. But this, says Kant, is the very nature of transcendent Ideas. Whenever we speak of something 'pure' or 'absolute' or 'infinite', as Derrida often does (the 'pure gift', 'absolute responsibility', the 'infinite other'), we are in the realm of transcendence, since we never encounter the pure or the absolute in our experience, it is never something that can be present to our experience. The Idea of a pure mother, for instance, would be the idea of a mother who would not be something other than a mother – not a daughter, not a lover, not a wife. We can *think* this Idea, but we don't encounter it in experience. (The Christian Idea of the 'Virgin Mary', as the mother of God, might be said to approximate this Idea of a pure mother.) The same holds for the logic of the pure gift, of justice, of democracy and so on. Indeed, in *Aporias*, Derrida explains that, when he was shopping around for a term to describe the formal status of his concepts – or rather his 'quasi-concepts' – he initially thought of adopting the Kantian term 'antinomy', but finally decided to use the Greek term 'aporia' instead (Derrida 1993a, 16).[19] The reason is that he wanted to distance himself from Kant, since their respective problems, as he explains, are *analogous* but not identical (the difference, in part, lies in their temporal structure). The fundamental aporia or antinomy, for Derrida, is that the 'condition of possibility' for, say, a 'gift' or a 'decision', is its very *impossibility*, which is why he describes his list of quasi-concepts as 'so many aporetic places or dislocations' (Derrida 1993a, 15).

But if the notion of the 'pure gift' is by definition a transcendent Idea, the immanent concept that corresponds to it is, precisely, *debt* (since any gift that is given is immediately incorporated into the cycle of exchange and indebtedness). This is in fact what one encounters in Deleuze's work: an immanent analysis of debt, and not a transcendent analysis of the pure gift. In this, Deleuze follows Nietzsche, whose own immanent critique of morality – the *Genealogy of Morals* – was grounded in an analysis of debt. It was in the debtor-creditor relation, Nietzsche writes, 'that one person first encountered another person, that one person first *measured himself* against another'.[20] In this regard, a certain compatibility exists between Derrida and Deleuze. Deleuze would no doubt agree that the condition of possibility for the 'pure gift' is its impossibility, and that the gift itself has an 'aporetic' status. But this simply points to the transcendence of the concept, and the need for an immanent analysis of gift giving insofar as it is always enmeshed in the immanent relations of exchange and debt. Derrida and Deleuze each modify Kant's notion of 'conditions of possibility' in formulas that sum up their philosophical projects. Derrida defines deconstruction as the experience of the possibility of the impossible – that is, the (impossible) possibility of the impossible 'marks an absolute interruption in the regime of the possible' (Coward and Foshay 1992, 290).

Such is the formula of transcendence. Deleuze, for his part, defines his philosophy, not as a search for the conditions of possible experience, but rather the conditions of *real* experience. Such is the formula of immanence.

This distinction between the two different theories of Ideas one finds in Deleuze and Derrida is necessarily carried over into two different theories of desire. Plato had already linked Ideas to the theory of desire (Eros). In Kant, the *Critique of Practical Reason* is presented as an analysis of a 'higher' faculty of desire that is determined by the representation of a pure form (an Idea) – namely, the pure form of a universal legislation, or the moral law. This same linkage is carried over in Deleuze and Derrida. For a certain period of time, Deleuze was characterised (at least in France) as a 'philosopher of desire', in part because one of the aims of *Anti-Oedipus* (1972) had been to develop a purely *immanent* conception of desire. For our purposes, however, it is perhaps more useful to examine Deleuze's analysis of the contrasting *transcendent* conception of desire, since it anticipates, *mutatis mutandis*, the theory of desire one finds in Derrida. The transcendent theory of desire can be summarised in three distinct moments. First, if I desire something, it is because I lack that something. But whereas *need* is a relative lack that is satisfied as soon its object is attained, *desire* has traditionally been defined as an irremediable ontological lack which, by its very nature, is unrealisable – precisely because its object is transcendent, or absolutely other (Good, One, God, Moral Law). From Plato and Augustine to Hegel and Freud, desire has been defined, ontologically, as a function of a field of transcendence, in relation to transcendence (as expressed in an Idea). Desire thus presents us with a 'tragic' vision of humanity: as humans, we are incomplete and riddled with deficiencies, and ontological desire is the sign of our incompleteness, of our 'lack of being'. The 'moral' of this vision, in turn, is that we need to *acquire* our being: in Plato, for instance, we need to make our desire coincide with the order of the Good, an order which desire itself furthers (*Symposium*); in St Augustine, desire aims at God, an impossible desire (in this life) which accounts for the perpetual 'restlessness' of the soul (*caritas* versus *cupiditas*). Hence, finally, the 'dramatic' dimension of desire as expressed in the theme of the quest, the incessant search: the initial postulate of our lack of Being is pregnant with a series of intermediate postulates that lead to the ultimate postulate of a recovered Being.

But there is a second and third moment to this transcendent theory of desire. If desire aims at a transcendent object that is by nature unattainable, then what is it that comes to satisfy this desire? The answer: what satisfies this transcendent desire, and gives it a kind of immanence, is akin to what we call a state of *pleasure*. But this pleasure is, alas, a false immanence, a pseudo-immanence, a kind of delusion or illusion. Desire is calmed for a moment –

but then begins again. In Freud, for instance, desire is experienced, energetically, as a disagreeable tension, a kind of 'charge'. To get out of this disagreeable state, a *discharge* is necessary, and this discharge is experienced as a pleasure. Humans will then have peace, their desire will be calmed – but only for a moment, for desire is reborn, and a new discharge becomes necessary. Pleasure, at this level, becomes the only immanent unit capable of measuring desire. The final moment: if desire is an 'intentionality' that aims at what it lacks, and is measured in terms of a unit (pleasure as discharge) that is not its own, then we must say that these states of pleasure – such as orgasm or ecstasy, whether mystical or otherwise – only provide illusory or apparent satisfactions to desire; its 'true' satisfaction is never present, but is infinitely delayed, infinitely deferred. The irreducibility of desire to states of pleasure must be reaffirmed under another mode: it is the relation (as Lacan puts it) between an 'impossible *jouissance*' and death. In other words, as long as desire is defined as a function of transcendence, as a desire for the other, then the condition of possibility for desire is its very impossibility. In Deleuze's analysis, then, the transcendent theory of desire comprises three moments: (1) desire is the mark of our 'lack' of being, since the object of desire is transcendent; but (2) one can only hope for illusory discharges of desire in acts of pleasure; and thus (3) desire is pursuing a *jouissance* that is ultimately impossible.[21] In this manner, says Deleuze, the theory of desire is completely ensnared in a field of transcendence.

This is a quick summary of the analysis of desire presented in *Anti-Oedipus*, but it is not difficult to ascertain the degree to which Derrida participates in this tradition, and indeed pushes it to its limit. Not only does Derrida conceptualise a purely formal structure of transcendence under the guise of the 'absolute other' or the *tout autre* (moreover, if the absolute other is irreducible to a concept, or a word, for example, it is because it transcends the orders of conceptualisation, or language); he also undertakes a persistent exploration of the *experience* of this transcendence, which he often expresses, in terms almost identical to Deleuze's analysis of desire, as an 'interminable experience', 'the experience of the impossible', a 'double bind'. What does it mean to 'live' the aporias of the gift or justice? Can one 'experience' the impossible? Derrida replies: yes. 'If the gift is another name for the impossible, we still think it, we name it, we desire it. We intend it. And this even if or because or to the extent that we *never* encounter it, we never know it, we never verify it, we never experience it in its present existence or its phenomenon' (Derrida 1992c, 29).

What then is the nature of this 'experience of the impossible'? Derrida replies: *a double bind*. The Idea of justice is *not* deconstructable, for Derrida, because it is an *infinitely transcendent* Idea that is unknowable: it provides no knowledge, and is independent of any determinable context.[22] This means, on the one hand, that we can only experience the Idea of justice *practically* as a *call*, as a call to justice, as an absolute demand for justice; but it also means, on the other hand, that the Idea of justice provides us no rule for determining when a decision is just or unjust. Hence the double bind of the aporetic experience: the condition of possibility for acting justly is grounded in the impossibility of ever knowing when or if an act is just. And as Derrida comments, 'a double bind cannot be assumed; one can only endure it in a *passion*' (Derrida 1998, 36).[23] What then is the 'passion' or 'desire' specific to the experience of the impossible? It is a desire for the absolute other, and hence a desire that is *infinitely suspended*, whose fulfilment is *infinitely deferred*:

> Isn't it proper to desire to carry with it its own proper suspension, the death or the phantom of desire? To go toward the absolute other, isn't that the extreme tension of a desire that tries thereby to renounce its own proper momentum, its own movement of appropriation? . . . And since we do not determine ourselves *before* this desire, since no relation to self can be sure of preceding it, to wit, of preceding a relation to the other, . . . *all* reflection is caught in the genealogy of this genitive (i.e., 'desire of . . .'). (Derrida 1995c, 37)

Thus, for Derrida, the possibility of *openness* or *invention* (e.g., the possibility of 'an other justice', 'an other politics', and so on [e.g., Derrida 1997a, 24]) is necessarily linked to the transcendent Idea of the *absolutely* other. The 'disruptions' Derrida introduces into thought are the movements of this formal structure of transcendence. One can see clearly how Derrida's notion of desire, in relation to, for example, the 'infinite Idea of justice', recapitulates the three moments of the transcendent theory of desire outlined by Deleuze: (1) the 'call' to justice has as its object an 'infinite' Idea that is unrealisable, and that transcends any determinable context; (2) what comes to fulfil the call to justice are 'decisions' (e.g., by judges in a court of law), but these 'decisions' as such cannot be determined to be just, so the call to justice is continually reborn; hence (3) the call to justice can never be fulfilled or satisfied, it is the experience of something that is fundamentally impossible. Derrida not only seeks to disengage a formal structure of transcendence (*différance*), but to describe the desire or passion of that transcendence (defined as a double bind or experience of the impossible). For his part, Deleuze agrees with Derrida's analyses, and provides variations of his own, but they are always a prelude to eliminating transcendence and providing an *immanent* account of the same phenomenon: an immanent ontology (univocity), an immanent theory of Ideas (defined in terms of multiplicities and singularities), and an immanent theory of desire (defined as the prolongation or synthesis of singularities).

No matter which formulation one considers, then, one finds Derrida and Deleuze following diverging philosophical trajectories, marked by these two vectors of transcendence and immanence. First, in the tradition of subjectivity, transcendence refers to what transcends the self (the other, the world) – or more profoundly, to the subject itself, as that which transcends the pure 'flux of consciousness' or 'flow of experience'. One can critique the status of the subject by appealing to the transcendence of the Other, or by appealing to the conditions of the immanent flux of experience that the subject itself transcends (theory of intensity). Second, with regard to the question of ontology, transcendence refers to that which is 'beyond' or 'otherwise than' Being – or, in its more contemporary form, to relations to the other that 'interrupt' Being, or erupt or intervene within Being. Whereas Deleuze defines both Being and beings immanently in terms of a genetic principle of difference, Derrida defines *différance* transcendently as 'originary' difference that is beyond both Being and beings. Finally, from the viewpoint of a Kantian (or neo-Kantian) epistemology, transcendence refers to those Ideas of objects that lie outside the immanent realm of possible experience. Deleuze attempts to formulate an immanent theory of Ideas and desire, while Derrida attempts to define a purely formal structure of transcendence and the passion of the double bind that it entails. In each of these areas, Deleuze's and Derrida's projects move in very different directions, despite so many surface similarities and affinities.

But this leads to an obvious final question: How should one *assess* this difference? Can one say that the trajectory of transcendence or of immanence is 'better' than the other? This is a difficult question, perhaps reducible, in the end, to what one might call philosophical 'taste'. My own view is that the 'philosophy of the future' (to use Nietzsche's phrase) needs to move in the direction of immanence, for at least two reasons. The most obvious reason is that the validity of a critique of transcendence above all stems from the theoretical interest to expose its fictional or illusory status – this has been a constant of philosophy from Hume through Kant to Nietzsche, its 'demystificatory' role. But the more important reason has to do with practical philosophy, with ethics and politics. Kant, Levinas and Derrida, along with many others, while perhaps denying transcendence a constitutive status, are nonetheless willing to assign it a *practical* role (regulative, imperative, communicative, and so on). For Deleuze, this is equally illegitimate, but it seems to have been a source of genuine perplexity to Deleuze. There is a curious passage in *What is Philosophy?* where Deleuze and Guattari more or less ask: What *is* it with immanence? It should be the natural acquisition and milieu of philosophy, yet such is not always the case. Moreover, the arguments brought to bear against immanence are almost always *moral* arguments. Without transcendence, we are warned, we will fall into a dark of chaos, reduced to a pure 'subjectivism' or 'relativism', living in a world without hope, with no vision of an alternate future. Indeed, the two philosophers who pushed followed the trajectory of immanence the furthest – Spinoza and Nietzsche – were condemned by both their contemporaries and successors, not only for being atheists, but, even worse, for being 'immoralists'. The potent danger that was sensed to be lurking in the *Ethics* and the *Genealogy of Morals* was precisely the danger of immanence. 'Immanence', Deleuze writes, 'can be said to be the burning touchstone of all philosophy . . . because it takes upon itself all the dangers that philosophy must confront, all the condemnations, persecutions and repudiations that it undergoes. This at least persuades us that the problem of immanence is not abstract or merely theoretical. At first sight, it is not easy to see why immanence is so dangerous, but it is. It swallows up sages and gods' (DG 1994b, 45; trans. modified).

From this practical point of view, Spinoza poses the most interesting test case of the position of immanence. Heidegger himself wrote notoriously little on Spinoza, which is a surprising omission, since Spinoza's *Ethics* is a work of pure ontology that explicitly poses the problem of the ontological difference in terms of the difference between the infinite substance (Being) and its finite modes (beings). Derrida too has written little on Spinoza. By contrast, Deleuze's reformulation of ontology in Spinozistic terms not only allows him to push the Heideggerian heritage in an immanent direction (rather than Derrida's transcendent direction), but also to understand that ontology in explicitly ethical terms. Like Spinoza, Deleuze defines beings immanently in terms of their intensity or 'degree of power', a degree which is actualised at every moment in terms of the whole of one's 'affections' (which are nonetheless in constant variation). The fundamental question of ethics is not 'What *must* I do?' (the question of *morality*) but rather 'What *can* I do?' Given my degree of power, what are my capabilities and capacities? How can I come into active possession of my power? How can I go to the limit of what I 'can do'? The political question follows from this, since those in power have an obvious interest in separating us from our capacity to act. But this is what makes transcendence an eminently pragmatic and ethical issue. The ethical themes one finds in transcendent philosophies such as those of Levinas and Derrida – an absolute responsibility for the other that I can never assume, or an infinite call to justice that I can never satisfy – are, from the point of view of immanence, imperatives whose effect is to separate me from my capacity to act. From the viewpoint of immanence, in other words, *transcendence represents my slavery and impotence reduced to its lowest point*: the absolute demand to do the absolutely impossible is nothing other than the concept of impotence raised to infinity. This is why transcendence itself poses precise and difficult ethical problems for a philosophy of immanence: If transcendence represents my impotence (power = 0), then under what conditions can I have actually been led to *desire* transcendence? What are the conditions that could have led, in Nietzsche's words, to 'the inversion of the value-positing eye'? How could I actually reach the point where I desire my slavery and subjection as if it were my salvation? (In a similar way, immanence poses a precise and difficult problem for a philosophy of transcendence: How can one bridge the interval that separates the transcendent from the immanent – for instance, the interval between the undeconstructability of justice from the deconstructability of the law?)

In short, the difference between the two philosophical trajectories of immanence and transcendence must be assessed and evaluated, not simply in the theoretical domain, but in the ethico-political domain. In part, this is because the speculative elimination of transcendence does not necessarily lead to its practical elimination, as one can see already in Kant. But more importantly, it is because it is at the ethical level that the difference between transcendence and immanence appears in its most acute and consequential form. On this score, it is perhaps the difference between Deleuze and Levinas that presents this contrast most starkly. For Levinas, ethics *precedes* ontology because it is derived from an element of transcendence (the Other) that is necessarily 'otherwise' than Being (and hence privileges concepts like absolute responsibility and duty). For Deleuze, ethics *is* ontology because it is derived from the immanent relation of beings to Being at the level of their existence (and hence privileges concepts such as *puissance* (power or capacity) and affectivity). This is why Spinoza entitled his pure ontology an *Ethics* rather than an *Ontology*: his speculative propositions concerning the univocity of Being can only be judged practically at the level of the ethics they envelop or imply. Put summarily, for Levinas, ethics is derived from transcendence, while for Deleuze, transcendence is what prevents ethics. It seems to me that it is at this level – at the practical and not merely speculative level – that the relative merits of philosophies of immanence and transcendence need to be assessed and decided.[24]

Notes

1. See Agamben 1999, 239. Edith Wyschogrod (1990, 191, 223, 229) distinguishes between philosophers of difference (Levinas, Derrida, Blanchot) and philosophers of the plenum (Deleuze and Guattari, Genet), but this distinction seems far less germane than Agamben's.

2. See Sartre 1972 as well as Deleuze 1990, 98–9; 343–4. Deleuze will retain the notion of an impersonal transcendental field, but strips it of any determination as a constituting consciousness.

3. See DG 1994b, 46: 'Kant discovered the modern way of saving transcendence: this is no longer the transcendence of Something, or of a One higher than everything (contemplation), but that of a Subject to which the field of immanence is only attributed by belonging to a self that necessarily represents such a subject to itself (reflection).'

4. See Deleuze 1997, 137: 'The poisoned gift of Platonism was to have reintroduced transcendence into philosophy, to have given transcendence a plausible philosophical meaning.' Deleuze is here referring primarily to ontological transcendence.

5. See also Heidegger 1982, 4: ' "Christian God" also stands for the "transcendent" in general in its various meanings – for "ideals" and "norms", "principles" and "rules", "ends" and "values", which are set "*above*" Being, in order to give Being as a whole a purpose, an order, and – as it is succinctly expressed – "meaning".'

6. In this, Derrida is certainly more faithful to Heidegger, and is attempting, in an explicit manner, to carry forward a trajectory already present in Heidegger's work: the immanent question of being and its transcendental horizon (time), which is posed in *Being and Time*, comes to be progressively displaced by the transcendent themes of *Ereignis* (the 'event') and the *es gibt* (the 'gift' [*Gabe*] of time and being). The trajectory is continued in the Derridean themes of revelation and promise. See Derrida 1992e, 122–4.

7. See Derrida 1978, 117, where history is characterised as 'the very movement of transcendence, of the excess over the totality, without which no totality would appear'.

8. See also Derrida 1981b, 10: one must 'borrow the syntaxic and lexical resources of the language of metaphysics . . . at the very moment one deconstructs this language'.

9. Derrida 1981a, 168: '*Différance*, the disappearance of any originary presence, is *at once* the condition of possibility *and* the condition of impossibility of truth.'

10. Significantly, Derrida says the first question he would have asked Deleuze would have concerned the term immanence – a term 'on which he always insisted' (Derrida 2001a, 195).

11. For Deleuze's interpretation of Platonism, see in particular 'Plato and the Simulacrum' in Deleuze 1990, 253–66 (though the concept of the simulacrum developed there assumes less and less importance in Deleuze's work).

12. Levinas 1969. Deleuze never discusses Levinas' work directly, except as an instance of Jewish philosophy (DG 1994b, 233n5). See, however, Badiou 2001.

13. For their respective discussion of the divine names traditon, see Deleuze 1992; Derrida, 1995c.

14. For Thomas Aquinas' formulations of analogy, see *Summa Theologiae* 1.13.5. The great modern proponent of the way of affirmation is Charles Williams (1994).

15. See Schürmann 1978, especially 72–192. While recognizing Eckhart's affinities

with immanence (see 176; 252n56) and with an immanent causality (177), Schürmann attempts to provide a qualified analogical interpretation of his teachings (179).

16. Derrida characterises the nature of deconstruction itself in terms derived from the tradition of negative theology. See Derrida 1988a, 5: 'What deconstruction is not? everything of course! What is deconstruction? nothing of course!'

17. See Kant 1929, A236–7/B294–5: 'We have now not merely explored the *territory* of pure understanding, and carefully surveyed every part of it, but have also measured its extent, and assigned to everything in it its rightful place. This domain is an island, enclosed by nature itself within unalterable limits. It is the land of truth – enchanting name! – surrounded by a wide and stormy *ocean*, the native home of illusion.'

18. Derrida himself draws the analogy between Kantian Ideas and his own concepts at numerous points throughout his work. For instance, the structure or logic of the gift, Derrida tells us, has 'a form analogous to Kant's transcendental dialectic, as relation between thinking and knowing. We are going to give ourselves over to engage in the effort of thinking or rethinking a sort of *transcendental illusion* of the gift' (Derrida 1992c, 29–30; emphasis added). Similarly, Derrida notes that 'I have on several occasions spoken of "unconditional" affirmation or of "unconditional" "appeal". . . . Now, the very least that can be said of "unconditionality" (a word that I use not by accident to recall the character of the categorical imperative in its Kantian form) is that it is independent of every determinate context, even of the determination of a context in general. It announces itself as such only in the *opening* of context' (Derrida 1988b, 152–3). To be sure, Derrida refuses to accommodate his own thought to Kantian formulations: 'Why have I always *hesitated* to characterize it [deconstruction] in Kantian terms, for example, or more generally in ethical or political terms, when that would have been so easy and would have enabled me to avoid so many critiques, themselves all too facile? Because such characterizations seem to me essentially associated with philosophemes that themselves call for deconstructive questions' (Derrida 1988b, 153).

19. See also Derrida 1993e, 84, where he is still hesitating between the two terms: 'The concept of responsibility [would be] paralyzed by what can be called an aporia or an antinomy.'

20. Nietzsche, *Genealogy of Morals*, Essay II, §8, as quoted at Deleuze 1983, 213–14.

21. For a summary of Deleuze's theory of desire, see his seminar of 26 March 1973, available on-line at <http://www.webdeleuze.com/sommaire.html>, English translation at <http://www.usyd.edu.au/contretemps/2may2001/deleuze.pdf>.

22. For the idea that the deconstruction of the law 'operates on the basis of the infinite "Idea of justice"', see Derrida 1992b, 25. That the Idea of justice implies 'non-gathering, dissociation, heterogeneity, non-identity with itself, endless inadequation, *infinite transcendence*' see Derrida 1997b, 17. On the Idea of justice being 'independent of all determinable contexts', see Derrida 1997a, 215–16.

23. My thanks to Andrew Montin for this reference.

24. An earlier version of this article was presented at the annual meeting of the

International Association of Philosophy and Literature at Erasmus University, Rotterdam, in June 2002. The ideas in this paper originated in discussions with Andrew Haas and Andrew Montin at the University of New South Wales and benefited greatly from suggestions from the editors of this volume.

CHAPTER 4

The Beginnings of Thought: The Fundamental Experience in Derrida and Deleuze

Leonard Lawlor

In his memorial text for Deleuze, Derrida speaks of a 'nearly total affinity' between his own philosophical content and that of Deleuze (Derrida 1995a; 2001a, 192; see also Lawlor 2000b). Here, Derrida is implying that there is only a formal difference between Deleuze's thought and his. Indeed, it seems as though Derrida is right. To understand the difference between Derrida and Deleuze one must focus on the concept of form, or more precisely, the concept of the 'informal'. Everything that follows in this essay will depend on a reflection on the informal. Such a reflection will allow us to determine 'the point of diffraction' between Derrida and Deleuze.[1] This point of diffraction is quite fine. Indeed, the 'nearly total affinity' constantly threatens to absorb the diffraction into its point. It is not the case that Derrida is the philosopher of pure transcendence and Deleuze the philosopher of pure immanence. Rather, and here we can see the diffraction disappear, both are philosophers of immanence.

Now, in order to keep the diffraction therefore from disappearing, we are going to insert four oppositions into it, which we will develop in the succeeding sections of this essay. First, Derrida is the true philosopher of unity, while Deleuze is the true philosopher of duality. Second Deleuze is the true philosopher of positivity, while Derrida is the true philosopher of negativity. Third, Deleuze is the true philosopher of the 'non-lieu', the non-place, while Derrida is the true philosopher of the 'mi-lieu', the halfway place. And lastly, Deleuze is the true philosopher of self-interrogation, while Derrida is the true philosopher of interrogation by another. We are saying 'true' here because appearances do not always support the divisions we are going to make. But regardless of whether we say unity or duality, positivity or negativity, non-place or halfway place, self-interrogation or other-interrogation, the entire thinking of both Derrida and Deleuze flows from one point, to which we now turn.

SIMULACRA

Although both Derrida and Deleuze will abandon later the idea of the simulacrum that they developed in the Sixties, it functions as their point of diffraction. In most general terms, the simulacrum is a repetition, an image, that has no model or original. Since the idea of the simulacrum consisted in lacking an original, both Derrida and Deleuze could use it in their project of reversing Platonism. For both, reversing Platonism consists in destroying the hierarchy of the image and original. In order to start to see the diffraction between Derrida and Deleuze, we must pay careful attention to the respective definitions of Platonism given in the texts of this period: Derrida's 'Plato's Pharmacy' (in Derrida 1972a; 1981a); Deleuze's 'Plato and the Simulacrum' (in Deleuze 1969; 1990), and Chapter 2 of *Difference and Repetition* (Deleuze 1968; 1994).

For Deleuze, the Platonic decision is one that subordinates *difference in itself* to the same.[2] This 'in itself' means that difference is conceived without any mediation whatsoever. This *unmediated difference* is why Deleuze insists on a 'difference in nature' between the simulacrum and the copy (Deleuze 1969, 297; 1990, 257). Copies or icons are 'good images', according to Deleuze, because they are endowed with resemblance to an idea, a Platonic idea (Deleuze 1969, 296; 1990, 257). The copies therefore have only one sense, the good sense coming from the idea. 'The simulacrum', in contrast, as Deleuze says in *The Logic of Sense*, 'is an image without resemblance' (1969, 297; 1990, 257). In *Difference and Repetition*, he says, 'in contrast to *icônes*, [the simulacra] have put resemblance on the outside and live on the basis of difference' (Deleuze 1968, 167; 1994, 128, cf. 1968, 87; 1994, 62). Here we must assemble the three characteristics of the Deleuzean simulacrum: singularity, in-formality, and becoming. First, since the simulacrum 'lives from difference' or since it is not based in resemblance, it has 'internalized a dissimilarity' (1969, 297; 1990, 258). It is what Deleuze calls a 'singularity' (1969, 69; 1990, 53; cf. 1969, 299–300; 1999, 260). To put this as simply as possible, a singularity, for Deleuze, is not a general form; it is an event. Thus, the Deleuzean simulacrum is always based in the abyss, in the formless, in chaos (1969, 192; 1990, 164). As Deleuze says, 'everything begins with the abyss' (1969, 219; 1990, 188). Yet, since the simulacrum is an image, it is formal and repeatable. Thus, second, the Deleuzean simulacrum – singularity – is defined by the 'in-formal'. 'In-formality' means that since the simulacrum begins from the formless (chaos), its repetition is always unformable (different), subject to events. Since the Deleuzean simulacrum is always subject to events, it is always becoming more and less. The 'simul' of the simul-acrum is always double. Simulacra go in two directions (*sens*) at once. In *The Logic of Sense*, Deleuze says that the simulacrum '*is* not more and less at the same time [*en même temps*] but *becomes* more and less at the same time' (1969, 9; 1990, 1; my italics). This difference between the 'is' and the 'becomes' means that the simulacrum is not defined by being but by *becoming*. Becoming is the third characteristic, and becoming for Deleuze only takes place at the surface. Thus, because Deleuze defines Platonism as the subordination of difference in itself to the same, reversing Platonism for Deleuze in fact means to make the simulacra rise to the surface (1969, 302; 1990, 262).[3]

Now, let us return to Derrida's definition of Platonism. The Platonic decision consists in being 'intolerant in relation to [the] passage between the two contrary senses of the same word' (Derrida 1972a, 112; 1981a, 99). The two contrary senses of the same word of course suggests that the 'simul' of the simulacrum, as in Deleuze, is double, the two senses or directions of the *pharmakon*. Yet, for Derrida, the Platonic intolerance means an intolerance to 'a blend [*mélange*] of two pure, heterogeneous terms', to 'a blend [*mélange*] and an impurity' (1972a, 146; 1981a, 128). Using the Neo-Platonic terms again, we must say that, for Derrida, the father (the unparticipated) is not the same but pure hetereogeneity, and the false suitor, the simulacrum, is not difference in itself but the same – but here understood as contamination. We must keep in mind that in *Voice and Phenomenon*, Derrida defines contamination by means of *la prise*.[4] Thus we must always be sensitive to Derrida's use of any word involving the verb 'prendre' such as 'comprendre', which means not only 'to understand', but also and more importantly 'to include'. Because Derrida defines Platonism as the subordination of contamination to pure heterogeneity, the Derridean simulacrum has a different set of characteristics. Unlike the Deleuzean simulacrum, the Derridean one has put resemblance on the inside, in 'the purity of the inside' (1972a, 147; 1981a, 128). In 'Plato's Pharmacy', Derrida maintains Plato's definition of the simulacrum (or writing, the *pharmakon*) as a copy of a copy (1972a, 159; 1981a, 138). Moreover, Derrida defines the simulacrum through *mimesis* or imitation (1972a, 157; 1981a, 137). As Derrida says in *Voice and Phenomenon*, 'everything begins with re-presentation' (1967b, 49n1; 1973, 45n4). Thus first, the Derridean simulacrum is not defined by singularity but by generality (cf. 1972b, 201; 1982, 168). It is not defined by an event or by the formless; rather it is defined by formality. To understand Derrida's formalism here, we have to recognise that Derrida is defining the simulacrum by the repetition of the word: two contrary senses '*in the same word*' (1972a, 111; 1981a, 98; Derrida's italics). The word is 'self-identical' (1972a, 130; 1981a, 114), 'is at once [*à la fois*] enough the same and enough other' (1972a, 195; 1981a, 168). There is a minimal unity to any word, its phonic or graphic form, that must be imitated or repeated if it is to function. In 'Plato's Pharmacy', Derrida calls this minimal form a 'type' (*typos*) (1972a, 119; 1981a, 104). It is this repeatable or iterable form that allows for the doubling of the sense. In fact, the Derridean simulacrum is doubled between presence and non-presence (1972a, 194; 1981a, 168). The non-presence of the Derridean simulacrum (or of writing, the *pharmakon*), we might say, is singular and formless (e.g., 1990a, 54; 1995e, 51). Therefore, second, the Derridean simulacrum is also defined by 'in-formality'. But, the simulacrum's non-presence implies that the Derridean simulacrum is defined *neither by being nor by becoming*. As Derrida says, 'writing (is) *epekeina tes ousias*' (1972a, 194; 1981a, 168; cf. 1992d, 259). This 'beyond being or presence', this non-presence or non-being – the third characteristic – is why Derrida also calls the simulacrum a trace (1972a, 119 and 176; 1981a, 105 and 152). That Derrida, however, must put the 'is' between parentheses indicates that Derridean doubling consists in a kind of mediation: the wholly other than being takes (*pris*) being *and* is taken by being. Thus, because Derrida defines Platonism as the subordination of contamination (the same or mediation) to heterogeneity, the reversal of Platonism for him does not mean to make the simulacra rise to the surface; rather it consists in 'displacing' them into the 'wholly other field' in which being and the beyond being mutually contaminate one another (1972a, 123; 1981a, 108).

We must make this diffraction more precise before it disappears back into the point. We were able to see that the simulacrum in both Derrida and Deleuze could be defined by in-formality. The simulacrum (in either Derrida or Deleuze) can never solely be defined by form and thus it is singular; but also it can never be defined as formless since it is a repeatable image. The diffraction therefore must occur in the *relation* between formlessness and formality. Their respective definitions of Platonism allow us to see how they are conceiving the relation. For Derrida, the relation cannot be one of heterogeneity; it must be a relation of contamination (another name for Derrida's famous '*différance*'). For Deleuze, the relation cannot be one of homogeneity; it must be a relation of difference in itself. With contamination, Derrida is trying to conceive difference with mediation, while, with difference in itself, Deleuze is trying to conceive difference without mediation. Because Derrida is trying to conceive difference with mediation, he defines the simulacrum by resemblance. Because Deleuze is trying to conceive difference without mediation, he defines the simulacrum by dissimilarity. Moreover, because Deleuze is trying to conceive the difference between form and formless as immediacy, he conceives the relation between – this place – as the surface. Because Derrida is trying to conceive the difference between form and formless as mediation, he conceives the relation as a field. The surface implies a duality (dissimilarity), while the field implies a unity (resemblance). For Deleuze, the surface implies an immediate duality within becoming; for Derrida, the field implies a mediate unity to the 'beyond being'. Here therefore is the most precise formula of the diffraction: Deleuze is the true philosopher of duality; Derrida is the true philosopher of unity. In *The Logic of Sense*, Deleuze says, 'This new duality of bodies or states of affairs and effects or incorporeal events [found in Stoic philosophy, which "dissociates" the effect from the cause] entails an upheaval in philosophy' (Deleuze 1969, 16; 1990, 6). In *Voice and Phenomenon*, Derrida says, 'But the strange *unity* of these two parallels [that is, the parallel in Husserl between the empirical life and transcendental life], which relates one to the other, does not let itself be distributed by them and dividing itself *solders* [*soude*] finally the transcendental to its other' (Derrida 1967b, 14; 1973, 14; my italics). No matter what, however, whether we speak of a duality or a unity of form and the formless, for both Derrida and Deleuze, this question of the relation refers us to language (Deleuze 1969, 16; 1990, 6; Derrida 1967b, 14; 1973, 15).

IMMEDIATE DUALITY, MEDIATED UNITY

When Derrida and Deleuze speak about language, they both use Husserl's concept of the noema to define sense. For both, what is important is that Husserl distinguishes the noema simultaneously from the physical object and from psychological lived experiences (Deleuze 1969, 32; 1990, 20; Derrida 1967b, 4–5; 1973, 6). To use Husserl's terminology, the noema is neither *real* nor *reell*, but *irreell*. For both, this non-regional existential status implies that the noema is a kind of an-archic repetition (Derrida 1967c, 243; 1978, 163; Deleuze 1969, 55 and 118; 1990, 41 and 97). Derrida and Deleuze also both refer to paragraph 124 of Husserl's *Ideas I* (Derrida 1967b, 19–20; Deleuze, 1969, 32; 1990, 20).[5] As is well known, in paragraph 124, Husserl describes the passage from intuitive sense to conceptual meaning. While here we have Husserl's distinction between *Sinn* and *Bedeutung*, we must recognise that sense is the broader term equivalent to the noema. There can be intuitive or perceptual sense and an expressive sense and a linguistic meaning which expresses the sense. Now, when Derrida looks at Husserl's description of the passage from intuition to meaning, what he focuses on is that, for Husserl, the passage is a 'coincidence' (*Deckung, recouvrement*) which is not a 'confusion' (Derrida 1972b, 199–200; 1982, 167).

Thus for Derrida the passage is a repetition of the intuitive sense in a conceptual meaning which is formal. But the very repetition of the intuitive sense in the conceptual form, the very formality without which expression would not be what it is, 'displaces' the intuitive sense (Derrida 1972b, 201;

1982, 168). Because of the formality (the *typos* of 'Plato's Pharmacy'), every expression is incomplete in relation to intuition or presence. To use the terminology of Husserl's First Logical Investigation, because every expression repeats the sense in the absence of intuition, every expression is therefore an index; it points to something absent.

Thus we have *Derrida's* critique of Husserl in *Voice and Phenomenon*, which consists in showing the indivision, thus the unity, of expression and indication (the index). For Derrida, Husserl does not recognise that expression and indication use the same form; he does not recognise the resemblance between them. As Derrida says, '*One and the same* phenomenon can be apprehended as expression or as index, as discursive or non-discursive sign. That depends on the intentional lived experience that animates it. The functional character of the description immediately presents us with the full extent of the difficulty' (Derrida 1967b, 20; 1973, 20; my italics). Derrida therefore is taking up Husserl's concept of indication, which is always defined by a pointing relation (1967b, 24; 1973, 23).

In contrast, Deleuze is taking up Husserl's concept of expression, calling sense or the noema 'the expressed'. What Derrida sees in indication is mediation (1967b, 41; 1973, 38), while what Deleuze sees in expression is immediacy (Deleuze 1969, 162; 1990, 137). Or, to put this another way – and we could see this already in the discussion of the simulacrum – for Derrida, the iterable ideality of the noema is more important than its event character (Derrida 1967b, 55; 1973, 50). Yet, for Deleuze, while 'dry reiteration' defines the noema, the event character is more important: sense, a repeatable form, is always an effect (Deleuze 1969, 87–8; 1990, 70).

Thus we have *Deleuze's* critique of Husserl in *The Logic of Sense*, which consists in showing the division, thus the duality, of expression from what causes it to be produced as an effect. Deleuze rejects Husserl's phenomenology as 'the rigorous science of surface effects' (Deleuze 1969, 33; 1990, 21), because Husserl does not recognise that sense is based in the formless; he does not recognise the dissimilarity between the cause of sense and sense as an effect (1969, 119; 1980, 97–8). The expression is not a mere 'shadow' that has the same 'thesis' as what generates it (1969, 147; 1990, 122). As Deleuze says, 'The foundation can never *resemble* what it founds' (1969, 120; 1990, 99; my italics, cf. 149; 123). This Deleuzean principle, which is perhaps *the* defining principle of all of Deleuze's philosophy, implies that the foundation of sense is nonsense. Similarly, when Derrida adopts the functional status of the difference between expression and indication, he is implying that the foundation of sense is nonsense. Given what we have seen so far, we can immediately construct two formulas: for Deleuze, nonsense is immediately sense, and yet is divided from sense; for Derrida, nonsense is mediately sense and yet is united with sense.

The problem of the relation between sense and nonsense leads both Derrida and Deleuze to make Husserl's noema converge with what Lévi-Strauss called a 'floating signifier' (Deleuze 1969, 64; 1990, 49; cf. Derrida 1967c, 423; 1978, 289). The floating signifier is always at once in default or is lacking and in excess in relation to the signified. In other words, it is at once sense (too much sense) and nonsense (not enough sense). For both Derrida and Deleuze, this relation is 'out of joint',[6] 'disjoined', 'out of correspondence', 'unequal', 'inadequate', or 'violent' (Deleuze 1969, 54; 1990, 39; and 1968, 119; 1994, 88; Derrida 1967b, 13; 1973, 13; and 1972a, 124; 1981a, 109). Thus the relation is defined by what Deleuze calls a 'paradoxical instance' (or 'element') (Deleuze 1969, 68; 1990, 53; and 1968, 157; 1994, 119)[7] or by what Derrida calls the 'supplement' (Derrida 1967b, 98; 1973, 88; and 1972a, 193; 1981a, 167).[8]

Yet, for Deleuze, this specific relation between sense and nonsense must be non-exclusionary or internal (Deleuze 1969, 89 and 99; 1990, 71 and 81). For Deleuze, what must be internal to sense is not logical absurdity (square circle), but rather the chaos and formlessness of the body, of the depth, of passions (Deleuze 1969, 114 and 92; 1990, 93 and 74). Deleuze is careful to distinguish nonsense from what he calls 'a-sense' or 'sub-sense' (1969, 111; 1990, 90). With a-sense, the body, passion, has absorbed all activity, all sense, all formality. While a-sense demolishes sense, nonsense grants sense, activity, what Deleuze calls 'superior forms' (1969, 131; 1990, 107). While nonsense is defined for Deleuze as being devoid of sense (formless), he is clear that this defect (*défaut*) does not mean that nonsense is the *absence* of sense. He says, 'Nonsense is that which has no sense, and that which, as it enacts the donation of sense, is opposed to the absence of sense' (1969, 89; 1990, 71). Because nonsense 'is opposed to the *absence* of sense', we must conceive Deleuzean nonsense as presence; indeed, he speaks of a 'co-presence' of sense and nonsense (1969, 85 and 87; 1990, 68 and 70). Although Deleuze uses a negation in the passage just quoted – 'nonsense is that which has *no* sense' – 'this negation no longer expresses anything negative, but rather releases the purely expressible with its two uneven halves' (1969, 161–2 and 148; 1990, 136 and 123). Deleuzean nonsense is not only presence but also a positivity. Without a negation in the middle, we must on the one hand see the paradoxical instance as consisting in an immediate relation between sense and nonsense. Yet, since they are both positivities, sense and nonsense do not resemble one another; there is a division between them: the in-formal. This double positivity – nonsense and sense are both positive, both presences – is why Deleuze defines the paradoxical instance as the 'aliquid', the something (1969, 84; 1990, 49).

In contrast, when Derrida in *Voice and Phenomenon* speaks of the parallelism between any of the oppositions that organise Husserl's discourse, he says that the 'nothing' (*rien*) is what separates the parallels (Derrida 1967b, 12; 1973, 12). Derrida's use of the 'nothing' to designate the same relation as Deleuze designates with a positive term implies that Derrida conceives nonsense by means of negation. Like Deleuze, Derrida does not define nonsense as logical absurdity (square circle) (1967b, 110; 1973, 98). A proposition like 'the circle is square', while lacking any possible object to which it could refer, nevertheless is meaningful. It is meaningful because its grammatical form tolerates 'a relation to an object' (1976b, 110–11; 1973, 99). As Derrida says, 'Here this aim [at an object] will always be disappointed, yet this proposition makes sense only because another content, put in this form (S is P), *would be able* to let us know and see an object' (1967b, 110; 1973, 99; Derrida's italics). Thus nonsense for Derrida is defined by 'non-presence', the lack of a presence of an object. Sense in turn would be constituted by its formal repeatability, but this very formal repeatability would always imply non-presence. Sense can and must be able to be repeated without an intuition of the object, in non-plenitude or non-fulfilment (1967b, 100; 1973, 90). If nonsense for Derrida is defined by the lack of intuitive presence, then sense is always necessarily taken (*pris*) by nonsense. This being taken by nonsense for Derrida means being taken by everything that is 'alien to expression', that is, by indication: 'the effectivity of what is pronounced, the physical incarnation of the *Bedeutung* [meaning], the *body* of speech' (1967b, 36; 1973, 34; my italics).

As with Deleuze, here in Derrida, the reference to the body means a kind of involuntariness or passivity (Derrida 1967b, 37; 1973, 34). However, Derrida is not here understanding the body (*Körper*) as divided from *Leib* or *Geist* (1967b, 37; 1973, 35). For Derrida, there is always a modicum of formality. Being repeatable, the form of the body always exceeds intuitive presence; the interiority of the body always remains non-present. The supplement makes up for – supplements – the lack of intuitive presence of the interior of the body. Like the index finger, it points to the missing presence. Thus what Derrida calls the 'supplement' (1967b, 98–9; 1973, 88–9) consists in a relation different from what we just saw in Deleuze's paradoxical instance. While the paradoxical instance unequally joins two presences, two positivities, the supplement unequally joins presence and non-presence. While the Deleuzean paradoxical instance is defined by an immediate division between sense and nonsense, the Derridean supplement is defined by a mediate unity between sense and nonsense. Despite this difference between the paradoxical instance and the supplement, we are still talking about a relation defined by the 'simul', the 'at the same time'. Thus, as Derrida says, 'sense [has] a temporal nature' (1967b, 95; 1973, 85).

When, in *Voice and Phenomenon*, Derrida examines Husserl's description of temporalisation, that is, of the living present, Derrida emphasises a tension.[9] On the one hand, Husserl's 'whole description is incomparably well adapted to [an] original spreading-out' (Derrida 1967b, 69; 1973, 61). In fact, for Husserl, as Derrida stresses, no now point can be separated from the 'thick slice of time'. On the other hand, 'this spreading out is ... thought and described on the basis of the self-identity of the now as a "source-point"' (ibid.). Derrida's analysis depends on the fact that Husserl makes the retention of the immediate past an irreducible component of the thick slice of time. No now point can be separated from retention. Husserl says, at one point in the descriptions, that retention is a 'non-perception'.

For Derrida, that Husserl calls retention 'non-perception' implies that Husserl recognises that 'the eye closes', that is, that retention consists in a non-presence. For Derrida, re-tention has always already re-peated something that is no longer present. As Derrida says, '... the ideality of the form (*Form*) of presence itself implies that it can be infinitely re-peatable, that its re-turn, as a return of the same, is necessary to infinity and is inscribed in presence itself' (1967b, 75; 1973, 67). The repetition of retention, 'repetition in its most general form', is, for Derrida, the 'constitution of a trace in the most universal sense' (ibid.). Thus, for Derrida, since the trace is necessarily inscribed in presence, there is not a 'radical difference', as Husserl wanted, between evidence and non-evidence, perception and non-perception, between presence and that which is given mediately through signs (1967b, 73; 1973, 65). Rather, there is 'a difference between two modifications of nonperception' (ibid.). This non-radical difference is what Derrida calls 'the same'.

The non-radical difference between the trace's non-presence and presence implies, for Derrida, that the living present is not simple in the literal sense (1967b, 68 and 74; 1973, 61 and 66); it is not 'folded once'. As Derrida says, 'the presence of the present is thought of arising from the fold [*le pli*] of a return, from the movement of repetition, not the reverse' (1976b, 76; 1973, 68). Because the difference between the trace and presence is the same, we must see that Derrida's fold is a folding-in. The trace's non-presence has included (*a com-pris*, that is, has contaminated) presence. Non-presence is implied (*im-pli-qué*) (1967b, 96; 1973, 86) in presence, and thus the fold is always 'du-pli-cated' (11; 11). We can describe Derrida's fold therefore as a knot twisted together around a point that is never fully present, a knot therefore always still loose, interwoven (20; 20), sewn together so that one cannot determine one side from the other, so that one side mixes with the other. Derrida's fold is what we earlier called the displaced field (as opposed to the surface). In a later essay Derrida calls this field a 'non-lieu', a 'non-place'.[10] But, because Derrida always emphasises the 'medium' (1967b, 85; 1973, 76), we must characterise his 'non-lieu' as a 'mi-lieu' (Derrida 1972a, 144; 1981a, 126), a halfway place, which never quite but almost gathers presence and non-presence into a unity: the same.[11]

As is well known, Deleuze too uses the image of the fold and characterises it as both a 'milieu' and a 'non-lieu' (Deleuze 1969, 194–95; 1990, 166). But, Deleuze's fold is not the same but divided. It is not chiasmatic;[12] it is un-folded (déplié) (1969, 31–2; 1990, 20). Deleuze says, 'Only by breaking open the circle, as in the case of the Möbius strip [the French word here is 'anneau': ring], by unfolding [dépliant] it lengthwise, by untwisting it, does the dimension of sense itself appear' (1969, 31; 1990, 20). In fact, Deleuze compares this 'unfolding' operation to making a purse out of handkerchiefs sewn 'in the wrong way' so that the outside surface and the inside surface are 'continuous' (1969, 21; 1990, 11). 'In the wrong way' means that they are not sewn into one another in order to form a medium. Rather they face one another continuously, immediately, 'unanimously' (Deleuze 1988a, 43; 1993, 30), and nevertheless, the two surfaces are du-pli-cated, divided. This unfolding, for Deleuze, defines time.

Like Derrida, Deleuze is trying to conceive time not in terms of the present. As he says in *Bergsonism*, 'We are too accustomed to think in terms of the present' (Deleuze 1966, 53; 1991a, 58). In *The Logic of Sense* therefore Deleuze speaks of 'side-stepping' (*esquiver*) the present. This 'side-stepping' can occur in two ways, what Deleuze calls 'Chronos' and what he calls 'Aion'. Chronos, according to Deleuze, 'side-steps' the present in the now, in a 'vast and thick' present that 'absorbs' or 'includes' (*comprend*) the past and future (Deleuze 1969, 190 and 193; 1990, 162 and 164). Chronos therefore side-steps the present by 'mixing' (*mélanger*) the past and future together. We cannot fail to recognise the similarity of Chronos to Husserl's living present and even to Derrida's analysis of it, and indeed when Deleuze describes Chronos he uses the phrase 'living present' (1969, 192; 1990, 164). Aion however side-steps the present in a different way. According to Deleuze, instead of the now, the instant 'without thickness' defines Aion: 'Instead of a present which absorbs the past and future, a future and a past divide the present at every instant, which subdivides it into past and future to infinity, in the two directions at once [*dans les deux sens à la fois*]' (1969, 192–3; 1990, 164). Because of this infinite division of the present, the instant cannot be identified with any 'assignable present' (1969, 193; 1990, 165). Literally, the instant is nowhere or everywhere; as we have already noted, it is 'atopon', the non-place, not the mi-lieu (1969, 195; 1990, 166). Aion breaks open the Möbius 'ring' and changes it into 'a straight line, limitless in both directions' (1969, 194; 1990, 165). This straight line is the Deleuzean surface. And Aion, for Deleuze gives us a 'lengthened, unfolded experience' (1969, 32; 1990, 20).

THE EXPERIENCE OF THE VOICE IS THE EXPERIENCE OF DEATH

These different places – the mi-lieu and the non-lieu – have different ontological statuses. The non-lieu in Deleuze is becoming, while the mi-lieu in Derrida is beyond being. Thus, as they themselves have done, we can return to the old scholastic ontological designations of univocity and equivocity. Indeed, Deleuze says that the Aion is the pure infinitive, the Verb (1969, 216; 1990, 184–5). When Deleuze speaks of 'the univocity of being' (1968, 57–61; 1994, 39–42, and 1969, 208–11; 1990, 177–80), the 'uni' here, the oneness, refers to immediacy. There is an immediate relation between the two sides of the surface, between nonsense and sense, between past and future. This immediate relation is the literally the 'verb', the voice. The verb for Deleuze is always the infinitive, which implies that the verb is the place of becoming. Thus the phrase 'the univocity of being' means 'the becoming of being', or, better, 'the immediate becoming of being'. Now the 'uni' of the two sides is accomplished by the voice, but the voice cannot be a vocal medium for Deleuze. Such a mediation would introduce equivocity. Therefore, according to Deleuze, only silence allows for an 'immediate communication' between the two sides (1969, 162; 1990, 137). Thus, as strange as this sounds, in *The Logic of Sense*, Deleuze says that the 'verb', literally, the voice, is silent (1969, 281; 1990, 241). To use the terminology of *Difference and Repetition*, the verb is the 'loquendum', that is, what is language and silence at the same time (Deleuze 1968, 186–7; 1994, 143). In *The Logic of Sense*, the *loquendum* is what Deleuze (appropriating Lewis Carroll) calls a 'portmanteau word', that is, a word that unifies two other words without a copula, in other words, unifies them with a silent verb, for example, 'slithy' (=lithe-slimy-active) and 'mimsy' (=flimsy-miserable) (Deleuze 1969, 61; 1990, 45). A portmanteau word is the paradoxical instance. Thus, in *The Logic of Sense*, Deleuze calls the silent verb 'the paradox of the voice': '[the voice] has the dimensions of a language without having its conditions; it awaits the event that will make it a language. It is no longer noise but not yet language' (1969, 226; 1990, 194).

As we saw, the paradoxical instance functions for Deleuze between two presences or positivities. We can see now that it functions between two sounds: noise and language. Noise, for Deleuze, is the noise of singularities, of the abyss, of the body, of passions (1969, 130; 1990, 106–7). It is 'the full voice of intoxication and anger' (1969, 130; 1990, 107). This noise is 'clamour' (cf. Deleuze 1968, 52, 114, 389; 1994, 35, 83–4, 304). This noise is the 'noisy events' of death (1969, 212; 1990, 163). As Deleuze says, 'sickness and death are the event itself' (Deleuze,1969, 131; 1990, 108), or 'every event [is] a kind of plague, war, wound, or death' (1969, 177; 1990, 151). Following Blanchot, Deleuze distinguishes between two kinds of death; death is double (1969, 177–8, 182–3, 258–9; 1990, 151–2, 156, 222; and 1968, 148–9; 1994, 112–13). On the one hand, death is personal: I am dying. It attacks my body in the present, causing me to cry and yell, forcing noise out of me. This noise is not yet language. On the other hand, death is impersonal: they (*on*) are dying. This death of them (*l'on*) is incorporeal since it is not grounded in my body. But this impersonal death also 'side-steps' the present. This death is the infinitive death of them in which *one* (*on*) never finishes dying. This second death is silent, or this silence is a dead space, in which nothing noisy happens, the non-lieu. Yet, for Deleuze, the silent death of them is the genuine event in which 'death turns against death' in order to produce an excess of life. This 'strangely impersonal death', Deleuze says, is 'always to come, the source of an incessant multiple adventure in a persistent *question*' (1968, 148; 1994, 112; my italics).

Thus by stressing this question, we can provide an example of the experience of the voice. It comes from *Difference and Repetition*: the police interrogation (Deleuze 1968, 255; 1994, 197). In a police interrogation, the detectives ask the questions. I am *powerless* in relation to them. I do not know the answer (cf. 1969, 220; 1990, 194). And if I say, 'Who are you to ask the questions?', the detectives reply by inflicting pain on me, on my own body. I am dying. Even though I am innocent, they impose an imperative: 'Answer the question!' When I asked, 'who are you to ask the questions', that was stupid. It relies on the voice of others: 'My father has lots of money. Who are you to ask the questions?' (cf. Deleuze 1969, 219–20; 1990, 193–4). But if there is 'simply a silence with only the noise of my own breathing' (cf. 1969, 180; 1990, 154), then thinking begins. Thinking begins in silence, when no longer relying on the voice of others – they are silenced – one begins to respond in one voice, the voice of everyone or no one: *On*. Then the transmutation of powerlessness into power occurs: one invents a response to the question. The experience of the voice in Deleuze therefore is the experience of being 'demolished' (1969, 180–9; 1990, 154–61). The police interrogation, for Deleuze, is an experience, a test, an ordeal, *une épreuve*.

While the Deleuzean voice is the voice of one, the Derridean voice is the voice of the other. The title of Derrida's 1967 study of Husserl, *La Voix et le phénomène* refers back to his earlier 1962 Introduction to his French translation of Husserl's 'The Origin of Geometry'. There (Derrida 1962, 104; 1977, 102),

Derrida realises that language consists in a double necessity or imperative. Simultaneously, language must be equivocal and univocal. We were able to anticipate this duplicity in Derrida, when we noted that for him indication, the relation of pointing to, defines language. Language for Derrida is always defined by a 'relation to'. By means of its repeatability, language must always be the same, univocal, and sent *to* an other who is not present, who is beyond being (beyond presence), equivocal. While for both Derrida and Deleuze, the verb defines language, for Derrida, the verb is always in the dative case; it always has an indirect object. Thus the 'verb', in Derrida, literally the voice, is always an address *to* me from the other.

This necessary equivocity of the other organises Chapter 7 of *Voice and Phenomenon*: 'The Voice that Keeps Silence'. Here Derrida is examining what Husserl says about the pre-expressive stratum of sense, 'the absolute silence of the self relation' (Derrida 1967b, 77; 1973, 69). Derrida therefore is examining the experience of auto-affection, of the fold. Inside myself when I speak to myself, I make no actual vocalisation. Thus auto-affection consists in a voice that keeps silence. In this experience, according to Derrida, I must hear myself speak at the very moment I speak. It is the same me speaking as hearing: uni–vocal. Yet, given that I am not the one speaking when I am the one hearing and vice versa, it is not the same me speaking as hearing: equi-vocal. Because there is always a retention inseparable from the now, from the very moment in which I am hearing, there is always an other in me, in the same, speaking to me (Derrida 1967b, 92–3; 1973, 82–3).

Earlier we encountered the fundamental principle of Deleuze's entire thinking (immediate duality): the ground can never resemble what it grounds. Now we encounter the fundamental principle of Derrida's entire thinking (mediate unity): I can never have a presentation of the interior life of an other, but only ever a re-presentation (never *Gegenwärtigung* but only ever *Vergegenwärtigung*). Derrida has taken this phenomenological insight from Husserl's Fifth Cartesian Meditation and generalised it to all experience, even my own internal experience. Even though this other is in me, is the same as me, I can only have a re-presentation of that other. Thus, while this other speaks to me, inside me, this other hides silence in the voice (*Vergegenwärtigung*). This other me is always already non-present, beyond being, thus dead.

For Derrida too, the experience of the voice is the experience of death. Again, in the earlier Introduction to Husserl's 'The Origin of Geometry', Derrida had realised that if sense is defined as indefinite re-iteration, then it required necessarily to be embodied in language, vocalised, and ultimately written down (Derrida 1962, 88; 1977, 90). Yet, if linguistic embodiment implied indefinite re-iteration, then whenever I speak, my disappearance in general is implied (Derrida 1967b, 60–1; 1973, 54–5). My death is implied even when I use an indexical such as 'me' (1967b, 108; 1973, 96–7); the very fact that it points to me across a distance implies that it does not require me to be present, up close to it. I am already other and absent from it. For Derrida, as for Deleuze, the experience of death is double. On the one hand, it is the death of me. Whenever I speak, when, for example, I say 'I am dead', this speaking constitutes a repeatable form that necessarily survives without me. On the other hand, for Derrida, death is also the death of an other. Whenever I speak, when, for example, I say 'I am alive', this speaking fills a repeatable form with presence, a repeatable form which has survived the death of countless others. Quoting the Biblical definition of Yahweh as 'I am He who is', Derrida says that this sentence is 'the *confession* [*l'aveu*] of a mortal' (1967b, 61; 1973, 54, my italics).[13]

Thus, by stressing this confession, we can provide an example in Derrida of the experience of the voice. It comes from *Voice and Phenomenon* (Derrida 1967b, 78–9; 1973, 70–1). Instead of a police interrogation, as with Deleuze, we have with Derrida, a self-interrogation. The experience of the voice in Derrida is not just any internal soliloquy. It occurs when I have wronged another. Thus the experience consists in me 'addressing myself to myself as to a second person whom I blame, exhort, call to a decision or a remorse' (1967b, 79; 1973, 71). When I say to myself, 'You have gone wrong, you can't go on like that!' (1967b, 78; 1973, 70), I become other. As an other, as an other no longer here, as an other speaking from the grave, wronged, I put myself in question. Again as in the police interrogation, the other asks the questions: 'Why did you act that way?' Again, I am *powerless* in relation to the other. I am caught (*pris*). When I ask this ghost who troubles me 'what am I to do?', he remains silent. Must I risk my life for the other who haunts me? I do not know what to do or say; I cannot decide. I do not know how to right this wrong, and, in fact, nothing can ever right it. But, if I believe in the voice of the other, then thinking begins. Then the transmutation of powerlessness into power occurs: even though it is impossible, one decides. The experience of the voice in Derrida therefore is the experience of bad conscience. The self-interrogation, for Derrida, is also an experience, a test, an ordeal, *une épreuve* (1967b, 111; 1973, 99).

CONCLUSION: THE BEGINNINGS OF THOUGHT

The point of diffraction in the great French philosophy of the Sixties is at its finest between Derrida and Deleuze. As we have seen, the *point* is the simulacrum understood through in-formality. If we can speak this way, the *diffraction* consists in Derrida emphasising the 'form' (repetition) and in

Deleuze emphasising the 'in' (event). This slight difference of emphasis between difference in itself and contamination allowed us to insert oppositions into the diffraction. For Deleuze, the relation between form and formless, that is, the 'simul' of the simulacrum, is a relation of immediate duality (dissimilarity). For Derrida, the same relation is a relation of mediate unity (resemblance). Two presences or two positivities (sense and nonsense) constitute the Deleuzean immediate duality. Presence and non-presence, a positive and a negative (sense and nonsense) constitute the Derridean mediate unity.[14] Thus going across the convergence between phenomenology and structuralism, between the noema and the floating signifier, we had the opposition between the Deleuzean paradoxical instance and the Derridean supplement. And this opposition led us to time – the 'simul' again – in which we were able to see that Derrida conceives the place between form and formless as a chiasmic fold, the mi-lieu (the displaced field) and Deleuze conceives this place as an untied fold, the non-lieu (the surface). The idea of the fold finally led us to the experience of the voice. Here, the opposition becomes the opposition between interrogation by another, the police interrogation in Deleuze, and self-interrogation, the confession in Derrida. But as we have just seen, this characterisation actually means that, in Deleuze, the interrogation by another is an interrogation by the self understood as the 'one', the 'dissolved self', as Deleuze would say. In Derrida, the characterisation actually means that the self-interrogation is an interrogation by an other.

But here we must be careful. This alterity in Derrida does not mean that he is a philosopher of pure transcendence; he is a philosopher of the same, of impure, that is, contaminated immanence. Perhaps we must conceive the dative relation in Derrida not as a pure 'à' ('to') but as an impure 'à même' ('right on'[15]): transcendence *à même* immanence. Similarly, the dissolved self in Deleuze is a dissolution into the other that comes from the outside, and thus perhaps we must conceive the lack of the dative relation in Deleuze as impure transcendence. Always the diffraction threatens to disappear into the point – even when we look at the more recent philosophy of Deleuze and Derrida. Deleuze abandons the idea of the simulacrum in favour of the idea of a multiplicity, while Derrida abandons the idea of the simulacrum in favour of the spectre. Yet, what maintains the continuity over their earlier and later works is the 'untimely' in Deleuze and the 'older' in Derrida. Both the untimely and the older, however, concern the future: *l'à-venir*. But, at least, we can see always that their point of diffraction consists in the experience of death. When I suffer the erosion of my thought, this impotence forces me to think. The experience of death is fundamental for Derrida and Deleuze.[16]

Notes

1. I investigate this and other aspects of the great French philosophy of the Sixties in Lawlor 2003.
2. One should keep in mind that Chapter 1 of *Difference and Repetition* is called 'difference in itself'.
3. One finds a similar statement at DG 1972, 323–4; 1984, 271. When Deleuze speaks of making the simulacra rise to the surface, as if they were buried in caves (Deleuze 1969, 304; 1990, 263), he is implying that the reversal of Platonism consists in a kind of philosophical archaeology. Similarly, in 'Plato's Pharmacy', Derrida defines reversing Platonism as the '*exhumation* of the conceptual monuments erected by Platonism' (Derrida 1972a, 122–3; 1981a, 107; my italics; see also 1972a, 149; 1981a, 129). We should keep in mind Deleuze's close connection to Foucault. It is possible to read *The Logic of Sense* as an extension of *Les Mots et les choses*. See Deleuze 1969, 83–4; 1990, 66–7. Furthermore, Deleuze uses the word 'archéology' to describe a double thinking (1969, 53; 1990, 39). Also, one should not overlook Derrida's constant use of the word 'archive'. See 1972a, 122; 1981a, 107; 1967b, 15; 1973, 15. See also Derrida's recent *Mal d'archive* (Derrida 1995b). It is at this point that we can see the connection to Foucault and even to the later Merleau-Ponty, as I show in Lawlor 2003.
4. Derrida 1967b, 20; 1973, 21. Because we are interested in the question of voice in Derrida and Deleuze, we are not going to use the standard English title, but rather *Voice and Phenomenon*.
5. See also 'Form and Meaning: A Note on the Phenomenology of Language', (Derrida 1972b; 1982).
6. Derrida begins *Spectres de Marx* with this phrase from *Hamlet* (1993d, 43–4; 1994b, 19–20).
7. Here Deleuze is calling the 'paradoxical element', 'the dark precursor'.
8. Eric Alliez points to this distinction in his 'Ontology and Logography', in this volume.
9. For a more detailed analysis of Derrida and Husserl see Lawlor 2002.
10. Derrida 1986, 181; 1979a, 138. This non-place is also, for Derrida, Plato's *chora*. See Derrida 1993b, especially p. 74, where Derrida plays on the word 'milieu'; 1995c, 116. Cf. also Wolff 1992, 245. For another use of this 'non-lieu', see Foucault 1971; 1998.
11. In his early writings Derrida uses Merleau-Ponty's figure of the chiasm to speak of this undecidable point; see Derrida 1972a, 145; 1981a, 127. Cf. also Derrida 1987a, 23–4; 1989b, 8–9. Here Derrida is speaking of the four threads he is following in his reading of Heidegger. He says, 'Following the trace of Heidegger's spirituality would perhaps approach, not a central point of this knot – I believe there is none – but approach what gathers a nodal resistance in its most economical torsion.'
12. Cf. Deleuze 1986, 119; 1988b, 112. Here Deleuze is speaking of the fold in Foucault. He says, '. . . being is between two forms. Is this not precisely what Heidegger had called the 'between-two' or Merleau-Ponty termed the 'interlac-

ing or chiasmus'? In fact, they are not at all the same thing. . . . Everything takes place as if Foucault were reproaching Heidegger and Merleau-Ponty for going too quickly.'

13. On the concept of 'aveu', see Derrida 1994a, 72–3; 1997a, 54–5.
14. For more on the positive and negative in Derrida and Deleuze, see Bearn 2000.
15. The French adverb 'à même' is quite difficult to translate into English; its closest equivalent is one thing being 'right on' the other. But this English translation lacks the reference to 'le même', the same.
16. This essay was first presented as a lecture at Universiteit voor Humanistiek (Utrecht) on 30 May 2001 with the title 'The Experience of Force, the Experience of the Other: The Philosophy of Difference in Deleuze and Derrida.' It also has a companion piece (Lawlor 2000a).

CHAPTER 5

Ontology and Logography:
The Pharmacy, Plato and the Simulacrum

Eric Alliez

(translated by Robert Rose and Paul Patton)

The world is its outside. (Maurice Blanchot)

At heart, the underlying question of this exchange is the question
of materialism. (Fragment of a letter from Jean-Louis Houdebine
to Jacques Derrida. (Derrida 1981b, 91))

In other words, what does Platonism as repetition signify?
(Jacques Derrida)

It is a deeper, more secret duality, buried in sensible and material
bodies themselves: a subterranean duality between what receives
the action of the idea and what slips away from this action.
(Gilles Deleuze)

DOUBLES

That this will not exactly be a communication is also to say that the exigencies
which determine the cost of subscribing to it do not seem to me likely to do
justice to the play (*paidia*) which Plato had to admit was inevitably present in
all philosophical writing. To exceed the carefully guarded logic of intended
meaning (*vouloir-dire*), the part of Platonic play – the play of the other in being
– was ontologically sidelined by the author of *Metaphysics, Book Gamma*, in
deciding in favour of an identitarian determination constitutive of the unity of
sense and of the consensus that grounds it in return. Without being altogether
ready to evaluate the scope of this reflection, it seems to me that the author-

function arises fully armed from this *originary scene* of the *Metaphysics* in which
Aristotle reduces to silence the polyphonic dramatisation of Socratic rejoinders
in the name of the new sense propounded by the *Philosopher*, and in the name
of a systematic philosophy that Plato had obstinately refused to produce.

According to the affirmation of *Letter VII*:

> one statement at any rate I can make in regard to all who have written or may
> write with a claim to knowledge of the subjects to which I devote myself – no
> matter how they pretend to have acquired it, whether from my instruction or
> from others or by their own discovery. Such writers can in my opinion have
> no real acquaintance with the subject. I certainly have composed no work in
> regard to it, nor shall I ever do so in future . . . If I thought it possible to deal
> adequately with the subject in a treatise or a lecture for the general public,
> what finer achievement would there have been in my life than to write a work
> of great benefit to mankind and to bring the nature of things to light for all
> men? (Plato 1961, Letter VII, 341 b-d).

'Thereupon', to follow the trail identified by Vincente Descombes (1971,
6–16), we will ask: did Plato really write the *Sophist* instead of the *Philosopher*
he announced (at 217a) because the desire of unification in a definitive book
imitating the model of the world fell under the stricture of the 'third man'
argument – that is, of an infinite doubling of books each of which in turn
divides in order to multiply the others? A *Philosopher* whose absence is perhaps
justified in Letter VII,[1] or even prescribed by the *Sophist* about whom it is said
that he exists only insofar as he partakes of a simulacrum of being or that 'he
meddles and insinuates himself everywhere'. The final definition of the Sophist
'leads us to the point where we can no longer distinguish him from Socrates
himself – the ironist working in private by means of brief arguments. Was it
not necessary to push the irony to that extreme?' asks Gilles Deleuze. 'Was it
not Plato himself who pointed out the direction for the overturning of Platonism?' (Deleuze 1969, 256; 1990, 295; trans. modified; cf. *Sophist* 268b–c).

In this direction, Platonism appears like the primitive scene of a modernity
haunted, since Nietzsche, by the rediscovery of the genetic and 'differential'
element of the simulacrum. In philosophy, as we know, it is with Nietzsche
that pure becoming once again finds the *force* to express the play of a ?-being
carrying all things to the condition of a simulacrum in the relationship of the
ungrounded to the groundless, 'the mad element that subsists and occurs on
the other side of the order that Ideas impose and that things receive' (Deleuze
1969, 20; 1990, 2).

As a result of this (onto)logic of sense, we can read aphorism 289 of *Beyond
Good and Evil* as standing in for the Platonic letter:

The hermit does not believe that a philosopher – supposing that a philosopher has always been first of all a hermit – has ever expressed his real and final opinions in books: does one not write books precisely to conceal what lies within us? Indeed, he will doubt whether a philosopher *could* have 'final and real' opinions at all, whether behind each of his caves there does not and must not lie another, deeper cave – a stranger, more comprehensive world beyond the surface, an abyss [*Abgrund*] behind every ground [*Grund*], beneath every 'foundation' [*Begründung*] . . . Every philosophy also *conceals* a philosophy; every opinion is also a hiding-place, every word also a mask. (Nietzsche 1990, 216)

I could have dispensed with citing this famous page, which counts as one of the most beautiful ever written by Nietzsche if, on at least two levels, the Nietzschean doubling did not profoundly dictate the reading of the Platonic Odyssey undertaken by Gilles Deleuze and Jacques Derrida.

1. First of all, we note the analogous procedure of unveiling the latent content hidden behind the manifest content. As a result, in each case, the Platonic distinction is displaced prior to the great Idea/image duality and becomes instead a distinction between two sorts of images, or two sorts of writing. Plato's text is thereby delivered over to a symptomatology, the principle of which consists in counter-effectuating its displacements of meaning from the point of view of the system of forces that gave rise to it, that motivate it and work through it. The motivation of Platonism is tracked in the same way that Plato tracks the sophist. The 'overly simple character of the overturning' – according to a formula borrowed from Derrida's *Positions* – is measured all along the length of this programme. The reason is that the forces are all the more dissimulated as they exceed the system of simple meaning [*vouloir-dire*]. Hence the necessity of doubling the *overturning* of the classical opposition by a general *displacement* of the system. 'It is only on this condition that deconstruction will provide itself the means with which to *intervene* in the field of oppositions it *criticizes, which is also a field of nondiscursive forces*' (Derrida 1972b, 393; 1982, 329; emphasis added).[2] Made explicit in *Positions*, the general strategy of deconstruction will strive to repeat indefatigably the text while *altering* it and 'adding' to it the genealogy of the conflictual and subordinate structure of the opposition in question. In turn, this leads to the irruptive emergence of nomad concepts, of undecidable concepts that correspond 'to whatever always has *resisted* the former organization of forces, which always has constituted the remainder irreducible to the dominant force which organized the – to say it quickly – logocentric hierarchy' (1972b, 393; 1982, 329–30). Like the *pharmakon*, some 'units of simulacra'

return to the surface to disorganise profoundly a textual field that had been until then regulated in a state of equilibrium, in order to submit the text to the becoming that is coextensive with it 'without ever constituting a third term'. In fact, Derrida writes in a thoroughly Deleuzean vein, 'I attempt to bring the critical operation to bear against the unceasing reappropriation of this work of the simulacrum by a dialectics of the Hegelian type [which internalises the self-difference of the recovered identity]' (Derrida 1972c, 56–9; 1981b, 43).

At this first level of a subversive reading of Platonism, we witness a veritable system of references and referrals (latent and manifest) between Deleuze and Derrida. Deleuze's 'Plato and the Simulacrum' refers to the unsettled relationship between writing and the Platonic *logos*, which is highlighted in Derrida's 'Plato's Pharmacy'. It is entirely an affair of subversion 'against the father' mounted by a simulacrum that no longer passes through the Idea of the Same, but through a 'model' of the Other, in order to produce an effect of resemblance or repetition on the basis of an internalised dissemblance (Deleuze 1969, 296–7; 1990, 257–8).[3] For its part, Derrida's '*Différance*' begins with a series of remarks on the possibility of an 'order which no longer belongs to sensibility', one that 'resists the opposition, one of the founding oppositions of philosophy, between the sensible and the intelligible' (Derrida 1972b, 5; 1982, 5) (and its overly simple overturning), in order to place itself under the rubric of a symptomatology that always diagnoses the detour or the ruse of an instance disguised in its *différance*'. *Différance* thereby refers to a force that only ever presents itself in the movement of differences among forces, bringing back 'all the others of *physis* . . . as *physis* deferred and differing. *Physis* in *différance*'. At this point, Derrida cites the following passage from Deleuze's *Nietzsche and Philosophy*: 'The difference of quantity is the essence of force, the relation of force to force' (Derrida 1972b, 18–19; 1982, 17; cf. Deleuze 1962, 49; 1983, 43). This passage is introduced by Deleuze in the following way: 'If a force is inseparable from its quantity it is no more separable from the other forces which it relates to' (Deleuze 1962, 49; 1983, 43).

For Deleuze, this means that the multiplicity of forces refers to the multiple being *of* force (as *difference* of potential constituting the intensive nature of the transcendental field)[4] to which we must relate the dualisms as though to an outside irreducible to any intralinguistic play of signifiers . . . to a 'formless outside . . . a turbulent stormy zone where singular points and relationships of force between these points are tossed about', to '*an outside which is farther* away than any external world and even any form of exteriority, which henceforth becomes infinitely closer' (1986, 129 and 92; 1988b, 121 and 86; trans. modified). A depth deeper than any bottom, a cave behind every cave. . . . this is Deleuze's profoundly ontological response to the question formulated by

Derrida at the end of '*Différance*': 'How to conceive what is outside a text?'
(Derrida 1972b, 27; 1982, 15).[5]

2. We pass here to a second, discordant level, that will fight against the
linkage of reading to writing in one of two ways: either in terms of *statements*
(*énoncés*), thereby relocating language within the domain of exercise of an
enunciative function. This implies that discourses are irreducible to the system
of language alone since 'events make language possible' (Deleuze 1969, 212;
1990, 181).[6] (Parenthetically, this move to the enunciative domain of statements is the 'more' [*plus*] that makes so ironic Foucault's title, *Les Mots et les
choses* (*Words and Things*)); or in terms of textuality, where 'everything becomes
discourse' as a function of a 'generalised structure of reference' endlessly
relaunched in the absence of a transcendental signified able to calm the play
'in the last instance'; and where force – like matter, which, as we read in
Positions, stands in 'a relationship of written concatenation' to other agencies
(Derrida 1972c, 91n27; 1981b, 106n37) – is no more than the series of its
effects deployed in the generalised writing of supplementarity. A graphology of
forces progressively reduces to silence the *primitive* affirmation according to
which 'the field of oppositions . . . is also a field of non-discursive forces'
(Derrida 1972b, 393; 1982, 329). And, beneath all the grounds [*fonds*], under
all the foundations [*fondations*], there is only an abyss that the statements of
ontology seek to fill by determining the sense of being as signified presence, a
first signification [*primum signatum*] amounting 'to a subordination of the
movement of *différance* in favour of the presence of a value or a *meaning*
supposedly anterior to *différance*' (Derrida 1972c, 41; 1981b, 29).[7]

It is for this reason that Jean-Michel Rey will entitle his very Derridean
book *Lecture de Nietzsche: l'enjeu des signes* (1971).[8]

So, to speculate on 'Plato' is to be referred to the 'effect' of a network of
relays the *primary position* of which (cf. the *thēsein* of the end of the *Sophist*,
268c) suggests that its constitutive function is to mask the indecision of the
sign (a non-'linguistic' sign, cf. *Cratylus*) as a means of producing sense. In this
self-reference, contemporary philosophy uses for its own ends the figure of
Socrates, he who doesn't write, as a curious pragmatics transcendental to its
own use. The Socratic 'refusal of theses' would be deployed as the baroque
theatre of the archi-text is written in order to be diffracted in an erased
economy of forces always already represented in another writing: that which
produces the trace as trace, to the extent that presence is irremediably
dissimulated in it.

All this implies that, after Nietzsche and Heidegger, and in the excess of
Nietzsche over Heidegger, the exchange of these Platonic letters circulating
between Jacques Derrida and Gilles Deleuze constrains us to recommence

from the beginning the phenomenology of the question of being, a question put (back) into play by 'the absence of the transcendental signified as limitlessness of play' (Derrida 1967a, 73; 1974, 50), minus the interiority of the soul as regulated within the Platonic system.

THE COLLAPSE OF PLATONISM

> What then? I cried with curiosity.
> *Who then*? you should ask!
> Thus spoke Dionysus; and then he became quiet in his peculiar way, that is, as a seducer does. (Nietzsche)

> Each time, until now, that one has declared: 'This is', an ulterior, more refined epoque has been found in order to reveal that these words only had one possible sense: 'This signifies.' (Nietzsche)

Since it was written, what has not been said about the inexhaustible character of the interpretation of the work that has reached us under the name of Plato? In so far as it falls short of the Aristotelian decision of the unity of sense that was supposed to overcome the Platonic embarrassment (if Parmenides, then Gorgias, therefore Socrates), Platonism is presented as the *elementary* point of implication and application of an *active linguistics* in its critical task of bringing to light the value judgements which dominate and articulate the logic of the concept. It is for this reason that particular attention is paid to the ironic and moral dimension of the Platonic dialectic[9] that cannot pose the question '*what is?*' without selecting the hereditary line of the '*who?*'. Who has the right to bear the name? To whom does the name revert? Who has the right to name according to a well-founded claim? In the Platonic dialogues, as Vincent Descombes remarks, 'everything happens as if the name [*le nom*] were always a *proper noun* [un *nom propre*]' (only Justice is just), as if the rivalry among pretenders had to do first and foremost with the name (those who are called just) (Descombes 1971, 53–4). It is for this reason that the dialectical statement of rivalry *profoundly* defines the Platonic modality of appropriating language by unveiling its inevitable *reference*: the will to distinguish the true from the false claimant pretender.

It remains to determine what permits the effective choice between rival forces. How does one choose in the absence of the mediating logic of a 'representable' *ratio* in things? This was Aristotle's great critique of Plato: you will never reach a well-founded specification of the concept by differentiating on the basis of inspirations from the Idea alone. . . . And the argument carries weight. Plato had to invent those great founding stories he needed in order to authenticate a pure, unrepresentable line of descent from the Idea . . . Only the recourse to 'myth' allowed the evaluation of claimants as a function of the degree of their elective participation in the *Imparticipable* that unequally gives to each something in which to participate. This proto-narrative of foundation designates the Idea as the appropriate foundation for discrimination at the moment when the dialectic discovers its genuine unity in myth. It appears here in the test of the selective foundation that resemblance to (the image of) the Idea is the elective repetition of the unicity of the Reference. In accordance with this writing, the selection begins by sidelining the philosopher's great rival, with his capacity for bringing forth a world, or being, by saying it – it is a question of the poet *insofar as he leads back to the element that produces and nourishes the sophist* (sophistry is poetry from the speculative point of view of its *phantastic* or logological doubling).

The foundation selects images as a function of an internal resemblance founded on the originary identity of the Idea that includes the relations and propositions constitutive of the essence. To establish the domain of representation on the model of the Same and the Similar, the method of division relates the Idea to the image, the original to the copy that it unifies in distinguishing them, as well-founded phenomena,[10] from the simulacrum and phantasm. In discovering the real distinction between two kinds of images in the *relationship of forces* between model and simulacrum, we finally attain the true motivation of Platonism 'erected on the basis of this wish to hunt down the phantasms or simulacra'. Namely, using difference in order to make the identical exist, declaring difference 'unthinkable in itself and sending it, along with the simulacra, back to the bottomless ocean' (Deleuze 1968, 166; 1994, 127) – 'This Platonic wish to exorcize simulacra', Deleuze concludes, 'is what entails the subjection of difference' (1968, 340; 1994, 265).

Here we have an iconological exorcism derived from a moral vision of the world that must be affirmed at least once in the light of day, in order that the categorical logic of the representation that will cover it up can be deployed. Because the world of representation is not a given, the Platonic statement allows a glimpse of the difference in *nature* between a copy ordered according to the model of Identity and a simulacrum grafted on a disparity which attacks both the notion of copy and the notion of model . . . It is *in itself* that it includes the differential point of view that brings forth in a lightning flash the terrible model of the Other in which rumbles the unlimited power of becoming, 'a becoming subversive of depths'. 'To impose a limit on this becoming, to order it according to the same, to render it similar – and, for the part which remains rebellious, to repress it as deeply as possible, to shut it up in a cavern at the bottom of the Ocean – such is the aim of Platonism in its will to bring about the triumph of icons over simulacra' (Deleuze 1969, 298; 1990, 258–9).

We see the *collapse of Platonism* as it states/announces the subversion of the world of representation starting with an *ontological overturning* determined by the positive power that raises the simulacrum back to the surface. It is in the direction of this differential and intensive element, where the play of the world finds its genesis *and its primary resistance*, that *Différence et Repetition* seeks the conditions, no longer of possible experience, but of real experience. The essential is that only differences resemble each other because imitation (of the Idea) gives way to repetition as the being *of* the sensible, as a play of the individuating difference of the simulacrum that is nothing other than the differentiator of difference assuming the whole of being (*l'étant*). Difference and repetition designate the secret of the eternal return which makes divergent series come back as divergent, and affirms the manifold being of force as 'the other of language without which language would not be what it is' (Derrida 1967c, 45; 1978, 27) – when being (*l'étant*), for its part, *is* simulacrum.

It is impossible here not to stop at a chiasmatic effect that makes us ask ourselves: is it certain that in multiplying the surface play of simulacra 'as in a "flow" of speech' ('a wild discourse that would incessantly slide over its referent without ever stopping' (Deleuze 1969, 10; 1990, 2)), Deleuze does not end up losing sight of the operation of the demiurge who bends and twists a *rebellious* material? Deleuze *executing* the ontological overturning by virtue of an effect of simulation purely logological – would it not be definitively that 'in this sense, the simulacrum and the symbol are one; in other words, the simulacrum is the sign in so far as the sign interiorizes the conditions of its own repetition?' (Deleuze 1968, 92; 1994, 67). Repeating that difference is the only origin, Deleuze refers to Derrida's *différance* (1968, 164; 1994, 125), as found in 'Freud and the Scene of Writing', where the motif of a repression and a suppression (*refoulement . . . répression*) of writing is taken up, a motif which has been, ever since Plato, in solidarity with the determination of the being of being (*l'étant*) as *presence*.

DIFFÉRANCE AND REPETITION

One plus one make at least three. (Jacques Derrida)

Consider 'Plato's Pharmacy', the author of which affirms that this essay is nothing other than an indirect reading of *Finnegan's Wake* (Derrida 1972a, 109n17; 1981a, 88n20; see also 1987d, 29; 1984b, 145–58), but not without having signalled beforehand that the archaeology of Platonism there proposed takes a turn so 'originary' (under erasure) that it imposes a veritable analogical structure that carries away the metaphysical surface in its entirety. In effect, the *pharmakon* plays a role analogous to that of the supplement in the reading of Rousseau, as we see in Derrida's note 40 to this essay; while note 56 tells us that, between presentation and representation, Husserlian phenomenology is systematically organised around an opposition analogous to the two forms of repetition in the *Phaedrus*. It is along this Plato-Rousseau-Husserl/Saussure axis that I see the Derridean enterprise unfold under the general rubric of a *rewriting of modernity*, in the double sense of the genitive that I borrow from recent work by J.-F. Lyotard on the 'postmodern condition'.[11] In fact, 'if everything is a sign, a coded reference . . . there is no longer a *real* opposition, only a functional one, between a sign and a thing; there is *nothing* left to replace, only signs to replace, only replacement (artificial, prosthetic), only places and sites'. Whence the question that Derrida seems to address to himself and that I will take up soon in this chapter: 'Completion of the "modern tradition" or postmodernity?' (Derrida, 1990b, 282).

This *Sign*, left in suspense at the moment of reading the Platonic prescription drawn up in the pharmacy, is written again in a footnote, as though in the back room of the text:

Plato condemns under the name of *phantasm* or of simulacrum what is being advanced today, in its most radical exigency, as writing. Or at any rate that is what one can call, *within* philosophy and 'mimetology' that which exceeds the conceptual oppositions within which Plato defines the phantasm. Beyond these oppositions, beyond the values of truth and nontruth, this excess (of) writing can no longer, as one might guess, be qualified simply as a simulacrum or phantasm. Nor can it indeed be named by the classical concept of writing. (Derrida 1972a, 173n58; 1981a, 138–9n63)

Let us translate as follows this note – the final word in the ordeal of the sign (cf. our note 8) – all the while risking a fold which would include the Deleuzean collapse: that which exceeds writing or, if you will, that writing which exceeds its classical concept as a *literary* image of speech, replaces the simulacrum in the *supplementary* putting into motion of the image. The image then no longer interiorises the dissimilitude of its constituting series ('the constituting *disparity in the thing* [emphasis added] from which it strips the rank of model': this is how Deleuze perceives that the simulacrum could be the symbol itself (Deleuze 1968, 92; 1994, 67)),[12] except by exteriorising the sole signifying trace of *différance* ('Writing would indeed be the signifier's capacity to repeat itself by itself, mechanically . . . without truth's *presenting itself* anywhere (Derrida 1972a, 138; 1981a, 111)). Thus, the ontological power of becoming, which affirms itself as being (*être*) in assuming the whole of being (*tout l'étant*) outside the world of representation, succeeds the pharmacological virtue of writing as an alogical milieu of forces. To be is to write and to be written in the ambiguous system of a language older than the arrested opposites *signified* by Plato.

The *pharmakon* is *agon* in its aneidetic undecidability: it de-limits the arena of combat between two repetitions and two writings, between the living inscription of the *eidos* of the absent Father repeated in the soul (*anamnesis*) and the parricidal writing of signs that have nothing to do with truth in the dialectical process of its presentation (*hypomnesis*). The latter is a writing which represents absence, which repeats the repetition opened by the declared parricide against Presence in order to allow a discourse to be maintained on the simulacrum and writing, or, to use Derrida's expression, that repeats the repeater. In the inversion of the traditional hierarchy between speech and writing, signified and signifier, the deconstruction of Platonism constitutes Platonism as *a textual system*. The text emerges from the 'play between two kinds of writing' where 'the good one can be designated only through the metaphor of the bad one' when all that mattered was distinguishing speech from writing (Derrida 1972a, 186; 1981a, 149). The text is born from a single stream that is both philosophical *and* literary, at the precise point where writing goes beyond the metaphysical interpretation of *mimesis*. 'Structure is a sort of writing', Derrida summarises (1972a, 202; 1981a, 162), which we can take to mean a play of writing in which 'an infinite number of sign-substitutions' are played out (1967c, 411; 1978, 280). *A writing in the land of the stand-in*[13] *where 'the simple origin is no more. Because what is reflected is doubled in itself* and not merely as an addition to the self of its image. The reflection, the image [writing, pure representation, the image of speech], the double–they all double what they double again. The origin of speculation becomes a difference' (Derrida 1967a, 55; 1974, 36).

According to the reading proposed – and this is one of the most fascinating nooks of the pharmacy – it is possible to determine the moment when logography invades the field of Platonic ontology. In effect, the question of the play of the other in being is enough for Plato to introduce the paradigm of writing 'in a discourse which would like to think of itself as spoken in essence, in truth, and which nevertheless is written. And if it is written *from out of the death of Socrates* [and out of the parricide of the *Sophist*], this is no doubt the profound reason for it' (Derrida 1972a, 204; 1981a, 163).[14] This new depth 'refers' to the graphic of supplementarity and to the ideality of the *eidos* in the same way as it does to the necessity of the repetition of the same that starts the movement of signifiers turning around an absent signified. A bastard Platonism determines its other in *arresting* the difference between signified and signifier. Aristotle will pick this up from Plato: once the identity of sense is determined in the signified, and being in the concept, all that remains to do is to put the sophist back on the structurally subordinated side of the signifier. But by the same token, is not *the unity of the system of this difference* 'the inseparability of sophistry and philosophy'?

Even though we do not draw exactly the same consequences, it is difficult not to agree with Derrida concerning the 'untenable and absurd' character of a simple inversion (of sign) of signifier and signified[15] *if the ultimate signified is nothing more than the very existence of the signifier that is extrapolated beyond the sign: its 'supplement' or its 'surplus'*. Precisely.

Camera obscura.

THE REPETITION OF THE DIFFERENT, OR WHAT HAPPENED?

Recall Bloom in the pharmacy. (Jacques Derrida)

The *différe/ance* that is introduced in relation to the Deleuzean interpretation can be measured when, at the surface of the Platonic text, the irruption of non-being as the other of the represented identity of being only *expresses* the event that made language possible by producing (non)sense[16] (the moment of the *Cratylus*) in so far as it *designates* the differential element as the alternative principle of the genesis of being in its univocity (the moment of the *Timaeus*). And it is because 'univocity means that it is the same thing which occurs and is said' (Deleuze 1969, 211; 1990, 180) that the heterogenesis of the Giver whose insistence remains undetermined if not by the very sparkling of the outside, breaks with the limitlessness of *signifiance*[17] in designating his undertaking as the effect of a given that would have conserved his transcendent origins in the immanence of language. *Eventum tantum* 'that exceeds the excess of the signifier' (DG 1980, 146; 1987, 116).

Let us return one last time to 'Plato and the Simulacrum', at the precise moment when Deleuze in his turn encounters the great letter of *Finnegan's Wake*, in order to approach the aesthetic conditions of the overturning of Platonism in the *complicatio* of the Joycean *antilogos*. From the work of art as experimentation to the theory of art as a reflection of real experience . . .

Three times (*temps*) are set free: (a) on the basis of the *coupling* between heterogenous series in a unity which results in a 'chaos always excentered' (b) a sort of *internal resonance* is produced between divergent series, as an asignifying surface effect which must be assigned to the very origin of the transcendental field; (c) this resonance induces a *forced movement* that overflows the series and produces sense by connecting elements that are not themselves signifying but 'differenciating'. This principle of the emission of singularities 'necessarily' includes a registry of ideal *events* that form a *story*. We will call a *signal* 'a structure in which differences of potential are distributed: '. . . the *sign* is what flashes across the boundary of two levels, between two communicating series' (Deleuze 1969, 301; 1990, 261). Now, in such intensive signal-sign systems, the series do not depend on the signifier and its effects; rather, the signifying chain depends on the amplitude of the series and on the climb to the surface of asignifying signs. Issued from the process of signalisation, they crush signifiers like signifieds, 'treating words as things' (DG 1972, 290; 1984, 244). But the essential is that all phenomena answer to the transcendental conditions of these differential systems of disparate, resonant series – and *express the functioning of the simulacrum* – in so far as they find their raison d'être in a dissymmetry, in a constitutive inegality that relates the different, and the same, and the similar, to Difference as though to a primary power[18] always displaced in relation to itself. For as such they always escape the world of representation, and therefore 'all physical systems are signals, all qualities are signs' (Deleuze 1969, 301; 1990, 261).

Thus, a letter can 'connect all the series in the world in a chaos-cosmos' that realises the overturning of Platonism and 'to overturn Platonism is first and foremost to relieve essences of their duties in order to substitute for them events as bursts of singularities' (1969, 54 and 69; 1990, 40 and 53; trans. modified).

And being (*l'être*), as the eternal return which brings back the immanent identity of chaos with the cosmos. An *ontological repetition* beyond the repetition of collapse.

At the end of this trajectory, the language of the world comes back to the surface. It no longer 'slips away' in the graphic of a generalised transcendental illusion; it no longer 'refers' as though to its double (*crossed-out*), or to the nihilistic subsumption of being under a methodology. (Neokantianism is the *historical* truth of 'postmodernity').[19]

Force, the outside as the milieu of forces; force as 'the pure experience of the outside'[20] gives itself for what it is – stronger than the text.

But the text, in turn, does not climb to the surface without changing its nature:

And now, to distinguish, between two repetitions . . .
Night passes. In the morning, knocks are heard at the door. They seem to be coming from the outside, this time . . .
Two knocks. . . . Four . . . .
. . . that other theater, those knocks from outside . . . (Derrida 1972a, 213; 1981a, 171).

Notes

1. Brisson 1987, 153–4.
2. See also '*Mes chances, Au rendez-vous de quelques stéréophonies épicuriennes*', where Derrida advances the notion of *marked insignificance*, which is different from the concept of the signifier insofar as 'its generality extends the mark beyond verbal signs and even human language'(Derrida 1988c, 31; 1984, 16). For the Nietzschean critique of 'the belief in the antinomy of values', see the beginning of *Beyond Good and Evil*, 2.
3. My *inter*vention, which is prescribed by *the necessity of a play*, pretends only to make visible the mirror play that folds these two pages where Deleuze's footnotes 2 and 3 are located: between the writing of the simulacrum and the model of the other. Between logography and ontology.
4. It is well known that Deleuze never hid his debt to the great book by G. Simondon, *L'Individu et sa genèse physicobiologique* (Simondon, 1964; cf Deleuze 1969, 126n3; 1990, 344n3). Mireille Buydens makes good use of this in the first chapter of *Sahara. L'Esthétique de Gilles Deleuze* (Buydens 1990).
5. Let us recall that Deleuzean ontology is dictated as much by the reading of Nietzsche as by Stoic thought with its two planes of being: 'on the one hand, *profound and real being, force* [emphasis added]; on the other hand, the plane of deeds that are played out on the surface of being and that constitute an endless multiplicity of incorporeal beings' (Bréhier 1928, 13; cited at Deleuze 1969, 14; 1990, 5).
6. For Deleuze, being is an infinitive verb (and the verb [*le verbe*] is the univocality of language).
7. Note that, not unexpectedly, in his *prefatory letter* to Buydens 1990, Deleuze rejects the notion of Presence ('too pious') in favour of 'conceiving of life as non-organic power'.
8. (*Reading Nietzsche: The Question of (or What is at Stake in) Signs*). Nietzsche, noted Derrida, 'far from remaining *simply* (with Hegel and as Heidegger wished) *within* metaphysics, contributed a great deal to the liberation of the signifier from its dependence or derivation with respect to the *logos* and the related concept of truth or the primary signified' (Derrida 1967a, 31–2; 1974, 19). Then, in a 'see saw' that is characteristic of the Derridean style of thinking, a note – 'This does not, by simple inversion, mean that the signifier is fundamental or primary' (1967a, 32n9; 1974, 324n9). We will refer to this note again.
9. Dividing a genre into species is only the superficial aspect of division (cf. the definition of angling) as long as the *profound opposition* of the pure and the impure, the authentic and the inauthentic, etc., does not intervene.
10. 'Laying claim is not one phenomenon among others, but the nature of every phenomenon' (Deleuze 1968, 87; 1994, 62). See also Foucault 1970b, 944–5; 1998, 344–5.
11. Lyotard 1988; 1987.
12. Worked out in all of its reasoning, this is the Deleuzean response to the problem that we brought up at the end of 'The Collapse of Platonism'. Insofar

as 'the thing is reduced to the difference that tears it apart and to all of the differences implied in the latter by those it passes through, . . . the simulacrum is the symbol itself ' (Deleuze 1969, 92; 1994, 67). Taking into consideration that the most rhetorical questions are not necessarily those to which the author responded to in advance . . .

13. I use here the expression of John Sallis (1990, 360). The perversion of writing is the inversion of the speech/writing hierarchy ('to the point that in the end it seems as if speech is an image of writing' (352)).

14. Concerning the paradigm of writing in its Platonic literality, see Goldschmidt 1947.

15. 'At the limit, that thought would destroy the entire conceptuality organised around the concept of the sign' (Derrida 1967a, 32n9; 1974, 324n9).

16. 'Nonsense is that which has no sense, and that which, as such and as it enacts the donation of sense, is opposed to the absence of sense' (Deleuze 1969, 89; 1990, 71).

17. 'It comes to the same thing to say that the sign refers to other signs ad infinitum and that the infinite set of all signs refers to a supreme signifier' (DG 1980, 144; 1987, 115). 'This is why, at the limit, one can forego the notion of the sign . . . The limitlessness of signifiance has replaced the sign' (1980, 141; 1987, 112).

18. 'In the reversal [overturning] of Platonism, resemblance is said of internalised difference, and identity of the Different as primary power. The same and the similar no longer have an essence except as simulated, that is as expressing the functioning of the simulacrum' (Deleuze 1969, 303; 1990, 262).

19. This was the sense of my presentation at the Centre International de Cerisy-la-Salle, at the colloquium *1790–1990: Le Destin de la philosophie transcendentale* (*Concerning the* Critique of Judgement).

20. Foucault defines thus the Nietzschean force in 'The Thought of the Outside' (Foucault 1966, 553; 1998, 154). See also his comment on the Nietzschean experience of the glittering of the outside, when he says that Nietzsche discovers 'that all of Western metaphysics is tied not only to its grammar (that had been largely suspected since Schlegel), but to those who, in holding discourse, have a hold over the right to speak' (1966, 550; 1998, 151). It is the reading of Nietzsche that determines the violence of the Foucault/Derrida confrontation (Foucault 1972, 1113–36; 1998, 393–417; in 'response' to Derrida, 1967c, 51–97; 1978, 31–63; see also, Derrida 1967c, 410–11; 1978, 292–3).

CHAPTER 6

Algebras, Geometries and Topologies of the Fold: Deleuze, Derrida and Quasi-Mathematical Thinking (with Leibniz and Mallarmé)

Arkady Plotnitsky

MATHEMATICS, QUASI-MATHEMATICS AND PHILOSOPHY

A certain mathematical stratum appears to be irreducible in philosophy. Or, at least, philosophy appears to contain an irreducible quasi-mathematical stratum, that is, something that philosophically intersects with mathematics but is not mathematical in its disciplinary sense. Conversely, the conceptual richness of mathematics gives it a quasi-philosophical – and even philosophical – stratum. Even leaving aside a tremendous general philosophical and cultural impact of mathematics throughout Western history, particular mathematical concepts can and have been converted into philosophical ones, just as certain philosophical ideas or arguments can be and have been converted into mathematics. The quasi-mathematical is defined by and defines this reciprocity, which thus also gives rise to both Deleuze's and Derrida's quasi-mathematics. The quasi-mathematical allows us to gain an understanding of a certain conceptuality that, while not mathematical, is irreducible in mathematics and perhaps makes it possible.

It is more difficult to speak of philosophical disciplinarity than of that of mathematics, or so it appears, since mathematical disciplinarity has many a complexity of its own. Here, I shall adopt Deleuze and Guattari's understanding (extending Leibniz) of philosophy, in *What Is Philosophy?*, as the creation of new, or even forever new, concepts, or, as the case may be, 'neither terms nor concepts', such as those of Derrida, for example, *différance*. The term 'concept' itself must be used in the specific sense given to it by Deleuze and Guattari rather than in any common sense of it, such as that of an entity established by a generalisation from particulars or 'any general or abstract idea' (DG 1994b, 11–12 and 24). A *philosophical* concept has a complex multilayered structure, and 'there are no simple concepts' (1994b, 16). It is a multi-component conglomerate of concepts (in their conventional senses), figures, metaphors, particular elements, and so forth.

I shall now explain my key tropes or concepts – algebra, geometry, and topology. I see 'algebra' as a trope, perhaps the ultimate trope, or concept of formalisation, whether we think of formalising systems (such as those of mathematics or, via mathematics, physics or other sciences), systems of concepts in logic and philosophy, or language, as in linguistics. 'Algebra' in this broad sense refers to a conglomerate of certain formal elements and of relations between them. There is of course a mathematical field known as 'algebra'. It is a highly developed and technical field. Conceptually, however, this algebra, too, can be seen in the general terms just explained. In this sense, one can speak of 'algebra' whenever we deal with this type of situation, for example, in mathematical logic (which encodes mathematical propositions themselves) or in calculus, both among the areas where Leibniz's contributions were crucial. Leibniz's work in differential calculus may be argued to involve algebra (in either sense) and to couple it to geometry more fundamentally than is done in Newton's work, which is dominated by the geometrical and mechanical perspectives. Leibniz (but not Leibniz alone, even if only because of Descartes's role) set into operation an immense programme of algebraisation, which extends to, among other things, modern mathematical logic, computer sciences and linguistics.[1]

Derrida's philosophical 'algebra', especially his algebra of undecidables, developed in part via Kurt Gödel's work, on the mathematical-scientific side, and that of Stephane Mallarmé's, on the literary side, has a Leibnizean genealogy. Derrida devotes to Leibniz an important section of *Of Grammatology*, entitled 'Algebra: Arcanum and Transparence' and dealing with the 'logical algebra' of *writing*, ultimately in Derrida's sense of the term, the algebra that leads Derrida, via Gödel, to his philosophical undecidability (Derrida 1974, 75–81).

'Geometry' and 'topology', while both concerned with space, are distinguished by their different mathematical provenances. Geometry (geo-*metry*) has to do with measurement, while topology disregards measurement or scale, and deals only with the structure of space qua space (topos) and with the essential shapes or structure of figures. Insofar as one deforms a given figure continuously (i.e., does not separate points previously connected and, conversely, does not connect points previously separated) the resulting figure is considered the same.

Leibniz's ideas concerning the possibility of making topology into a rigorous mathematical discipline (his term was 'analysis situs') were among his greatest contributions to mathematics. These ideas were developed into modern topology in the nineteenth century in the works of Karl Friedrich Gauss, Bernhard Riemann, Henri Poincaré, and others. Leibniz was crucially responsible for reshaping our ideas concerning spatiality, whether one speaks of geometry (where Descartes's work was, again, a crucial contribution), topology, or physics (especially in his critique of Newton's ideas concerning absolute space). It is a certain quasi-mathematical geometry and topology that Deleuze primarily takes from Leibniz and other thinkers just mentioned, especially Riemann.

Thus, Deleuze's 'geometry' or 'topology' and Derrida's 'algebra' can be traced to two different facets of Leibniz's thought, to which one can also trace the genealogy of both Riemann's geometrical ideas and Gödel's 'algebra' of mathematical logic. Mallarmé's work, too, links that of Deleuze and Derrida through the Leibnizean figure of the fold, as Deleuze and Derrida discuss it in, respectively, *The Fold: Leibniz and the Baroque* (Deleuze 1993) and 'The Double Session' (in Derrida 1981a). The fold is a Baroque and a Leibnizian figure and concept par excellence. The geometry and topology of the fold make it Deleuze's figure and in turn, a Deleuzean figure and concept. On the other hand, it appears to be the *algebra* of the fold that makes it Mallarmé's and then Derrida's figure. Deleuze offers us a *philosophically* geometrical/topological perspective on or approach to the fold, albeit not without some algebra to it, especially in the case of Mallarmé's fold. Derrida offers us a *philosophically* algebraic one, although this algebra entails a certain topology or at least spatiality as well.

This difference, I argue, extends to a more general view of their thought. Deleuze's key conceptuality and Deleuze's thought itself are more spatial, topological (including when dealing with the temporal), in contrast to Derrida's 'algebra', ultimately linked to that which is neither spatial nor temporal, nor, again, definable by any other terms. Naturally, this argument requires qualifications and sometimes (qualified) reversals. It is a question of the difference in distribution and balance (obviously subject to an interpretation) of algebra and geometry or topology in Deleuze's and Derrida's thought. In Deleuze, however, arithmetic and algebra appear ultimately to refer to the geometrical/topological formations, to spaces, for example, at certain key junctures of *A Thousand Plateaus* (DG 1987, 389–94 and 482–8), on which I shall comment below.[2] By contrast, in Derrida topology ultimately becomes a-topology (Derrida 1992a, 209). Both his reading of Plato's *khōra* and his discussion of *différance* would further confirm this point, as these concepts relate to the efficacity or (they are as multiple as are their effects) efficacities of any conceivable spatiality.[3] Analogous efficacities are also responsible for all conceivable temporal effects, or interactions between spatial and temporal effects, while remaining inaccessible to any spatial terms any more than any temporal ones, or to any other terms or concepts, including those of efficacity or chaos. It goes without saying that, while I believe in their pertinence and hope for their effectiveness, these 'mathematical' terms alone could not be sufficient to describe either Deleuze's or Derrida's work, or even the relationships between their work and mathematics.[4] In particular, as will be seen, a certain 'physics', and two different 'physics' (one more geometrical, in Deleuze, and another more algebraic, in Derrida) appear to be irreducible in their work.

THE FOLD: FROM LEIBNIZ AND MALLARME TO DELEUZE AND DERRIDA

The mathematical concept of manifold, mani*fold*, brings together geometry and topology and is crucial to all of Deleuze's philosophy, and may be argued to constitute the primary *quasi-mathematical* model for it (there are, again, other models).[5] While the idea could be traced to Leibniz as well, the concept is primarily due to Riemann. According to Deleuze and Guattari, 'it was a decisive event when the mathematician Riemann uprooted the manifold from its predicate and made it a noun, "manifold" [*Mannigfaltigkeit*]. It marked the end of dialectics and the beginning of a typology and topology of manifolds' (DG 1987, 482–3; trans. modified). A manifold is a kind of patchwork of (local) spaces, each of which can be mapped by a (flat) Euclidean, or Cartesian, coordinate map, without allowing for a global Euclidean structure or a single coordinate system for the whole, except in the limited case of a Euclidean homogeneous space itself. That is, every point has a small neighbourhood that can be treated as Euclidean, while the manifold as a whole cannot. These cartographic terms, crucial to Deleuze (or Foucault, whom Deleuze discusses from this perspective in his *Foucault* (Deleuze 1988b)), are not accidental and have a historical genealogy. Riemann's teacher, Gauss, whose work was crucial to Riemann, arrived at these ideas through his work in land surveying. Riemann primarily considered the so-called differential or smooth manifolds, which, roughly, mean that mathematically one can define differential calculus in such objects (the concept carries or mathematically refines a general sense of smoothness as well), and specifically the so-called Riemannian manifolds, which allow one to define a metric in them and, thus, measure distances between their points. This also gives a Riemannian manifold, or allows one to associate with it, algebra by virtue of the equations that formalise such measurements. One of Riemann's many great inventions, prepared by Gauss' work, was the concept of measurement in curved spaces (of dimension three and higher), which Einstein used so brilliantly in general relativity, his non-Newtonian theory of gravitation. It is, crucially, not a matter of curves in a flat space but of the curvature of the space itself. The concept of differential manifold and measurement in curved spaces is germane to the idea of non-Euclidean geometries, one of which, that of positive curvature, was discovered by Riemann. Gauss was a co-discoverer of the geometry of negative curvature, the discovery he suppressed for twenty years fearing (rightly) that he would be laughed at by philistines.

Riemann's concept of the manifold also offers Deleuze's and Deleuze and Guattari's visions, especially in *A Thousand Plateaus*, a complex interplay of the smooth and the striated, crucial to the argument of the book. Certain aspects of Riemann's theory of manifolds could be considered as a complex form of Descartes' analytic geometry (expressing geometry in terms of coordinates and algebraic equations), as well as an extension of differential calculus. The question is how one *inflects* the Cartesian or the Euclidean. In any event, it is the topological and specifically smooth (in Deleuze and Guattari's sense) and not the metric or striated character of Riemannian spaces that is more important for Deleuze and Guattari.[6] The reason for this significance is the irreducibility of the smooth in 'Riemannian spaces'. Deleuze and Guattari write, via Charles Lautman's analysis:

'Riemann spaces are devoid of any kind of homogeneity. Each is characterized by the form of the expression that defines the square of the distance between two infinitely proximate points . . . It follows that two neighboring observers in a Riemann space can locate the points in their immediate vicinity but cannot locate their spaces in relation to each other without a new convention. Each vicinity is therefore like a shred of Euclidean space, *but the linkage between one vicinity and the next is not defined and can be effected in an infinite number of ways. Riemann space at its most general thus presents itself as an amorphous collection of pieces that are juxtaposed but not attached to each other.*' It is possible to define this multiplicity without any reference to a metrical system, in terms of the conditions of frequency, or rather *accumulation*, of a set of vicinities; these conditions are entirely different from those determining metric spaces and their breaks (even though a relation between the two kinds of space necessarily results). In short, if we follow Lautman's fine description, Riemannian space is pure patchwork. It has connections, or tactile relations. It has rhythmic values not found elsewhere, even though they can be translated into a metric space. Heterogeneous, in continuous variation, it is a smooth space, insofar as smooth space is amorphous and not homogeneous. We can thus define two positive characteristics of smooth space in general: when there are determinations that are part of one another and pertain to enveloped distances or ordered differences, independent of magnitudes; when, independent of metrics, determinations arise that cannot be part of one another but are connected by processes of frequency or accumulation. There are the two aspects of the *nomos* of smooth space. (DG 1987, 485)

The mathematical model of the smooth in Deleuze and Guattari's sense is defined by the topology of the differential manifold, which need not entail a metric but which, in the case of Riemmanian metric spaces, is also responsible for the (globally) non-Euclidean character of Riemannian metric and of a corresponding striation. Thus, while every Riemannian space allows for and defines a certain striation, this striation irreducibly entails and is an effect of a *nontrivial smooth* space, in contrast to a flat Euclidean space (defined by a Cartesian striation), which is *only trivially smooth* (either in Deleuze and Guattari's or in a mathematical sense). Accordingly, a striation defined by a nontrivial Riemannian metric can only be translated into and entails a nontrivially smooth space.

This type of 'geometry' defines Deleuze's vision throughout his work and gives it a fundamentally spatial (geometrical and topological) character, ultimately as a vision of underlying connectivity and continuity. Deleuze acknowledges the necessary relationships between the continuous and the discontinuous, the smooth and the striated, the topological and the metric (or geometry and algebra, or arithmetic), or, concomitantly, the major and the minor, the state and the nomad, and so forth. This latter set of terms defines different artistic, mathematical or scientific, or other cultural, including political, formations and the relationships between and among them (DG 1987, 351–423; see also DG 1994a). The irreducibly heterogeneous, multifarious character of the Deleuzean smooth is crucial to his vision and must be kept in mind. The space of this vision is a kind of 'Riemannian space', multi-mapped and multi-connected, in accordance with the passage cited above. This passage also allegorically describes the 'space' of the 'The Smooth and the Striated' chapter of *A Thousand Plateaus*, with its multiple and multiply interactive models, maps and atlases, or the 'space' of the book itself, its potentially thousand plateaus.

Deleuze's concept of the Baroque is one of the major facets of this vision, to which it also gives a fundamental material dimension. The Baroque is defined, above all, by both a separation and an interactiveness of the material and the spiritual:

What makes the new harmony possible is, first, the distinction between two levels of floors, which resolves tension or allots the division. The lower level is assigned to the façade, which is elongated by being punctured and bent back according to the folds determined by a heavy matter, forming an infinite room for reception or receptivity. The upper level is closed, as a pure inside without an outside, a weightless, closed interiority, its walls hung with spontaneous folds that are now only those of a soul or a mind. This is because . . . the Baroque world is organized along two vectors, a deepening towards the bottom, and thrust toward the upper regions. Leibniz will make coexist, first the tendency of a system of gravity to find its lowest possible equilibrium where the sum of masses can descend no further and, second, the tendency to elevate, the highest aspiration of a system in weightlessness, where souls are destined to become reasonable. The coexistence resembles Tintoretto's paintings. That one is metaphysical, dealing with souls, and that the other is physical, entailing bodies, does not impede the two vectors from comprising a similar world, a similar house. And not only are they distributed as a function of an ideal line, which is actualized on one level and realized on another; a higher analogy endlessly relates the one to the other. (Deleuze 1993, 29)

'What is Baroque is this distinction and division into two levels or floors', divided by a fold. 'The Baroque contribution par excellence is a world with only two floors, separated by a fold that echoes itself, arching from the two sides according to a different order. It expresses the transformation of (the Neoplatonist) cosmos into a "mundus"' (ibid.). This architecture enacts a complex reciprocal interplay – interfold – of materiality and conceptuality, or phenomenality. According to Deleuze: 'The severing of the inside from the outside in this way refers to the distinction between the two levels, but [this distinction] refers to the Fold that is actualized in the intimate folds that the soul encloses on the upper level, and effected along the creases that matter brings to life always on the outside, on the lower level. Hence the ideal fold is *Zweifalt*, a fold that differentiates and is differentiated' (Deleuze 1993, 30). It differentiates between, and yet also relates, 'folds' together, the material and the phenomenal and is differentiated on each side. The relation between them takes place through reflection rather than connection, at least as a first approximation, since a certain (material?) efficacity is responsible for the effects of reflection.

At this juncture in *The Fold*, Deleuze introduced two key twentieth-century conceptions of the fold, those of Heidegger and Mallarmé, figures equally crucial to Derrida, who invokes Heidegger's 'fold' in his reading of Mallarmé (Derrida 1981a, 192). Deleuze writes:

When Heidegger calls upon the *Zweifalt* to be the differentiator of difference, he means above all that differentiation does not refer to a pregiven undifferentiated, but to a Difference that endlessly unfolds and folds over from each of its two sides, and that unfolds the one only while refolding the other, in coextensive unveiling and veiling of Being, of presence and of withdrawal of being. The 'duplicity' of the fold had to be reproduced from the two sides that it distinguishes, but it relates one to the other by distinguishing them: a severing by which each term casts the other forwards, a tension by which each fold is pulled into the other. (Deleuze 1993, 30)

There are, thus, two different – heterogeneous and yet interactive – folds, each of them incessantly differentiating in its own right, and yet at each point a difference between them continuously emerges. 'In Tintoretto the lower level shows bodies tormented by their own weight, their souls stumbling, bending and falling into the meanders of matter; the upper half acts like a powerful magnet that attracts them, makes them ride astride the yellow folds of light, folds of fire bringing their bodies alive, dizzying them, but with a "dizziness from on high": thus there are two halves of the *Last Judgment*' (ibid.). By contrast, Heidegger's *Zweifalt* need not be seen in these *vertical* terms, while it is defined by the same (Baroque) geometrical and topological structure. *Our* (rather than historical) Baroque, that of Klee, Heidegger, Mallarmé, Boulez, Stockhausen, Dubuffet or of Deleuze is defined by suspending the *vertical* movement of the fold, towards God, for example, and moving to the new *horizontal* and divergent harmonies. It moves from monadology and its vertical space (singular) to nomadology and its smooth space*s* (plural), with which Deleuze closes the book:

To the degree that the world is now made up of divergent series (the chaosmos), or that crapshooting replaces the game of Plenitude, the monad is now unable to contain the entire world as if in a closed circle that can be modified by projection. It now opens on a trajectory or a spiral in expansion that moves further and further away from a center. A vertical harmonic can no longer be distinguished from a horizontal harmonic, just like the private condition of a dominant monad that produces its own accords in itself, and the public condition of monads in a crowd that follows the lines of melody. The two begin to fuse on a sort of diagonal, where the monads penetrate each other, and modified, inseparable from the groups of prehension that carry them along and make up as many transitory captures.

The question always entails living in the world, but Stockhausen's musical habitat or Dubuffet's plastic habitat do not allow the difference of inside and outside, of public and private, to survive. They identify variation and trajectory, and overtake monadology with a 'nomadology'. Music has stayed at home: what has changed now is the organization of the home and its nature. We are all still Leibnizian, although accords no longer convey our world or our text. We are discovering new ways of folding, akin to new envelopments, but we all remain Leibnizian because what always matters is folding, unfolding, refolding. (Deleuze 1993, 137)

The chancier *horizontal* spiral of our Baroque replaces 'the *vertical* spiral' of Leibniz's Baroque: 'the line effectively folds into a spiral in order to defer inflection in a movement suspended between sky and earth, which either moves away from or indefinitely approaches the center of a curve and at each instant "rises skyward or risks falling upon us"' (Deleuze 1993, 17). This horizontal Baroque is also marked by a shift of emphasis, in part also by placing the emphasis on a certain 'algebra' (in 'divergent series' of differential calculus, Stockhausen's musical scores, and Dubuffet's works) vs a more pronounced geometrical/topological character of Deleuze's rendition of the vertical, hierarchical Baroque. The *horizontally* geometrical/topological determination itself appears to remain dominant.

Mallarmé is one of the initiators of this transition, both from vertical to horizontal and, closer to Derrida, from geometrical to algebraic, in part by virtue of his deployments of textuality and writing, ultimately in Derrida's (more 'algebraic') sense. Deleuze writes:

The fold is probably Mallarmé's most important notion, and not only the notion but, rather, the operation, the operative act that makes him the great Baroque poet. *Hérodiade* is already the poem of the fold. The fold of the world is the fan or 'l'unanime pli' (unanimous fold). At times the open fan makes all particles of matter, ashes, and fog rise and fall. We glimpse the visible through the mist as if through the mesh of a veil. Following the creases that allow us to see stone in the opening of their inflections, 'fold after fold', revealing the city. . . . Ultimately [however] the fold pertains to the sensitive [or phenomenal] side of the fan, to sensitivity itself, . . . and, from the other side of the fan that is now closed (*'le sceptre des rivages roses ce blanc vol fermé que tu poses'*) [the sceptre of the rosy shores . . . this white closed flight you pose], . . . the fold no longer moves towards pulverization, it exceeds itself or finds its finality in an inclusion, *'tassement en épaisseur, offrant le miniscule tombeau, certe, de l'âme'* [thick layerings, offering the tiny tomb, surely, of the soul]. (Deleuze 1993, 30)

One easily recognises the key elements of Leibniz's monadology here, insofar as each particle involved is defined by a micro interfold of pleated matter and folded spirit (each of which may be shown to be structured in Riemannian terms). At the same time, a certain more horizontal figuration ('the fan') of the fold begins to emerge, even if still in interaction with an up-

and-down movement, defining the vertical Baroque. In considering this movement, Deleuze is about to shift from the geometry to the 'algebra' of the fold,
through the (horizontal) textuality of both monads and Mallarmé's fold, and
by so doing about to bring both closer to Derrida. According to Deleuze, 'on
the other side, there are these folds of the soul, where inflection becomes
inclusion: we're no longer seeing, we're *reading*. Leibniz begins to use the word
"to read" at once as the inner act in the privileged region of the monad' (1993,
31).

This region is privileged for a good reason. There is perhaps no mathematics
without reading or writing, in a certain sense especially in the case of algebra,
but only in a certain sense, since (leaving aside notational elements without
which geometry is inconceivable) the points and lines of geometry are irreducibly inscriptive. They are written and are writing, the *point* made and implied
along many *lines* of Derrida's analysis of *writing*. Leibniz's pointedly algebraic
symbolism of calculus, to which he paid a special attention and which we still
use, confirms this argument. A graphic (in either sense) example in the present
context is his invention of his symbol $\int$ for the integral, a stylized Latin 'S', for
'sum', referring to a continuous summation and replacing the Greek Σ for
discrete (if possibly infinite) summations, used in the case of sums of (convergent) infinite series of differential calculus.[7] As Deleuze observes, 'it is well
known that the total book is as much Leibniz's dream as it is Mallarmé's, even
though they never stop working in fragments' (ibid.). Derrida tells us that this
is ultimately the only possible form of the book.[8] Deleuze concurs: 'Our error
is in believing that they did not succeed in their wishes: they made this unique
Book, perfectly, the book of monads, in letters [in either sense] and little
circumstantial pieces that could sustain as many dispersions and combinations'
(ibid.).

We are now confronting algebra, mathematical and quasi-mathematical, the
algebra of horizontal combinations of symbols and marks, or at higher levels a
combination of propositions (as in mathematical logic) or larger entities –
conceptual, textual or mathematical, including geometrical or topological
formations. Mallarmé's text tells us not only that textuality and, hence, the
fold can be read as a form of algebra, but also that mathematics, especially
algebra, is a form of writing. Ultimately this argument applies to geometry as
well (impossible without points and lines, and hence without *writing* in
Derrida's extended sense) and to topology, although certain topoi in Alexandre
Grothendieck's topos theory have no points. But they have algebra to them,
which can also be linked to the algebra of mathematical logic.

The concepts of the fold in Leibniz and, especially, in Mallarmé may, thus,
be given a Derridean, philosophically 'algebraic', character. As the operation
of the fold *writes* and, thus, enacts the workings of writing in Derrida's sense,

it also enacts the quasi-mathematical, and specifically quasi-algebraic, nature of writing and the *written* (in Derrida's sense) nature of mathematics in their mutual reciprocity. Deleuze argues that 'the monad is the book or the reading room' (1993, 31). But it has to be a combination of letters first. These 'combinatorics' ('combinatorics' also names a mathematical field) ultimately entail *writing* in Derrida's sense.

First of all, algebra is primarily defined by written or, in any event, written-like symbolism, whether actually materially written down, as is usually the case, or not. This was what Leibniz realised, which led him to his project of universal characteristic, the ultimate form of philosophical algebra. In the section 'Algebra: Arcanum and Transparence' in *Of Grammatology*, Derrida argues as follows (a classic deconstructive argument). On the one hand, Leibniz 'divorces' all mathematical writing, all 'algebra', from its connection to *phone* (speech and voice) and theological and onto-theological determinations defined by this connection. On the other hand, even while bypassing *phone*, Leibniz reinstitutes this link at the level of concepts or ideas, whose meaning and/as organisation his, or at least God's, algebra of logical propositions would control. In other words, it would calculate the undecidable. More accurately, it would aim to calculate what would appear as undecidable from a Derridean perspective. It is hardly surprising that Leibniz would not think in terms of undecidability. His quasi-Platonist model of philosophy was based on the always decidable, at least in principle, truth of mathematics (see Derrida 1979b, 98–9).

It is remarkable that, in examining the mathematically rigorous versions of this type of propositional calculus (rich enough to contain the propositions of arithmetic), Gödel arrived at a mathematical demonstration that it contains strictly undecidable propositions, propositions neither provable nor disprovable as true by means available within the system. One such undecidable proposition concerns the consistency of any such system itself, which makes it impossible to prove this consistency by means of the system. In other words, if the system is consistent, this consistency is unprovable by means of the system. Such a system, for example, arithmetic, may, on the other hand, be discovered to be inconsistent. This is an extraordinary mathematical fact: *any mathematical system, based on a consistent set of axioms and rich enough to contain arithmetic, is either ultimately inconsistent or, if consistent, its consistency is unprovable.* Gödel's proof was inspired by Leibniz's universal characteristic, the project of symbolically (algebraically) mapping the propositions of logic or philosophy and the well-formed rules for deriving them. Gödel's 'symbols', mapping the propositions of arithmetic, are numbers themselves, with an unexpected outcome that certain well-formed statements about numbers can never be ascertained to be either true or false; they are undecidable. Gödel's findings fundamentally undermine the belief that mathematics could provide an impeccable model of truth and proof, as it has done often from the pre-Socratics to Leibniz and beyond.

On the other hand, a very different mathematical model and a new mathematical and quasi-mathematical starting point emerges, in quasi-mathematical terms quite possibly well before Gödel, for example, in Mallarmé's writing (in either sense). Derrida introduces a certain *philosophical* version of undecidability, specifically in 'The Double Session' and then 'Dissemination' of *Dissemination*, in the context of, respectively, Stéphane Mallarmé's and Philippe Sollers' work.[9] Gödel's mapping of the propositions concerning numbers by numbers appears in the first sentence of his essay on Sollers: 'These *Numbers* enumerate themselves, write themselves, read themselves', and by so doing bring in undecidables and make them unavoidable (Derrida 1981a, 290). One must, again, keep in mind the differences between mathematical and quasi-mathematical conceptualities involved and the limits these differences impose upon quasi-mathematical thinking, the point stressed by Derrida and Deleuze alike (Derrida 1981a, 217; Deleuze 1995a, 129). In particular, within the proper mathematical limits, every proposition is assumed to be in principle either true or false, or undecidable, and in principle, if not in practice, provable as such. It cannot be in general disseminated or iterated otherwise, in contrast to what obtains in the Derridean situation, as exemplified by Mallarmé's *writing*. Most of Derrida's undecidable propositions, such as, say, that of positioning Mallarmé's text between philosophy and literature, are only *ultimately* undecidable, on both counts – that of their ultimate undecidability and that of the possibility or necessity of a certain (locally) decidable positioning of Mallarmé's text or some of its elements as either literary, philosophical, or as undecidable in this respect. In this sense, Derrida's undecidability extends Gödel's. It goes without saying that it is not a question of abandoning logic, but of establishing the limits within which logic would apply and of exploring the areas where one must operate beyond these limits (but never absolutely outside them).

The outcome of Mallarmé's operation and the fundamental diacriticity of its *writing* is 'a certain inexhaustibility which cannot be classed in the category of richness, intentionality, or a horizon', but, Derrida adds, against Jean-Pierre Richard's (thematic) reading of Mallarmé, 'whose form would not be simply foreign to the order of mathematics' (Derrida 1981a, 258). We can now see why such is the case. Most fundamentally, it is because mathematics is indissociable from and is even made possible by *writing*, even though, within its disciplinary limits, mathematics can contain certain radical effects of this inscriptive machinery. Derrida explains this inexhaustibility of writing in terms of undecidability immediately upon introducing Gödel's findings (1981a, 219).

He also explains the radical nature of his quasi-mathematical undecidability and, they are correlative, the inexhaustibility in question proceeding via Plato and Hegel, with some recasting of Freud added on (1981a, 220–1; 221n.32). This discussion recapitulates in terms of undecidability the nature of his standard operators, for example, supplement and dissemination (1981a, 262).

These terms name different aspects of this 'operation' or indeed different operations, which can be given no single name or containable set of names. This naming is itself subject to the uncontainability, inexhaustibility, dissemination and so forth here in question, which fact is reflected in Derrida's, by definition, interminable network of terms, including those just mentioned (*différance*, supplement, trace and hymen are among them as well). By the same token, none of these terms could be seen as absolutely indispensable. This structural dispensability is itself part of the difference between Derrida's dissemination or Mallarmé's hymen and Hegelian decidable pluralities (designated by such terms as *Aufhebung, Urteil, Meinen, Beispiel*, etc.) and other containable philosophical calculi of the plural. 'Between [*entre*]' becomes a strategic Mallarméan marker of this situation, although it must be seen as subject to the irreducible possibility of its own suspension as well (1981a, 220–1). These structures themselves form a certain complex quasi-Gödelian undecidable 'algebra' or 'calculus' and to some degree an 'algebra' of undecidables, insofar as most propositions involving them are undecidable as concerns their truth or falsity. Thus, the *ultimate* positioning of Mallarmé's text between, that is, as a *différance* of, philosophy and literature, between Plato (or Hegel) and Mallarmé would be undecidable in this sense, and it is this *différance* that defines the in-between [*inter*] the ultimately irreducible undecidable in-between – 'Hymen: INTER Platonem et Mallarmatum' – that Mallarmé's text inscribes (1981a, 181). The same undecidable 'hymenology' would govern the in-between of philosophy and linguistics, or literature and logic, or literature and mathematics, or philosophy and mathematics. (One could also remix these.) It would also govern conceptual (rather than 'field') hymens, in particular those of identity and difference or chance and necessity. These hymens are themselves linked by way of a kind of double-hymen to the hymen of philosophy and literature by Mallarmé's textual, inscriptive algebra (1981a, 277).

Mallarmé's inscription is, reciprocally, both investigated by Derrida by means of his algebra or calculus of undecidables and shapes this algebra (1981a, 220–1). Mallarmé's text becomes an enactment of *writing* in Derrida's sense and of its undecidable calculus, practised at every level of Mallarmé's textual machinery. The fold participates in this enactment, especially insofar as it is seen as an 'operation', as it is by both Deleuze and Derrida, with undecidability added to it. 'All this is the movement of a fan. The polysemy, actually dissemination, of "blanks" and "folds" both fans out and snaps shut, ceaselessly' (1981a, 251). This 'algebra', however, could only be reached if we read the blanks and folds, or 'notations' and diacritics, as algebra, to begin with, that is, not in terms of content but in terms of inscription. Algebra has no content in the philosophical, metaphysical sense, and may thus be devoid of connection to voice or ultimately any logos. If Leibniz would reinstate this link, Mallarmé takes the general textuality of algebra, or algebra of textuality, to their arguably ultimate and most radical limit. Accordingly, the most crucial and most profound is the general quasi-algebraic inscriptive structure or operation of Mallarmé's text or of Derrida's algebra of undecidables (which algebra is inscriptive in turn). This operation applies to elements – marks or blanks – of Mallarmé's or Derrida's *writing*, or reading (theirs and ours), regardless of the overtly mathematical character of the signifiers or spaces involved. Indeed it is often more fundamental elsewhere, for example, when 'literature' itself is at stake, as it is throughout Mallarmé's text and Derrida's reading of it.

Consider the case of 'or', the most essential logical operator, if indeed it is in any way simpler than any given propositional chain (hardly possible in Mallarmé's case). Thus 'or' joins two signifiers O and R, read for example, as zero, ze*RO* (the opposite of OR), nothing, and reality (everything?) or zero and real numbers (collectively designated as R) in mathematics. The OR of Mallarmé's *Or* involves and branches into these elements through the same type of dissemination. 'Or' is the French for gold, but, it can be shown that the English 'or' is part of Mallarmé's disseminating play, often taking place between French and English, their *différance* and dissemination into each other. English 'therefore' (coupled to Mallarmé's famous '*igitur*', technically meaning 'therefore') is part of the same play – 'for', 'or', or 'fort-da', in Derrida, thus adding hymens coupled to 'psychoanalysis' (psychoanalysis and literature, psychoanalysis and philosophy, and so forth) to the algebra of undecidable conjunctions in question. It is tempting to see 'or' as a quasi-minimal case of dissemination, which, once it enters, and this entry is not preventable, cannot be stopped. The blank space between O and R is itself not decidable (at least not once and for all), as to whether O and R, 'nothing' and 'all', are joint or disjoint. In part by virtue of this undecidable functioning, '*blanc*' is in turn a key figure for Mallarmé. Indeed, while it may seem as always the same, it is also a figure of difference. Every 'blank', including every actual blank space, let alone every signifier, may be different, even ultimately must be different each time, physically and conceptually – in a *différance*, along with dissemina-tion of empty space – although certain effects of sameness, which allow us to treat such blank spaces as the same or equivalent, are produced. It is towards the *différance* of blanks and marks, and their folds, that Mallarmé's text directs our gaze.

This is a crucial point, especially since it also reminds us that there is at least a topology, if not geometry, to algebra, and that, to begin with, there is the interaction of the materiality of (the marks or black) and the phenomenality in the processing of all this mathematics and quasi-mathematics. No algebra would be possible without this topology of the interplay of symbols and other written marks and blank spaces. Mallarmé's text takes advantage of the possibilities that this impossibility of algebra without topology in its graphics offers, as do many of Mallarmé's followers from the Dadaists on to concrete poetry and beyond. Certain arrangements of marks on the page or between pages are part of Mallarmé's fold. The figure of a painted, marked, fan and its folding and unfolding is an example of this arrangement, or indeed a figure of a more primordial topology of marks and blank spaces, with which I am primarily concerned at the moment. This topology is the precondition of any writing, mathematical writing included; and it is of some interest that Kant appears to associate something akin to this topology with, in de Man's terms, a certain 'material vision' of poets, and makes it a precondition of the sublime in the Third *Critique*.[10] Mallarmé's fold or, correlatively, Derrida's *writing* and all that it involves or that involves it (particularly *trace*, '*the différance*which opens [all?] appearance (*l'apparaître*) and signification' (Derrida 1974, 65)), relates to this folding, unfolding, and refolding, and their undecidable interplay – the interplay of marks and blanks, of algebra and geometry or topology, of material and phenomenal, of visual and verbal, of form and content, and so forth. Neither is, accordingly, ever reducible to algebra, any more than any other algebra, or any geometry to geometry, or any topology to topology. The signifiers themselves of 'blanc' or 'pli', or their interplay (their undecidable *inter*-play) become subject to this structure and hence, again, could never be irreducibly primary (Derrida 1981a, 253; 257–8). However, they do play a strategically crucial role in Mallarmé's and Derrida's undecidable algebra-geometry-topology. As Derrida observes:

These plays (on '*plume*', on 'winds' [unfolding the fan], etc. [we must also add fold, *pli*] are anathema to any lexicological summation, any [decidable] taxonomy of themes, any deciphering of meaning. But precisely, the crisis of literature, the '*exquisite crisis, down to the foundations*', is marked in a corner of this cast off excess. The [undecidable] figure of the *corner [le coin]*, with which we began, would testify to this in all the recastings and retemperings that have marked its course (an angle, an open recess, a fold, a hymen, a metal, a monetary signifier, a seal and superimpositions of marks, etc.). The *coin-entre*. (277; emphasis added)

There is, thus, a complex folding of algebra and geometry, figural and textual, including physical (turning a corner of a page), to Mallarmé's textual practice and even to his algebra, and ultimately to any algebra. The 'exquisite crisis, down to the foundations', which could serve as an exquisite description of the impact of Gödel's findings a few decades later, is the crisis of undecidability in and of literature (for example, in relation to philosophy, or linguistics, or rhetoric, or other arts, such as dancing, that of Mallarmé's *Mimique*, for example). The nature of this crisis is defined by the inscriptive undecidability of Mallarmé's *writing* and folding. The latter must be seen as part of Mallarmé's practice of *writing*, even though and because folding (of pages, of wings, of the fun) reciprocally (for example, physically) also defines this practice. According to Derrida:

> Rhyme – which is the general law of textual effects – is [transformed by Mallarmé into] the folding together of an identity and a difference. The raw material for this operation is no longer merely the sound effect of the end of a word: all 'substances' (phonic and graphic) and all 'forms' can be linked together at any distance and under any rule in order to produce new versions of 'that which in discourse does not speak'. For difference is the necessary interval, the suspense between two outcomes, the 'lapse of time' between two shots, two rolls, two chances. Without its being possible in advance to decide the limits of this sort of propagation, a different effect is produced each time, an effect that is therefore each time 'new' [*neuf*], a game [*jeu*] of chance forever new, a play of fire [*feu*] forever young [*jeune*] – fire and games being always, as Heraclitus and Nietzsche have said, a play of chance with necessity, of contingency with law. A hymen between chance and rule. (1981a, 277)

Thus the Mallarméan-Derridean hymens, beginning with that of Derrida and Mallarmé, the hymen of undecidable philosophy and undecidable literature, are brought together. Among them are those of philosophy and literature, of philosophy and linguistics, of literature and linguistics, of reading and writing, of philosophy and mathematics (or algebra and geometry, algebra and topology, geometry and topology within it), of literature and mathematics, and of chance and necessity.[11] In part through the interplay of chance and necessity, coupled to materiality, some physics or biology and its 'genetic program' inevitably enter this algebra of undecidables as well and enable us to form new hymens (Derrida 1981a, 285). Indeed this description is almost strictly that of the quantum mechanical epistemology, in which we always deal with an effect and chance always new, whose efficacity, while in turn each time unique, is each time irreducibly inconceivable. This bringing together establishes a very complex algebra of relations – an immense programme set into operation by Mallarmé and the task he set himself. It is not coincidental and momentous in its implications that this algebra links literature (and all its hymens) to the Democritean-Heraclitean-Nietzschean hymen of chance and necessity, primarily a physical hymen, but also the hymen inherent in all writing or perhaps defined by writing, by virtue of its inevitably Derridean character. For, 'it is neither the natural arbitrariness nor the natural necessity of the sign, but both at once, that obtains in *writing*. It must be written. And sometimes the very gambols of Language itself bring this to the attention of the poet "or even the canny prose writer"' and Mallarmé also wonders whether 'strict observance of the principle of contemporary linguistics will yield before what we call *the literary point of view*' (Derrida, 1981a, 279).

'The crisis of verse (of "rhythm", as Mallarmé also puts it) thus involves all of literature', and much beyond, linguistics and philosophy, if not mathematics, included. 'The crisis of a *rythmos* broken by Being (something we began spinning off in a note toward Democritus) is "fundamental". It solicits the very basis of literature, depriving it, in its exercise, of any foundation outside itself' (Derrida 1981a, 279–80). That is to say, it also deprives it of any foundation qua foundation, inside or outside itself, altogether. This is how 'Literature, all along, in its exquisite crisis, shivers and flaps its wings, and goes trembling through the great divestment of a winter' (Derrida 1981a, 280). After a few more pages of algebraic ('signifier') pyrotechnics around 'i' and 'r' of *literature and crisis* (beginning with the key titles, *Crise de vers, Mimique, Or, Igitur; vers libre* and blank verse, in English words, *mots anglais*, such as I/je, also the I of the Idea; Plato's or Hegel's), Derrida closes his long text as follows:

> In a hymen depending on the verse, blank once more, composed of chance and necessity, a configuration of veils, folds, and quills, writing prepares to receive the seminal spurt of a throw of dice. If – it were, literature would hang – would it, on the suspense in which each of the six sides still has a chance although the outcome is predetermined and recognized after the fact as such. It is a game of chance that follows the genetic program. The die is limited to surfaces. Abandoning all depth, each of the surfaces is also, once the die is cast [*après coup*], the whole of it. The crisis of literature takes place when nothing takes place but the place, in the instance where no one is there to know. (1981a, 285)

An irreducibly untranslatable 'Personne – ne sachant – avant le coup – qui le déjoue en son échéance – lequel des six dés – chute', roughly, 'No one – knowing – before the throw – which undoes one [it/he] in its outcome – which of the six dies – falling', and, posterior epigraphs from Mallarmé and Artaud are added (1981a, 285–6; translation modified). While intermixing and ultimately suspending algebra and geometry or topology, and physics and biology, along with philosophy and literature, the foundational deprivation is what brings in and perpetuates, or brings in perpetually, the *crisis* of literature. 'Literature' enacts the ultimately irreducible undecidability of the demarcation of the inside and the outside of literature, or indeed of anything. It enacts it 'in its exercise', in its operation, in its logic or 'mathematics' – its hymenology, the calculus of hymens as undecidable, or in its 'physics', one is almost tempted to say, quantum physics, of the interplay of chance and necessity. Bringing these together or hymenologically interlinking them or, reciprocally, the disciplinary hymens – of literature (or other arts), philosophy, linguistics, mathematics and physics – makes this perpetual crisis *exquisite*. The conjunction, in *literature*, or a hymen of the logical-mathematical undecidability and the physical or, again, quantum-physical materiality (it has its algebra, too), defined by the chance-necessity hymen, may well be the most exquisite hymen and crisis of all.

CONCLUSION: WRITING CHAOS

As Mallarmé was undoubtedly aware, Lucretius in his vision of chaos and the emergence of order out of chaos in *De Rerum Natura* compares the atoms to letters of the alphabet, literally *litera*, the origin of '*literature*'. Accordingly, he maps his physics and geometry (trajectories, vortexes, etc.) of chaos by a kind of literary (in either sense, of using letters and as literature) algebra, coupled to a 'mechanics' and 'analytic geometry' of chaos. Thus, he also poses, a question of how we read or indeed write chaos, spatially-geometrically (even dealing with temporal and dynamic processes) or algebraically, and what is the representational or, conversely, non-representational character of such a writing. The argument here presented suggests two among possible answers: a Deleuzean and a Derridean.

Building upon Deleuze's earlier ideas concerning the virtual in *Difference and Repetition*, Deleuze and Guattari offer a highly original geometrical-spatial vision of chaos and its dynamics: 'Chaos is defined not so much by its disorder as by the infinite speed with which every form taking shape in it vanishes. It is a void that is not a nothingness but a *virtual*, containing all possible forms and drawing out all possible forms, which spring up only to disappear immediately, without consistency or reference, without consequence. Chaos is an infinite speed of birth and disappearance' (DG 1994b, 118). Chaos is seen by Deleuze and Guattari as the ultimate enemy of thought. Philosophy, mathematics and science, literature and art, are all our (different) means of keeping chaos at bay at least up to a point, which, however, does not prevent them from still spatio-temporally imagining chaos, at least in principle (1994b, 202–18). It is

important that we are dealing with a spatio-temporal dynamics rather than
with a strictly spatial, topological or geometrical, static configuration. In other
words, we are dealing with a certain 'physics', material or phenomenal – virtual
– of chaos. But this temporality and this physics are conceived in certain
spatio-temporal and thus, at least in principle, visualisable and even specifically
continuous formations. This vision, I would argue, follows that of classical
physics, from Newton's mechanics (or Descartes's and Leibniz's more continuous conceptions, or even Lucretian, if not Democritean, physics) to the
statistical physics of ensembles (or analogous ideas in molecular chemistry) to
chaos theory and, via Riemann's ideas, Einstein's relativity. These are all
conceptions that are persistently invoked and quasi-mathematically or quasi-
scientifically deployed by Deleuze, along with and often processed through a
more Leibnizean and Riemannian topological vision.[12] Even though some of
these theories, relativity and chaos theory, in particular, are often associated
with new physics, I see them as classical physics for epistemological reasons.
Most significant among them is giving a spatio-temporal conception or conceivability, at least in principle, to the processes in question that these theories
usually imply. This conceivability and even conception, I argue, also defines
Deleuze's (thus ontological) vision, including that of the virtual of chaos. One
might argue that this conception or Deleuze's earlier ideas concerning the
virtual in *Difference and Repetition* derive from the idea of the so-called virtual
particle formation (birth and disappearance) in quantum theory, specifically
quantum field theory. This *vision* is thus based on at least a potentially possible
spatio-temporal visualisation or intuiting on the model of classical physics,
however impossible an actual imagining or 'capturing' of the situation may be
due to the complexity of the multiplicities involved or the speed of such virtual
processes.

   This epistemology and ontology linked to it are in sharp contrast to certain
forms of the irreducibly non-visualisable and, in general, non-ontological
epistemology of quantum theory, such as Niels Bohr's, which leaves such
processes beyond any possible visualisation or indeed conception, and which
is closer to Derrida's epistemology and the vision, that is, un-vision of chaos it
implies.[13] Here is Derrida's undecidable algebra of chaos, which ultimately
defines all of Derrida's key concepts or neither terms nor concepts, from
différance to his reading of Plato's choral 'space', and beyond:

> Form (presence, self-evidence) [ultimately spatial concepts] would not be
> the ultimate recourse, the last analysis to which every possible sign would
> refer, the arche or the telos. Or rather, in a perhaps unheard-of-fashion,
> morphe, arche, and telos [all again, topological notions] still signal, in a
> sense – or a non-sense – that which metaphysics would have excluded from

its field, while nevertheless remaining in a secret and incessant relation with this sense, form in itself would already be the trace (*ikhnos*) of a certain nonpresence, the vestige of the un-formed, which announces-recalls its others, as did Plotinus, perhaps, for all metaphysics. The trace would not be the mixture, the transition between form and the amorphous, presence and absence, etc., but that which, by eluding this opposition, makes it possible in the irreducibility of its excess. (Derrida 1982, 172n16; see also 26–7; 66–7)

Is there algebra for this 'excess'? Yes, perhaps; but it would irreducibly involve the materiality of physics of *physis*, of matter. This has to do with the utmost reaches of modern physics, quantum field theories. These theories deal with how the ultimate constituents of matter, elementary particles, are made and disappear, incessantly all the time, that is, if we can apply this language, which is rather closer to Deleuze's vision of chaos than to what Derrida suggests here, and under the Derridean conditions we ultimately cannot. One may instead speak, as I have done earlier, of the epistemology of certain 'effects', whose ultimate efficacity or (they are always plural even if each time unknowable) the 'agencies' producing such manifest 'effects', lies beyond any possible conception, spatio-temporal (geometrical or topological), or algebraic, or philosophical, literary, linguistic, or any others. All of these names, 'efficacity' included, or any other names are themselves ultimately inapplicable here.

On this point, one would need to rethink the whole fabric of the relationships between geometrical vs arithmetical thinking, mathematical thinking and thinking, speech and writing, or thinking, painting and writing, and in Platonism and (not the same) in Plato. That includes the figure of artist-demiurge, *zographos*, 'a painter who comes after the writer', in the *Philebus*, with which Derrida begins his reading of Mallarmé in 'The Double Session'.

A Deleuzean-Derridean figure, perhaps. For whatever epistemology one ultimately adopts, it is not a matter of dispensing with either type of vision, even assuming that this is possible. At the very least, at the level of effects, the more topological, spatio-temporal, type of epistemology is necessary. We certainly need Deleuze's topological-geometrical and in (among others) this sense more intuitive and imaginative philosophy as much as Derrida's more rigorous algebra, which is more suspicious, indeed structurally, irreducibly suspicious of all spatio-temporal or other intuitions. Naturally, I am not suggesting that there is no work of thought against chaos in Derrida's algebra – quite the contrary. This 'algebra' is defined by this work, as is any algebra in mathematics, in spite and because of undecidability, and, as will be seen, both algebras depend on some geometry and topology. Nor, conversely, can Deleuze's thought quite keep chaos at bay, or, as I said, avoid algebra any-

more than Derrida can topology or geometry. For the moment, we may begin
to think in the way, to return to Kant's idea, poets, such as Mallarmé, find the
sublime – poets, who are mortal gods, and no gods are immortal any more.
They do it by arranging the written marks on a blank page, or rather, marks
and blanks which constitute the page of poetry, which is not reducible to
merely material pages but where neither materiality nor phenomenality are
ever reducible. This algebra, topology and geometry are indeed not foreign to
the order of mathematics, but they always irreducibly exceed this order. But
then, so does, inevitably, mathematics itself to itself, or physics itself to itself,
or philosophy itself to itself, linguistics itself to itself, or literature itself to itself.
They always exceed themselves, are inevitably invaded by 'chaos', and in this
excess they always mix with each other. But, however mixed, they could not
approach or even in any way relate to that 'chaos' which is neither chaos nor
order, nor *anything else*, but of which *everything else* is ultimately an effect, to
which one could relate. To that 'chaos' this last proposition or, again, the
name 'chaos' would be no more applicable than any other proposition or
name. Could then our thought live with this unthinkable un-chaos? Could it
live without it?

Notes

1. These ideas have their genealogy in medieval thought, specifically that of
   Raymond Lulle (1235–1316).
2. One finds of course algebraic elements and references to algebra in Deleuze,
   for example, in *The Logic of Sense* (Deleuze 1990), and in *Difference and
   Repetition* (1994). However, beyond the fact that such elements are often
   expressly linked to geometry or even refigured geometrically, their appearance
   does not in itself amount to quasi-algebraic (vs quasi-topological or quasi-
   geometrical) *philosophical thinking*; and, as I said, in question here is a relative
   balance of different quasi-mathematical elements, rather than a decidable
   determination.
3. On *khōra*, see Derrida 1995c.
4. See Deleuze and Guattari's discussion of different 'models' at DG 1987,
   477–500.
5. I have discussed the subject at Plotnitsky 1993, 56–65.
6. A metric is not the same as a striation, for example, a coordinate striation,
   although they may be defined correlatively in certain cases.
7. The concept of infinite series is a persistent reference in *The Fold* and elsewhere
   in Deleuze, via Leibniz, Karl Weierstrass and others. For example, '[Leibniz's]
   God does not determine the total quantity of progress either beforehand or
   afterwards, but eternally, in the calculus of the infinite series that moves
   through all increased magnitudes of consciousness and all the subtraction of
   the damned' (Deleuze 1993, 75). Divergent series (roughly those whose sums

are either infinite or not definable unambiguously) invoked by Deleuze in the passage cited earlier may be seen as irreducibly algebraic mathematically (1993, 137). They cannot correspond to any geometrical object (not all convergent series do either), and their mathematical legitimacy is a complex issue. They could, however, be considered and manipulated formally, and have been, from Leibniz's to the twentieth-century mathematics. Considered as potentially infinite 'horizontal' combinations of symbols, they could, thus, be seen in terms of algebraic writing. On the other hand, it appears that Deleuze's appeal to divergent series has a greater topological than algebraic import, as the passage just cited suggests, especially in terms of *conceptual* topology. (See Note 2 above.) The subject, however, requires a separate treatment.

8. The argument opens *Of Grammatology*, whose first chapter is famously entitled 'The End of the Book and the Beginning of Writing' (Derrida 1974, 6–26), and is made specifically in the context of the trope of 'the book of nature', highly relevant here. It is followed by Derrida throughout *Dissemination* (1981a) and elsewhere.

9. It is of some significance in the context of this essay that Deleuze and Guattari appear to be suspicious of undecidability (as concerns the determination of Oedipus) in *Anti-Oedipus* (DG 1984, 81). This type of undecidability would not be denied by Derrida, but would be linked by him to dissemination and its undecidable algebra.

10. De Man 1996, 82–3. I discuss the subject in Plotnitsky 2000.

11. This is a crucial theme in Derrida's work. See especially Derrida 1982, 7; and 1984a.

12. It is significant that, following Michel Serres, Deleuze and Guattari give a more continuous, rather than discrete, reading of Lucretius' atomicity (DG 1987, 489–90).

13. I have considered the epistemology of quantum theory in Plotnitsky 2002.

CHAPTER 7

The Philosopher *and* the Writer:
A Question of Style

Gregg Lambert

Can we today any longer imagine a philosopher who doesn't entertain an essential relationship to the question of style? Can we imagine a philosopher who didn't write? Of course, one can say that Hegel wrote, or that Kant conceived of his system in writing, that both were great composers of written works. But is this the same thing as the *philosopher as writer*? Hence, the question of writing must be understood to be both more general and more particular (one could say 'historical') than the philosophical problem of representation *as such*, since the contemporary philosopher (or the one who professes to 'do philosophy' in its current form and institutional setting) is someone who must reflect on the formal, but also the material, conditions of his or her philosophical project as also a project of writing.[1]

The above statements can be readily supported in the opening pages of the early (and perhaps most systematic) reflections on the relationship between philosophy and writing in, respectively, *Différence et Repetition* and *De la Grammatologie*. Deleuze writes: 'Perhaps writing has a relation to silence altogether more threatening than that which it is supposed to entertain with death' (Deleuze 1994, xxi); while Derrida writes: 'Perhaps patient meditation and painstaking investigation on and around what is still provisionally called writing, far from falling short of a science of writing or of hastily dismissing it by some obscurantist reaction, letting it rather develop its positivity as far as possible, are the wanderings of a way of thinking that is faithful and attentive to the ineluctable world of the future which proclaims itself at present, beyond the closure of knowledge. The future can only be anticipated in the form of an absolute danger' (Derrida 1974, 4).

In the above passages, written at the very commencement of their philosophical projects, both philosophers seem to express a certain foreboding around the question of writing, which appears to one as an 'altogether threatening silence', and to the other as an 'absolute danger'. For each, the limit (or horizon) of knowledge will henceforth bear an ineluctable relationship to 'the experience of writing', which is to say, to *ex-perience itself.*

Do the above statements, however, also imply that writing has replaced death as the absolute border of silence (non-being) and finitude? If so, what is its specific threat or danger – a harmless supplement, a secondary appendage to speech, a mere automaton? After *Of Grammatology,* at least, no one can so easily dismiss the question of writing as that point where its all too self-evident meaning dissolves in favour of movement that necessarily exceeds conscious-ness, thereby dislocating the unity of the work with regard to its former end, goal or *telos.* As a consequence of Derrida's interrogation, no one today can (or rather should) approach the question of writing *innocently.* Its sign, as Derrida announces very early on, is always *presented* as a sort of 'monstrosity'.

This is not merely a sign of the times, according to Derrida, but rather of the 'inflation of the sign itself, absolute inflation, inflation itself' (Derrida 1974, 6). Today, in fact, we can still perceive all the symptoms of this inflation (of language, of writing) in the manner by which the subject (including every aspect of this subject's so-called activity – including its culture, politics, knowledge, economy) is absolutely *comprehended* by an order of signs, one might even say *pre-comprehended,* in a manner that necessarily exceeds con-sciousness. Thus, the weight and measure of the subject's own activity and experience has disappeared under the gravity of another measure that takes the form of a writing that the subject barely understands, even though it already animates every perception, action, feeling or thought. As Derrida writes:

> There is not a single signified that escapes, even if recaptured, the play of signifying references that constitute language. The advent of writing is the advent of this play; today such a play is coming into its own, effacing the limit starting from which one had thought to regulate the circulation of signs, drawing along with it all the reassuring signifieds, reducing all strongholds, all the out-of-bounds shelters that watched over the field of language. This, strictly speaking, amounts to destroying the concept of the 'sign' and its entire logic. (Derrida 1974, 7)

If one does not enter into this dangerous and insane game of writing lightly today, this is because the border that separates our knowledge from our ignorance has been eclipsed. Thus, as Deleuze remarks, '[w]e write only at the frontiers of our knowledge, at the border which separates our knowledge from our ignorance and transforms one into the other. Only in this manner are we resolved to write' (Deleuze 1994, xxi). All the old reference points are gone (or, at least, strangely dislocated); once we enter the game, there are no more 'time-outs', and what's worse, we only come to discover that we were always already playing and being played. Given the gravity of this 'new' situation, therefore, it would seem plausible that one could (even should) simply choose not to enter into the game, to continue speaking of and from that former limit, to hold on to all the old reassuring signifieds, to cling to a concept of the 'sign' as spoken, intentional, ordered, most of all, 'logical'. However, if the future introduced by the advent of writing exposes one to the measure of a certain insanity (one that necessarily exceeds Hegelian 'bad infinity'), then the avoidance or reduction (perhaps even the 'foreclosure') of this moment only exposes one to another, potentially more dangerous and violent, form of madness.

My last statement can be readily illustrated by the following observation: if, as suggested above, the boundary- or limit-concept of knowledge has been transmuted from death into 'writing', then the reduction of the question of writing (again) to a former position of 'secondariness' would be comparable to reducing the question of finitude (again) to the status of mortality of the 'creature' (*ens creatum*). It is not by chance that we see in this response the nostalgic reassertion of a certain theological solution, since, as Derrida has remarked many times, the production of theology (in the West) has always taken place by means of a certain repression of the limit first introduced by writing (although one could also say in this context by a certain history of writing, or even the repression of history *as such*, which can be defined as 'the total movement of the trace').[2] Thus, Derrida writes, 'in its origin, to be sure, one can already suspect that an origin whose structure can be exposed as 'signifier of the signifier' conceals and erases itself in its own production' (Derrida 1974, 7).

The above exergue on the question of writing only served to demonstrate what, upon first glance, might seem all too obvious: Derrida and Deleuze are philosophers who write. It is difficult to judge which activity grounds the other, in the sense of which provides the necessary conditions for the other activity to take place – philosophising or writing? But then, assuming that this distinction makes sense any longer, can we imagine philosophers who are not also writers? Again, can we imagine today a philosopher who didn't write? Of course, the answer would be, 'yes', but only, I would argue, in the same way that one might imagine pink elephants and unicorns, since this would be a philosopher who would be virtually anonymous – or, at least, exceptionally rare. In order to account for this fact, certainly one factor would be the evolution in the systems of writing, publication, archiving, or, more generally, the dispersion of the public functions of discourse (especially written discourse), including all the civil and legal codes – here one might recall Foucault's descriptive genealogy of the author as a discursive function – that determine the circulation of written works and their relationship to proper, identifiable individuals. This has certainly become a constant, even obsessive, theme in Derrida's writings concerning the signature, the proper name, the enunciating dimension of the speech-act or performative statement (such as the promise or oath). One cannot account for this series of themes except to say that they mark the limits and the tertiary borders of a properly philosophical (demonstrative) discourse. They form the outside of philosophical representation, an outside that re-appears as the very condition of philosophy in its contemporary mode – the wildly different appropriations of the term 'deconstruction' already attest to this – and thus become occasions for Derrida's own interrogation concerning the various convergences and, more often, the 'destinerrance' of his body of work.

A second factor for understanding the emergence of the question of writing in philosophy is a certain 'contamination' that has taken place between the genres of philosophical and literary discourse in the modern period, after Nietzsche in particular. One might argue that this has always been the case (for example, Plato's dialogues, or Hegel's 'philosophical *Bildungsroman*'), but there is something distinctly modern in the emergence of 'literature', and in the concept of writing that accompanies it, as distinguished from the earlier forms of rhetoric, poetry, or 'belles lettres'. It is around this development that the question of writing is especially marked and around this question, I would argue, that the most dizzying and contracted dialogue between 'the philosopher' and 'the writer' has ensued in the contemporary period. At a moment of near identification, we can locate many places in both Deleuze and Derrida's work where the philosopher emerges to assert that what he is doing is not 'merely literature' – e.g., 'Those who accuse me of reducing philosophy to literature or logic to rhetoric . . . have visibly and carefully avoided reading me' (Derrida 1995d, 218) – or conversely, where the style of writing sometimes appears to ground (and thereby to 'authorise') the entire philosophical system. Yet, it is precisely this confrontation and even struggle around the question of writing that for both Derrida and Deleuze the question of philosophy has re-commenced in the modern period.

In the interview 'Is there a philosophical language?' Derrida addresses this 'contamination' of a 'properly philosophical language' and a 'purely literary discourse' in the following passage:

This explanation between 'philosophy' and 'literature' is not only a difficult problem that I try to elaborate as such, it is also that which takes the form of writing in my texts, a writing that, by being neither purely literary nor purely philosophical, attempts to sacrifice neither the attention to demonstration or to theses nor the fictionality or poetics of languages. In a word,

. . . I don't believe that there is a 'specifically philosophical writing', a sole philosophical writing whose purity is always the same and out of reach of all sorts of contaminations. And first of all for this overwhelming reason: philosophy is spoken and written in a natural language, not in an absolutely formalizable and universal language. That said, within this natural language and its uses, certain modes have been forcibly imposed (and there is here a relation of force) as philosophical. (Derrida 1995d, 218–19)

Consequently, it is by means of the proliferation of many experiments on the level of form – *Dissemination*, *Glas*, *The Post Card* and *Circumfessions* are perhaps the most notable examples – that Derrida has constantly called into question the supposed naturalness of a certain mode of philosophical discourse. There is a politics of style, and by means of this experimentation, style becomes a political question, since '[e]ach time a philosophy has been opposed, it was also, although not only, by contesting the properly, authentically philosophical character of the other's discourse' (ibid.). Moreover, there is a certain violence, at least the visibility of 'force', that Derrida's writing causes to appear, precisely in not obeying the traditional and institutional norms that always command the reproduction of an entire historical apparatus (of authorities, protocols, linguistic and discursive norms, national differences, etc.). 'A philosophical debate is also a combat in view of imposing discursive modes, demonstrative procedures, rhetorical and pedagogical techniques' (ibid.). It is precisely this combat between force and signification, which was invisibly present in the tradition of philosophy (constituting its 'white mythology'), that Derrida's style manifests as a *phenomenon* that must now be incorporated into its total signification.

As for Deleuze, it goes without saying that his work is prone to experimentation with regard to the normative conventions of a properly philosophical discourse, perhaps even to a hyperbolic degree in the case of the experimental performances of *Anti-Oedipus* and *A Thousand Plateaus*, both written with Guattari, or the two volumes on cinema. Even his more 'traditional' philosophical commentaries are extremely deceptive, and no less experimental in terms of innovating the genre (as in the case of *The Fold*). Of course, this programme or 'style' of experimentation is already foreshadowed in the preface to *Difference and Repetition*, where Deleuze writes:

The time is coming when it will be hardly possible to write a book of philosophy as it has been done for so long: 'Ah, that old style . . .' . . . It seems to us that the history of philosophy should play a role roughly to that of *collage* in painting. The history of philosophy is the reproduction of philosophy itself. In the history of philosophy, the commentary should act as a veritable double and bear the maximum modification appropriate to a double. (One imagines a *philosophically* bearded Hegel, a *philosophically* clean-shaven Marx, in the same way as a moustached Mona-Lisa.) (Deleuze 1994, xxi)

Given that the question of writing and a certain strategy of experimentation are fundamental traits in both philosophies of difference, could we then say that the difference between Derrida and Deleuze could be reduced to the question of 'style'? But then, this then begs a more preliminary question: 'what is style?'

In the penultimate chapter of his work on Proust (Deleuze 2000b), Deleuze defines the function of style as *the form of the communication of the whole within the work*. Its function is to unify a multiplicity of viewpoints, even at the level of the sentence, without thereby submitting this unity to a closed totality. 'But just what is this form, and how are the orders of production or truth, the machines organized within each other?' Deleuze asks. 'None has the function of totalization' (2000b, 161). In several places, Deleuze even refers to style as an 'essence', despite the inappropriateness some might ascribe to this word, since it allows a viewpoint to open up onto the work as a whole: 'an individuating viewpoint superior to the individuals themselves, breaking with their chains of associations' (2000b, 162). Thus, the essence of essence, of style as the essential viewpoint in the work, is 'syntactic' or 'conjunctive': 'essence appears *alongside* these chains, incarnated in a closed fragment, *adjacent* to what it overwhelms, *contiguous* to what it reveals' (ibid.). Alongside, adjacent and contiguous – style, nevertheless, expresses unity, which is the unity *of* this multiplicity of fragments, tissues, and parts.

At the same time, style must also be defined as the unifying trait that is produced after the work, at its end – one might say as the gesture of a final brushstroke or word – but which nevertheless continues to exist alongside the work. The fact that this unity continues to exist 'alongside the work', contingently related, possibly undergoing further permutations, is what makes style an object of criticism. Each critic seeks to grasp the unity of a work (of a given author) by discovering the most stylistic element that defines the work's genetic structure and its essential idea. The fact that most critics fail to discover this element of style, or that it is open to such intense disagreement and even conflict, is what makes the function of style so interesting, since it opens the question of the work's unity (its genetic or formal history) to a seemingly endless number of appropriations. It is by this trait that 'style' functions like a foreign language within language, and as a second-level order of signification, or new convention by which the work is determined, even if this determination is only 'contingently' fixed and can undergo further translation or repetition.

Does this mean that style is external to the work? The translation of the work's meaning into another, so-called secondary, and descriptive language, like a foreign language borne within the work, but abutting its external representation? Each work, according to Umberto Eco (who is cited by Deleuze in this context), 'produces new linguistic conventions to which it submits, and itself becomes the key to its own code' (Deleuze 2000b, 168). Later, Deleuze will rename this 'foreign language within language' or this 'transversal dimension' (the very *element* of style) as, very simply, 'the outside'. For example, I cite the following passage from 'He Stuttered' concerning style:

> When a language is so strained that it starts to stutter, or to murmur or to stammer . . . then language in its entirety reaches the limit that marks its outside and makes it confront silence. When language is strained in this way, language in its entirety is submitted to a pressure that makes it fall silent. Style – the foreign language in language – is made up of these two operations. (Deleuze 1997, 113)

Finally, according to Deleuze, it is through this 'outside' or 'transversal dimension' that the work is able to communicate with other works by the same writer, even those that do not yet exist, in addition to the works of other writers or artists.

> For if the work of art communicates with a public and even gives rise to that public, if it communicates with the other works of the same artist and gives rise to them, if it communicates with the works of other artists and gives rise to works to come, it is always within a dimension of transversality, in which unity and totality are established for themselves, without totalizing objects or subjects. (Deleuze 1997, 168–9)

Following this definition, for example, one can see that it is an element of style that allows Beckett as the writer of *Molloy*, for example, to communicate (belong to the same series) as the Beckett of *The Lost Ones*, *Waiting for Godot*, *Krapp's Last Tape* and even *Quad*. It allows all these Becketts to communicate via the singular expression of a style, as so many perspectives or viewpoints opening to a whole which is not, for that matter, closed off or contained by the totality of Beckett's œuvre.

In addressing the same issue (the definition of the work, of its manner of unifying itself, the existence of a unique idiom or style), Derrida also speaks to a certain 'unity without totalization', a unity that exceeds the identity of the signature, or the individuating viewpoint of the writer (i.e., the limited chain of associations):

There is a legal copyright and a civil identity, texts signed by the same name, a law, a responsibility, a property, guarantees. All this interests me very much. But it is only one stratum of the thing or the singular adventure called a work, which I feel is at every moment in the process of undoing itself, expropriating itself, falling to pieces without ever collecting itself together in a signature. I would be tempted to retain from the old concept of work the value of singularity and not that of identity to itself or of collection. If anything repeats itself in me in an obsessive fashion, it is this paradox: there is singularity but it does not collect itself, it 'consists' in not collecting itself. Perhaps you will say that there is a way of not collecting oneself that is consistently recognizable, what used to be called a 'style'. (Derrida 1995d, 354)

Yet, echoing the passage by Deleuze quoted above, the condition of this singularity, the condition of the 'recognition' of style – whether this is attributed to the work or to the writer, it is difficult to say – is *the other*. One can never recognise one's own style, or rather, this only occurs when the writer is already located in the position of *the other*, which is to say, at a certain distance and according to a measure and technique that is highly determined. Following Derrida's comment concerning style, any such nomination or viewpoint always comes from the other whose apprehension provides the very basis of the work's communication. Derrida writes:

This can be perceived only by the other. The idiom, if there is any, that by which one recognizes a signature, does not reappropriate itself, as paradoxical as that may seem. It can only be apprehended by an other, given over to the other. Of course, I may think I recognize myself, identify my signature or my sentence, but on the basis of an experience and of an exercise which I have undertaken in which I will have been trained as other, the possibility of repetition and thus of imitation, simulacrum, being inscribed at the very origin of this singularity. (1995d, 354–5)

It seems that we have located the essence of style in this event of expropriation of a singular and unique idiom, from the moment that this idiom is already handed over to the powers of repetition or imitation, revealing instead a discourse that is strangely divided from itself at its very origin. On the basis of this observation concerning the possibility of a singular or unique instance of 'I', it is interesting to remark that even to speak of the works of 'a Deleuze' and 'a Derrida', we are speaking from a pure convention, a fiction that belongs more to the history of the signature, the proper name, the bounded determination of the work as a property that belongs to an attested civil identity. It is even from this viewpoint that Derrida or Deleuze could be said to imitate or repeat themselves from the moment that they begin writing, since they themselves are marked or limited by the same institutional conventions that determine their civil identities and that define the very conditions of written enunciation. One can see why the works written with Guattari, where the status of the signature and the proper name is constantly frustrated by a writing process that refuses to obey the normative conventions of authorial identity, continue to trouble most of Deleuze's commentators – and perhaps this constitutes Deleuze's *and* Guattari's most radical experiment, one that transgresses not only philosophical conventions, but the underlying conventions of written forms.

The earlier mention of Beckett was not merely by chance. Perhaps no other writer obsessively created from a search for the zero degree of a style. He pushed this search to an extreme state, in which each moment 'he wrote' is only recognised from the position of the other. This is particularly evident in the trilogy, in the series of characters (Molloy, Jacques Moran, Malone and the unnamable), each of which is marked by a vague memory of *the other*, and of themselves as larval identities of the earlier characters, like worms that might have infested or inhabited the other characters, or have been cocooned and sleeping (and each one of Beckett's hilarious journeys begins in sleep). The 'narrative voice' (for lack of a better term) is itself only a variable mouthpiece of 'someone speaking'; all of the action occurs by means of what Deleuze calls 'inclusive disjunction', by which everything divides into itself. And yet, there is no totalisation or collection of individual identities within one final term (the self, the Ego), and the process itself ends only by exhausting all the possibilities that belong to the 'he said', 'he invents', 'he says'. Hence, in *The Unnamable* for example, the 'of me I must speak now' becomes 'it is not I, about me, it is not about me'; 'No, I have no voice, and if I have said anything to the contrary, I was mistaken . . . unless I am mistaken now' (Beckett 1997, 331).

Returning to the essay 'He Stuttered', Deleuze often speaks of 'a non-style', which is made up from 'the elements of a style to come, which does not yet exist' (Deleuze 1997, 113). In a certain sense, modern philosophy (after Nietzsche) has always concerned itself with the question of non-style, the discovery of a variable that will 'make difference' by means of a new species of repetition, one that assembles together all the elements of the 'not yet' and the 'to come'. Non-style, therefore, can be defined as virtual, suspended between the tensors of the 'to come' and the 'not yet', scattered and fragmentary. On the other hand, Deleuze also defines style as essentially economical. 'Style is the economy of language' (ibid.). However, this sentence would be misunderstood if 'economy' is conceived as an order in equilibrium and balance; rather, economy must now be redefined as the duration perched between *boom* and *bust*, as an order of profound disequilibrium. As Deleuze asks,

> Can we make progress if we do not enter into *regions far from equilibrium*? Physics attests to this. Keynes made advances in political economy because he related it to a situation of a 'boom', and no longer equilibrium. This is the only way to introduce desire into the corresponding field. Must language then be put into a state of *boom*, close to a *crash*? (1997, 109)

Likewise, we might think of Derrida's programme along the same lines: to introduce the question of language into a region far from equilibrium. In this manner, Derrida poses as his fundamental gesture the question of writing as an essential disequilibrium within what he names as the logo-centric tradition. As he summarises this strategy in the interview 'A "Madness" Must Watch Over Thinking', 'the act of writing or rather, since it is perhaps not altogether an act, the experience of writing . . . gives one a way that is better than ever for thinking the present and the origin, death, life, or survival' (Derrida 1995d, 347). Finally, in this context, allow me to recall a very early passage by Derrida, almost at the beginning of his work. He speaks about a certain *boom* that will inevitably lead to the *bust* of language. He writes:

> The devaluation of the word 'language' itself, and how, in the very hold it has upon us, it betrays a loose vocabulary, the temptation of a cheap seduction, the passive yielding to fashion, the consciousness of the avant-garde, in other words – ignorance – are evidences of this effect. (1974, 5)

My emphasis on these passages from the works of both philosophers is not merely to produce an analogy of themes based upon the repetition of the economic metaphors of 'boom' and 'crash' (or 'bust'), but rather underscores the redefinition of an economy of difference and repetition that no longer is related to the equilibrium of a certain return of the same (of metaphysics, identity, self-presence, etc.). Thus, the economy of disequilibrium is defined either as the point where the being of language cracks, shudders, and when language itself is pushed to a state of boom, close to a crash; or is revealed as expressing all the inflationary signs of a crash – one that is perhaps even 'immemorial'. In turn, this raises the question of silence in the region of language. There are actually two silences: one that is peaceful, marking a pause, a breath, which is already made possible by the order of speech. In fact, this is not silence at all, since it is already 'impregnated' by the signifier that speaks through it and replenishes its significance. The other silence, one might say, can never be heard. It is not peaceful, but essentially brutal; it does not mark a pause between two words, but the rupture of language with itself. In this second silence, no breath is possible, since it is not made for the breath, but for the eye. It is this other silence that is announced earlier on by Deleuze as 'altogether more threatening' and by Derrida as a 'dangerous future', a silence that is introduced by a philosophy of difference *and* repetition.

And yet, there is also a divergence present here between the two manners of reaching this point, and it is on this ridge line or border that we can sharply distinguish the philosophical projects of Derrida and Deleuze. Whereas Derrida will trace the effects of this profound disequilibrium of a difference 'that speaks everywhere throughout language', Deleuze will understand it as an act or activity of creation: to place language in a situation of a boom, close to a crash. For the latter, difference is essentially, and perhaps 'supremely', created difference and not the effect of some flaw or crack, some essential lapse, in the orders of being and language. It is here that we might locate a difference in style between these two philosophers, or rather, between the style of these two major philosophies of difference today. To put it succinctly, and recalling the above passages, while I would say that Deleuze is a philosopher of the *boom*, Derrida is the philosopher of the *crash*.

For Deleuze, the boom: in language, by creativity to push syntax to its limit, to the point of stuttering; in desire, to crack desire itself up to the point of causing it to multiply its objects and states of becoming, beyond Oedipal familiarity; in politics, to break from the individual and the fascist collective organisation alike, in order to cause the very phenomenon of collective assemblages to become more supple, molecular, and even experimental. All these mark the traits of a Deleuzean style of the critical (as the moment of turning, *krinein*, or crisis). Of course, the crisis of every boom is the risk of a crash. Thus, as Deleuze often warns, desire risks becoming trapped, or blocked; a schizoid process risks becoming schizophrenic; the body without organs risks becoming petrified, the vitrified body of a junkie filled with refrigerator waves. As for language, there is the risk of it falling silent, and non-style can easily come to resemble all the trademarks of an all too familiar style. The point, it seems, is to keep on moving, that is, creating. The moment one stops, difference risks becoming un-creative, static, (non) Being.

For Derrida, on the other hand, one could say that the crash is itself the creative moment par excellence, and one does not approach it by dint of force, much less by exceptional or creative effort. One can find this axiom supported as early as 'Force and Signification', where Derrida already announces the critical forces of this crash: 'The force of our weakness', he writes, 'is that impotence separates, disengages, *and emancipates*. Henceforth, the totality is more perceived, the panorama and the panoramagram are possible' (1978, 5;

my emphasis).[3] Moreover, the crash – of a certain metaphysical epoch, a logo-centric tradition, a certain subject of representation, of a certain idea of science and writing – has already happened. This is already evident in a passage from the essay 'Force and Signification' where this approach or strategy is method-ologically announced (what would later be baptised as a 'deconstructive operation') in terms of a certain solicitude or solicitation of the whole:

> Structure can be *methodically* threatened in order to comprehend more clearly not only its supports but also that secret place in which it is neither construction nor ruin but labiality [one might say at its fringe, margin or border – terms that Derrida will make much use of from this point onward, but already in *Of Grammatology*]. This operation is called (from the Latin) *soliciting*. In other words, *shaking* in a way related to the *whole* (from *sollus*, in archaic Latin, 'the whole', and from *citare*, 'to put in motion'). The structuralist solicitude and solicitation give themselves only the illusion of technical liberty when they become methodological. In truth, they repro-duce, in the register of method, a solicitude and solicitation of Being, a historical-metaphysical threatening of foundations. It is during the epochs of historical dislocation, when we are expelled from the *site*, that this structuralist passion, which is simultaneously a frenzy of experimentation and a proliferation of schematizations, develops for itself. (1978, 6)

In this passage, one can already detect in the italicised terms all the earmarks of a Derridean style of critique that would be *methodologically* deployed in subsequent works. More importantly, we might note the transformation mid-passage that occurs when Derrida ascribes the structuralist moment, their 'method' as well as their 'passion' for form, to a more original cause. Thus, the structuralist gesture is not original, but already a reproduction or response to an ontological becoming that has resulted in the shaking of foundations of science and knowledge. In truth, 'the structuralist activity', as Barthes once defined it, is here described as a supreme passivity, an openness to and a vibration with a more original event having to do with 'our historical disloca-tion'. Today, one is left only to demonstrate its 'taking place', to allow its event to unfold throughout all its ramifications, a task of demonstration that requires an infinite patience of a Derridean style of criticism (one that, by the way, demands an equal degree of patience among his listeners or readers). Here, the character of the *krinein*, the crisis demonstrated by means of the critique, bears a negativity that speaks to a secret affiliation between the Derridean style of critique and Heideggerian *Gelassenheit* (as a 'letting be' or 'opening to' the eventuality of the event of difference), but which also opens to the dimension of the 'not yet' or 'to come', a dimension of 'non-style'.

It is significant to note that Derrida never completely renounces the word 'critique', whereas Deleuze never really takes it up. This cannot be stressed enough.

> The *critical* idea, which I believe must never be renounced, has a history and presuppositions whose deconstructive analysis is also necessary. In the style of the Enlightenment, of Kant, or of Marx, but also in the sense of evaluation (esthetic or literary), *critique* supposes judgment, voluntary judgment between two terms; it attaches to the idea of *krinein*, or of *krisis*, a certain negativity. (Derrida 1995d, 357)

In other words, as illustrated in the above passage from the interview 'A "Madness" Must Watch Over Thinking', Derrida understands his project in the tradition of a certain style of 'Enlightenment' (*Aufklarung*); the problem with the earlier philosophical works in this tradition (that of Kant, certainly, but also Hegel, Husserl and Heidegger) is that their understanding of critique was not critical enough. The crash has not been understood in all its ramifications, has not nearly come into its own; we have *not yet* exhausted its potential effects, particularly those effects that will have already taken place, but which are *still to come*. The point is to push the possibilities of the critique further, to make it 'hyperbolique', to become 'hyper-critical', and finally, to constantly refuse the point where the labour of negativity congeals into simple negation, or turns to reveal the resemblance of a properly metaphysical entity. (Is this not Derrida's constant criticism of Kant's heliocentricism, Hegel's Eurocentricism, of Husserl's logo-centrism, of Heidegger's spiritualism?) As Derrida remarks, 'This thinking perhaps transforms the space and, through aporias, allows the (non-positive) affirmation to appear, the one that is presupposed by every critique and every negativity' (1995d, 357).

Stepping back from this extremely shorthand sketch of a major distinction in these two philosophies of difference, one can now glimpse the reason behind Derrida's hesitation over 'the [Deleuzean] idea that philosophy consists in "creating" concepts' (Derrida 2001a, 193). For Derrida, the task of philosophy is largely demonstrative, and while the creation of a new concept can serve to demonstrate a shift or transformation of the old ground (or closure), it cannot become the highest definition of philosophical activity. In fact, this supreme act of creativity, 'this frenzy of experimentation and proliferation of schematization' as Derrida would say, is only the effect of a more primordial dislocation, which becomes the condition of any subsequent 'play' and 'creation'. Although the force of creativity is often characterised as a power (for example, as a power of imagination and affection), in fact it is the power of a fundamental passivity, weakness, impotence, disengagement – *critique* and *emancipation*.

Consequently, deconstruction is not an act of creation, but rather the demonstration (*monstration*, or the bringing to manifestation) of a silent lapsus that *insists* in any order of signification, marking the very opening of this order to what exceeds it. In this way, *différance* can be better likened to the manifestation of the *lapsus calumi* that Freud discovered in *The Psychopathology of Everyday Life*.[4] What happens when a slip of the tongue or pen occurs is an event where the literal meaning of the text is opened to another text, another production or logic of signification. The slip, the error, the lapse – all interrogate this order, which can never close upon itself finally to assign identity, or meaning. In a certain sense, one can say on the basis of the above that Derrida also believes with Deleuze that the nature of the unconscious is productive, although this production is not for that reason located in an 'unconscious' as an agent of production and creativity. Rather, the unconscious is the name for the silent lapse that strikes against the being of language. What is the other name for this silence but writing?

In conclusion, I return to my initial question. Can we imagine a philosopher today who didn't write? In response, I would pose another question: is there anything more pitiful than writing? Anything more deluded, more helpless, more in error. The one who writes is not to be admired. He (or she, but what difference does this make, except the trait of a final anthropomorphism to the concept of writing?) only suffers from a delirium, that is, from a lack of style. Style, then, could represent a partial solution to the 'altogether threatening silence' that strikes against the being of one who writes 'Unquestioning. I, say I. Unbelieving'(Beckett 1997, 331).

Notes

1. Of course, this generalisation would certainly be more accurate for a certain tradition of 'continental philosophy' than for so-called 'analytical philosophy', for which writing still functions to a great degree as a secondary and externalised means of reproducing 'arguments' and 'theses'. In an interview, Derrida once remarked on this tendency (though not specifically addressing any school or institution of philosophy): 'Those who protest against all these questions [of writing in general] mean to protect a certain institutional authority of philosophy, in the form in which it was frozen at a given moment. By protecting themselves against these questions and the transformations that these questions call for and suppose, they are also protecting the institution against philosophy' (Derrida 1995d, 218).
2. Derrida writes: 'The "theological" is a determined moment in the total movement of the trace. The field of the entity, before being determined as a field of presence, is structured according to the diverse possibilities – genetic and structural – of the trace. The presentation of the other as such, that is to say the

dissimulation of its "as such", has always already begun and no structure of the entity escapes it' (1974, 47).

3. Derrida immediately goes on to define the structuralist panoramagram, which he is in the process of defending for its excessive formalism, by citing *Littré* which states that it was a device invented in 1824 'to obtain immediately, on a flat surface, the development of depth vision of the objects on the horizon' (1974, 5).

4. We should recall that Derrida particularly emphasised the function of *lapsus calumi* in the early essay 'Freud and the Scene of Writing', where he recommends as a potential line of inquiry 'a *psychopathology of everyday life* in which the study of writing would not be limited to the interpretation of the *lapsus calumi*, and, moreover, would be more attentive to this latter and to its originality than Freud ever was' (1978, 230).

CHAPTER 8

Active Habits and Passive Events or Bartleby

Branka Arsić

> But subjectivation to what? To common sense which, turning away
> from mad flux and anarchic difference, knows how, everywhere
> and always in the same manner, to recognize what is identical? But
> what if we gave free rein to ill will? What if thought freed itself
> from common sense and decided to function only in its extreme
> singularity? (Michel Foucault)

NEITHER PASSIVITY NOR ACTIVITY BUT PASSIVITY

Why Bartleby?

There is no answer to this question because Bartleby is neither a literary
character nor a 'figure'; neither a metaphor nor a proper name; neither a
question nor an answer but a problem; a problem in the Deleuzean sense of
the word. In this sense of the word the problem escapes what Foucault, in his
interpretation of Deleuze, calls 'the neurosis of dialectics' insofar as such a
neurosis cherishes differences but does so only under the weak light that shines
from the star of the negative, 'as an instance of nonbeing': 'What is the answer
to the question? The problem. How is the problem resolved? By displacing the
question. The problem escapes the logic of the excluded third, because it is a
dispersed multiplicity; it cannot be resolved by the clear distinctions of a
Cartesian idea, because as an idea it is obscure-distinct; it firmly disobeys the
Hegelian negative because it is a multiple affirmation; it is not subjected to the
contradiction of being and nonbeing, since it is being. We must think problematically rather than question and answer dialectically' (Foucault 1998, 359).
Thinking problematically means having to think 'differently' or having to think
differences differently; no longer neurotically, no longer in a way that enables
thought to gather all its contradictions into a unity thanks to the activity of its
labour of self-appropriation, but according to Bartleby's thinking which remains

passive without being arrested into a motionless, stupid equilibrium of self-sameness. This different thought would, therefore, address passivity in a different way: not as a frozen, immobile, sleepy or lazy moment of a thinking that does not want to think and that is in opposition to activity conceived of as a labour of overcoming of contradictions and of the reconciliation of differences, but as a passivity that would be beyond the difference between activity and passivity. The stakes in this game of inventing a new thinking would be at least twofold: to escape the dialectical strategy of subjectivation or, to put it differently, to 'discover' an impersonal pre-individual singularity; and to think differences as a 'multiple affirmation' of being and not as an instance of non-being.

To think passively does not mean only to try to escape 'a simple confrontation between opposing, contrary or contradictory propositions', which is a 'long perversion' that 'begins with the dialectic itself, and attains its extreme form in Hegelianism' (Deleuze 1994, 164). In other words it does not mean simply subverting the thinking that appropriates itself by reabsorbing differences into its identity thus constituting itself into the subject. Rather, it means trying to subvert the traps in which the thinking that wanted to escape this 'long perversion' was caught. The traps that held Leibnizian passive genesis.

For even though Leibniz went a long way along the path of inventing impersonal singularities (or monads) he ended up with passive or static ontological genesis that reintroduced individuation of substances: 'Leibniz went very far in this first stage of the genesis. He thought of the constitution of the individual as the center of an envelopment, as enveloping singularities inside the world and on its own body' (Deleuze 1990, 111). But precisely this invention of the impersonal force of expression, that envelopes singularities within itself thus constituting itself into a 'centre' of expression, foreclosed the possibility of establishing a radically impersonal field of a thought that thinks impersonally, without appropriating itself. The whole problem with Leibniz's solution was not the impersonal force of expression itself but the fact that this force was 'inscribed' into each monad (as transcendence immanent to immanence) in such a way that for their part monads had to express it and through this expression to actualise themselves or to 'individualise' themselves. In other words, since every monad is already the expression of the 'highest' monad that expresses itself as a totality of all expressions or as a force that actualises (actualities and potentialities), then *even completely motionless and 'passive' substance is the activity of expression*. Passivity and activity are therefore only different degrees of activity of expression. Of course, the individual substance can express more or less, it can act or suffer more or less, it can be more or less active or passive, it can have the will to will or the will not to will. But the individual substance cannot not express, for the possibility of an absolute absence of expression would mean that the individual has a power greater than the power of force or the power of the infinite monad. It can will the absolute absence of expression, absolute passivity or indifference but this 'willing' is always already a failure for it is always enveloped within the activity of force. Even substances at the 'bottom' of the Leibnizian pyramid (those impersonal monads without intellect and will) express, perceive and have appetites. Even the passive, impersonal monad expresses predicates thus *'personalizing' itself, enveloping itself within itself*. By expressing its attributes the individual substance remains within itself and its expression is, therefore, its self-expression. Individual substance emits its expressions as an emission of singularities, but these singularities affect it, which is to say that it 'embraces' them again, that it envelops them thus enveloping itself within itself. Expression of the impersonal force thus became the self-expression of a personalised, individuated substance that expresses transcendence immanent to itself.

That is why this form of genesis is called by Deleuze 'static ontological genesis': what is impersonal, what is 'passive' in the sense of not working on its self-appropriation nevertheless appropriates itself, constitutes itself into a 'centre' or envelope of expressions. This is the final outcome of static ontological genesis and it represents Deleuze's fundamental problem with this genesis. For if it is 'true' that according to this version of passive genesis 'individuals are constituted in the vicinity of singularities which they envelop', then the whole problem resides precisely in the fact that those 'envelopes' of singularities are in fact the 'sites' of individuation that transform an impersonal envelope into a subject and singularities-expressions into predicates: 'To the extent that what is expressed does not exist outside of its expressions, that is, outside of the individuals which express it, the world is really the "appurtenance" of the subject and the event has really become the analytic predicate of a subject' (Deleuze 1990, 112). Or, to put it differently, even though the static ontological genesis subverts that 'long perversion' according to which the subject becomes the subject only insofar as it transcends itself remaining immanent *to* itself (thus appropriating itself *for* itself), it nevertheless institutes the subject insofar as the 'impersonal envelope' expresses transcendence that is immanent to it. The static ontological genesis is another version of a long perversion based on the labour of 'to' and 'for', based on a labour of de-appropriation that re-appropriates itself.

TO-ING AND FRO-ING

One could therefore say that this 'long perversion' is based on different versions of the relationship between the prepositions 'to' and 'for': transcendence is immanent to immanence (which would be the Hegelian solution according to which the subject transcends itself thus constituting itself for itself), or immanence is immanent to pure consciousness (the Kantian version that reads as follows: the transcendental subject transcends its receptivity which is going to 'remain' immanent to the act of transcending by which the subject establishes itself); or immanence is the 'primordial transcendence' (the Leibnizian solution that inscribes transcendence into the immanence of individuals as the impersonal force of self-expression). But is it possible to think without 'to' and 'for'? That is to say: is it possible to think the transcendental field without (self)consciousness insofar as it is that which produces the 'to' either by the unification or by the identification of itself or the object?

The possibility of such a transcendental field is Deleuze's main problem, the fundamental effort of his philosophy: 'We seek to determine an impersonal and pre-individual transcendental field, which does not resemble the corresponding empirical fields, and which nevertheless is not confused with an undifferentiated depth. This field cannot be determined as that of consciousness' (Deleuze 1990, 102). Deleuze tries to establish the transcendental field without depth and without consciousness; he therefore attempts to change completely the relationship between thought and being, to think thinking differently, to think being differently. He tries to establish what Leibniz failed to establish: a surface or ground made of multiplicities of little knots or loops of pre-individual singularities. But what does it mean, how is it possible to think the transcendental field without consciousness and how are those loops of pre-individual singularities bound? Such a binding is possible only when and if *passive syntheses* are substituted for the static geneses that always presuppose active syntheses. Only when constituent passivity that is neither passive nor active is substituted for passive genesis.

According to Deleuze the first kind of passive synthesis or the first level of its synthesising is made of two components. There is a ground or a surface, the pure force, made of impersonal motion of cases, elements, agitations or 'homogenous instants' which could be of different natures (organic or inorganic: the motion of particles of water or sand or sperm, the motion of sensations of hunger or thirst; but the succession of homogenous instants could also be composed by the ticking of a clock). And then, there is the contemplation which is neither self-expression nor (self-) reflection. The absence of reflection is the absence of mirroring, of the distance between contemplated and what contemplates. In that sense one can talk neither about the subject nor about the object of contemplation (that would mean talking about reflection). Instead of the subject of contemplation there is simply contemplation (or what Deleuze, using classical Renaissance terminology, calls the contemplative soul, which is neither spirit nor mind but an impersonal sensible plate through which animations pass). As a result of the abolition of the distance between contemplated and what contemplates, contemplation does not know that it contemplates and therefore does not know itself and its object but is or becomes what it contemplates: an impersonal contemplation contemplates. However, passive synthesis is neither the motion of homogenous instants nor contemplation. Passive synthesis emerges as the impersonally established 'link' between those two elements, it emerges when a motion of elements passing through the sensible plate causes a little spasm, a contraction. *Contraction is passive synthesis.* Contraction 'contracts cases, elements, agitations or homogeneous instants . . . however, this is by no means a memory, nor indeed an operation of the understanding: contraction is not a matter of reflection' (Deleuze, 1994, 70). Contraction takes place independently of any consciousness or will: there is a smile, there is a face, there is a contraction and there is a smiling face. Or: there is a tear, there is an eye, a contraction happens and a crying eye appears.

Let us consider the way these contractions operate in Bartleby's case. As the attorney discovered Bartleby lives on ginger: 'He lives, then, on gingernuts, thought I; never eats a dinner, properly speaking; he must be a vegetarian, then; but no, he never eats even vegetables, he eats nothing but gingernuts. My mind then ran on in reveries concerning the probable effects upon the human constitution of living entirely on gingernuts. Gingernuts are so called because they contain ginger as one of their peculiar constituents, and the final flavoring one. Now, what was ginger? A hot, spicy thing. Was Bartleby hot and spicy? Not at all. Ginger, then, had no effect upon Bartleby' (Melville, 1990, 12–13). But the attorney's reasoning is precisely what Deleuze tries to subvert. It is a reasoning that is always of the opinion that somewhere, in some depth, there is a 'true' nature of the individual that is either open to what is in accordance with it (hot and spicy welcomes what is hot and spicy) or that absorbs (negates) what is different from it into its sameness (the hot and spicy ingredient vanishes in the depths of a cold nature). However, the fact is that ginger contains certain doses of zingiberene and bisabolene, ginerols and shogaols, which are the volatile oils that make of it a carminative, antispasmodic, antiemetic, expectorant, analgesic, rubefacient, diaphoretic and emmenagogue. What is more, those main ingredients of ginger are used in the treatment of cases of 'motion sickness', dizziness and vertigo, they free the body from spasms and contractions as well as from hyper-motor activity. Bartleby, who lives on ginger, is therefore an organism that is slowed down, relieved of spasms or pain thanks to the narcotic effects of volatile oils. Without those 'ingredients' Bartleby would be the movement of vertigo, pain or pleasure, spasms and effortless walking – pure motion.

Exposed to volatile oils Bartleby is, therefore, simply an addict, a junkie who, drugged, and thanks to the contractions caused by those oils ('homogenous instants'), changes the configuration of the relationship between immanence and transcendence by means of effects similar to those of opium: 'Opium ensures a weightless immobility, the stupor of a butterfly that differs from catatonic rigidity and far beneath it establishes a ground that no longer stupidly absorbs all differences but allows them to arise and sparkle as so many minute, distanced, smiling and eternal events' (Foucault 1998, 363). Under the effect of drugs (under the effect of agitation of homogenous instants) a different passivity is produced, for which 'ground' or being does not have the heaviness that absorbs differences because it has become the surface of the sliding events or partial thoughts (or contractions) of which that very surface is composed. To put it simply: there is a gingernut, there is a composite that we call Bartleby's body made of the surfaces of his skin, of his organs, etc., the ginger passes through his body and causes a thousand tiny little contractions every-where on his skin, on his eyes, on internal or external surfaces of his internal organs, etc. There is neither the thought that penetrates being nor the being that embraces thought, neither immanence immanent to transcendence, nor transcendence immanent to immanence but only surface-ground, thought-being, the weightless passivity of an eternal, smiling papilionaceous event; only surface of contractions.

Each of these little contractions or passive syntheses constitutes what Deleuze names the impersonal passive self or the larval subject. What we call 'we' or 'I' is a provisional world populated by those contracting larval selves. Needless to say, contraction is not 'perceptive synthesis', it does not lead to the active synthesis of the unification of the sensible but 'refers back to syntheses which are like the sensibility of the senses; they refer back to the primary sensibility that we are. We are made of contracted water, earth, light and air – not merely prior to the recognition or representation of these, but prior to their being sensed' (Deleuze 1994, 73). Our laughter is never the outcome of our decision to laugh; but what is more important, we can feel that we are crying only if we are already crying: laughter is laughing, crying is crying, little smiles are smiling. That is what we are: a bunch of laughter, tears, smiles or anger. A bundle of contractions. A constituent passivity.

The question or problem we are facing here is already clear. For certain cases are repeated (the repetition of tick-tocks of the watch), it is always the same ginger, the same voice of the same attorney; simply: contractions repeat themselves as contractions. But if we are made of repetitions how then is the thesis that constituent passivity is nothing other than the repetition of the same to be avoided? How to avoid the unification of the repetition? The repetition of contractions as contractions produces habit. This is not to say that a will or an understanding decides to repeat the same activities by following certain decisions or rules or customs; on the contrary, it means that little selves are awaiting the repetition of contractions: the body waits for opium, an orgasm, water or ginger. The habit of contraction is impersonal and to the extent that we are contractions we are habits; the passive synthesis of contraction 'constitutes our habit of living' (Deleuze 1994, 74). In that sense, Bartleby is the being of repetition or the being of habit: 'I prefer not to dine today', said Bartleby, turning away. 'It would disagree with me; I am unused to dinners' (Melville, 1990, 32).

I am what I am used to, a series of contractions, a series of habits. Bartleby's repetition of his 'formula' should be, therefore, understood as the repetition of a habit: 'I prefer not to' because I am the habit of repeating that sentence, or because I am the habit of preferring not to; life is a habit of living, the I is a habit of saying I (DG 1994b, 48). But this impersonal habit, precisely because it repeats contraction or spasms, is the repetition of the same (of contractions) from which habit draws difference: 'habit draws something new from repetition – namely, difference' (Deleuze 1994, 73). How does this drawing of difference take place? Repetition, of course, does not change, or does not have to change anything in the repetitive element. It could always be the same wall or table or attorney but the contraction caused by the repetition always has a different intensity, it produces a new quality in the contemplative soul, new little impersonal selves, a change – an event: 'The repetition . . . changes nothing in the object or the state of affairs AB. On the other hand, a change is produced in the mind which contemplates: a difference' (Deleuze 1994, 70).

And all of a sudden everything is different thanks to that difference. Those qualities or events are pre-individual singularities, and a provisional network (disjunctive synthesis) of singularities constitutes an impersonal series of habits, an anonymous subject ('except that there is no longer any subject', says Deleuze), a Ulysses. A bundle of contractions and their different intensities traverses the network of larval selves thus changing it completely, making of it a constantly changing nomadic singularity (Deleuze 1990, 107). Being a nomad does not mean to move a lot; it means to be stationary while being traversed and changed by different degrees of intensities: 'The nomad has a territory; he follows customary paths; he goes from one point to another; he is not ignorant of points (water points, dwelling points, assembly points, etc.) . . . Although the points determine paths, they are strictly subordinated to the paths they determine' (DG 1987, 380). Even though the habits determine intensities they are strictly subordinated to them; even though being determines differences it is strictly subordinated to them. This is the paradox of repetition: 'Does not the paradox of repetition lie in the fact that one can speak of repetition only by virtue of the change or difference that it introduces into the mind which contemplates it?' (Deleuze 1994, 70). The Deleuzean concept of being therefore reads as follows: being would always be said in the same way but it would always say difference. Being is the repetition of difference. Stationary being, the repetition of habits, is the being that by means of that repetition always repeats differences, it is the being of differences, the nomadic being. That is why Bartleby is a nomad.

The path towards the other passive synthesis is now open. What is repeated in the repetition of contraction is precisely the 'now' of contraction. However, because contemplation is impersonal and not mediated by synthesis it is also always hidden and 'since it "does" nothing . . . it is easy to forget it' (Deleuze 1994, 76). The 'now' of contemplation is, therefore, oblivion. It is always already past and it has passed into the past that never happened (even though there was a contraction). It was the past while it was happening, during its own now (this is what constitutes the first paradox of the second passive synthesis: 'the contemporaneity of the past with the present that it *was*') (1994, 81). All 'nows', which are not only always past but which, because they are always past never happened, constitute a gigantic past that never happened. Passive synthesis is the synthesis of an absolute oblivion of 'now', it is virginal and virginity, as is well known, renews itself without complaining; it is innocent, it is the 'inexperienced experience' and its 'principle' is: nothing ever happened because everything is always already synthesised in the passive synthesis of the past that never happened and that repeats itself as what never happened. This repetition is a repetition by which time repeats itself as a past that never took place.

But if being is repetition, if it is the coexisting totality of all contractions that never happened, then, by that very repetition what has already passed will be repeated, it is something that will be: the past that never happened will be repeated as a 'now' that exists only as always already past past. This is the concept of the immemorial past that Deleuze takes over from Blanchot: 'Is it at Midnight that "the dice must be cast"? But Midnight is precisely the hour that does not strike until after the dice are thrown, the hour which has never yet come, which never comes, *the pure, ungraspable future, the hour eternally past*' (Blanchot 1989, 116). The dice are thrown only at midnight but the hour of midnight never strikes at midnight, it strikes only when the dice are thrown, it is the past that is happening only after the 'now' of the throw, it is the past that is the future, the pure unknown that is already past in the moment of its happening, the hour eternally past.

That is why being, which repeats what happened as what will happen, as what is unknown and unpredictable, is the being of chance that in every single dice throw affirms the totality of chance:

By virtue of its splintering and repetition, the present is a throw of the dice. This is not because it forms part of a game in which it insinuates small contingencies or elements of uncertainty. It is at once the chance within the game and the game itself as chance; in the same stroke, both the dice and rules are thrown, so that chance is not broken into pieces and parceled out but is totally affirmed in a single throw . . . If being always declares itself in the same way, it is not because being is one but because the totality of chance is affirmed in the single dice throw of the present. (Foucault 1998, 366)

This other kind of passive synthesis that repeats the past as the difference of chance enables a different 'reading' of the first kind: the repetition of the habit that is difference repeats itself as the repetition of chance. The repetition of habit is the repetition of chance; habit is chance. The stationary being of a nomad is exposed to the chance of dice throws, of their *coups*, of the strikes of intensities that can blow them apart. In that sense and to the surprise of stupidity, nobody lives more 'dangerously', is more exposed to chance, than Bartleby.

This is what the transcendental field now looks like: the manifold of impersonal habits repeated by chance. There is no depth, there is no consciousness, only the pure transcendental field. But where there is no consciousness the transcendental field can no longer be called the transcendental field: 'Were it not for consciousness the transcendental field would be defined as a pure plane of immanence because it eludes all transcendence of the subject and of the object' (Deleuze 2001, 26). The transcendental field becomes the plane of immanence made of the repetition of contraction-habits repeating difference: 'a *habitus*, nothing but a habit in a field of immanence' (DG 1994b, 48). The plane of immanence is the haecceity of the 'nows' of contractions, habits, little spasms, laughters, smiles and cries, in a word of singularities that constitute a life. For what is a life (impersonal, indefinite) if not the haecceity of those singularities. 'We will say of pure immanence that it is A LIFE, and nothing else. It is not immanence to life, but the immanent that is in nothing is itself a life. A life is the immanence of immanence, absolute immanence: it is complete power, complete bliss' (Deleuze 2001, 27).

The plane of immanence is the Leibnizian world taken to its extreme: to its extreme because there are no more individual substances but only pre-individual singularities and their series (series are disjunctive syntheses, singularities are in relation of non-relation, they are not mediated by the synthesis of conjunction). Those series could be contiguous or divergent. Every contiguous series forms a world (the temporary world of a network of habits) and the points of their intersection are the points of their convergence or divergence (a series could dissolve another series, a poison could dissolve a body, etc.). The points of intersections mark the beginnings of new worlds. Leibniz's concepts of compossibility and incompossibility are thereby endowed with new meaning:

> This convergence defines 'compossibility' as the rule of a world of synthesis. Where the series diverge, another world begins, incompossible with the first. The extraordinary notion of compossibility is thus defined as a *continuum* of singularities, whereby continuity has the convergence of series as its ideational criterion. It follows that the notion of incompossibility is not reducible to the notion of contradiction. Rather, in a certain way, contradiction is derived from incompossibility. (Deleuze 1990, 111)

Every series is a compossible world or a plane of immanence and the incompossibility of compossible and incompossible worlds is the plane of immanence as the multiplicity of planes of immanences, the 'open' totality of all contractions and habits, a rhizome. Every plane of immanence, which is the distribution of singularities, is a unique network of singularities, a *'universal singularity'* made of interleafing habits; each plane of immanence is an 'each' (DG 1994b, 50) and the indefinite and infinite totality of those 'eaches' is *a* plane of immanence, a pure impersonal life.

The possibility of a Deleuzean reading of Bartleby emerges. For example: the fact that Bartleby is living on a rhizome could be interpreted now as a compossibility of two series that through contractions and habits produce another rhizome, the rhizome of Bartleby's body, the becoming-rhizome of Bartleby that enables the 'local renovations' of his body. The same goes for his 'formula'. It would be wrong to reduce Bartleby to the agrammaticality of 'I would prefer not to'. For Bartleby is not only the repetition of the agrammaticality of this 'formula' but also the repetition of grammaticality, he is not only the nothingness of the will but also a wilful affirmation of being, an agrammaticality that affirms being: '*I would prefer to be* doing something else' (Melville 1990, 30); and he is not only 'the negativism beyond all negation' (Deleuze 1997, 71), but also the pure affirmation beyond all affirmation even when he negates: '*I prefer to give* no answer'(Melville 1990, 19). In other words, he is simultaneously yes and no and neither yes nor no, he is beyond every yes and no, he is the incompossibility of different worlds each of which repeats difference. He is the plane of immanence, being or a life.

This is the meaning of Deleuze's determination of Bartleby according to which Bartleby is 'being as being and nothing more' (Deleuze 1997, 71). Bartleby is a series of convergent and divergent series of contractions, habits, propositions, spasms, gazes which, taken all together make non-sense, but each of which taken as a singular contraction makes sense (thus confirming Deleuze's thesis that non-sense is the donation of sense). He is the network and intersection of events and differences: a pure life; or he is a divergence of series and therefore the disconnection of 'words and things, words and actions' (1997, 73); he is not subjected to the principle of contradiction but to the principle of in-compossibility; that is why he is completely impersonal or neutral. Bartleby is 'the modern-day Ulysses' (1997, 74), he is No one, which should be understood literally: he is not one, he is the repetition of differences, pure anonymity, the neutrality of that anonymity.

Bartleby's 'I am not particular' therefore does not only mean 'I am easy', I don't have preferences, I can do it both ways, but also 'I am not particular because I am singular', neuter, which is another concept that Deleuze takes from Blanchot. However, he does not call this neutrality and anonymity *Il* but, following Ferlinghetti, 'the fourth person singular' (Deleuze 1990, 103), thus trying to preserve the neutrality of the impersonal singularity, to preserve its smoothness or evenness that is smooth precisely because it is without identity, without particularities: Bartleby is without particularities: 'he is too smooth for anyone to be able to hang any particularity on him. Without past or future, he is instantaneous' (Deleuze 1997, 74). But this instantaneousness is an instant of a 'now' that was never present, which is always the 'yet to come' of an always already past past. He is the smoothness of a surface that is not only impersonal and passive but impassive because passive and neutral: the neuter surface of the neutrality of events repeating themselves.

However, the repetition of differences causes fatigue. Habit gets tired, the passive synthesis gets worn out. What is more, fatigue is the fundamental, real component of habit. 'Fatigue marks the point at which the soul can no longer contract what it contemplates, the moment at which contemplation and contraction come apart', thus 'announcing' that tiredness has reached the point of an 'extreme satiety or fatigue' (Deleuze 1994, 77). Bartleby's 'giving up', therefore, should not be understood simply as his 'giving up' of this or that, but as his getting progressively tired, as his getting tired of copying, of staring at the wall, of ginger, of water, the passive synthesis getting tired even of sitting against the banister until it finally lies down on that bench where Bartleby lay down and where contemplation and contraction came apart. This is not to say that the movement of singularities (of elements, cases, sensations, agitations) is going to be arrested. It means that it will no longer be contemplated on the sensitive plate of Bartleby's contemplative soul or, to put it differently, that Bartleby will step out from that 'each', from the plane of immanence of a singular network of habits of which he was made and will enter into *a* plane of immanence, into a pure life that is dying. For dying is nothing other than a life, pure impersonal life, bare life reduced to itself, a life that lives. A life or dying is a life that is living between life and death, a life playing with death: 'Between his life and his death, there is a moment that is only that of *a* life playing with death. The life of the individual gives way to an impersonal and yet singular life that releases a pure event freed from the accidents of internal and external life' (Deleuze 2001, 28).

However, this dying or this life is not simply a dying that precedes death. This is another key concept that Deleuze takes from Blanchot: 'Dying is, speaking absolutely, the incessant imminence whereby life lasts, desiring. The imminence of what has always already come to pass' (Blanchot 1995, 41). By saying this Blanchot is not referring to the dying that is always enveloped in life and according to which we are constantly dying as we approach death. He is referring to a dying that is 'the dark side of life, the far side with no action, the beyond without being – *life without death'* (ibid.). *A* life, therefore, pure life of the neuter, a plane of immanence. Melville leaves open the possibility of this 'reading'. Bartleby has stepped out into an impersonal life and he lives as the life without brunches or dinners, he has lain down on the bench and now he 'lives without dining' (Melville 1990, 33), says the attorney (or he is asleep with counsellors, sleeping and henceforth living).

This is the end or the beginning of the story of Bartleby, he lives finally listening to the music of pure silence, as life or as dying, like the mortally wounded soldier described by Deleuze who is 'no longer brave or cowardly, no longer victor or vanquished, but rather so much *beyond*, at the place where the Event is present, participating therefore in its terrible impassibility. "Where" is the battle?' (Deleuze 1990, 101). The battle is neither here nor there, neither in an interiority nor in an exteriority, it is outside. The outside is the plane of immanence. For the outside is not exterior *to* something. Only exteriority is exterior to interiority and by its exteriority constitutes and affirms the interiority of interiority. The outside is however outside of any exteriority as well as of any interiority, the outside is the outsideness beyond the difference between exteriority and interiority, beyond the being *for* exteriority of an interiority. The outside does not know of pre-positions that are the condition of possibility of positions, there are no positions 'in' an outside, no substantives, no adjectives, only a circulation of events, an 'absolute outside – an outside more distant than any external world because it is an inside deeper than any internal world: it is immanence . . . the incessant to-ing and fro-ing of the plane, infinite movement' (DG 1994b, 59) of the events or of a life or of dying or of becoming.

Deleuze's first and last word, as it were, the plane of immanence, *the outside*, derives from Blanchot and the latter's determination of the outside as an impersonal dispersal into a space that is always already past time, into 'the vertigo of spacing' therefore, 'where contrariety has nothing to do with opposition or with reconciliation, and where the *other* never comes back to the same. Shall we call it becoming?' (Blanchot 1993, 46). That is what Deleuze calls it: when Bartleby lies down on the bench he lies down 'into' a dying, 'into' a life, he goes away 'into' outsideness, he finally becomes the outsider. He enters the future that already happened as a past that never happened, he enters the Dead Letter Office, the office without address or the impersonal world of addressing without address: he goes away into the Outside.

However, and in accordance with Deleuze's thesis that sense is always double, this going away is a form of arriving, for it produces effects in the world of those who are active agents in the offices of New York City, who are overwhelmed by the good-sense idea that life needs external active stimulants in order to be felt as life and who, like Turkey and Nippers, regularly dine 'out' (this or that restaurant, a glass of wine or beer, let us hear the noise of the city) accompanied by their ambitions, tensions and nervousness. But the agricultural minds for which the city is an irrigated field of food and drinks that stimulate life or 'relax' it when needed will all of a sudden be caught in the logic of the neuter, passive 'I would prefer not to': 'As he opened the folding door to retire, Nippers at his desk caught a glimpse of me, and asked whether I would prefer to have a certain paper copied on blue paper or white. He did not in the least roguishly accent the word prefer. It was plain that it involuntarily rolled from his tongue. I thought to myself, surely I must get rid of a demented man, who already has in some degree turned the tongues, if not the heads, of myself and my clerks' (Melville 1990, 20). 'Involuntarily' because this becoming-Bartleby comes about through passive syntheses, through the impersonal 'little' repetitions of habits of which nobody knows anything, for contemplation escapes reflection. Impersonal neutrality spreads like a contagion over New York City, turning the tongues if not the heads of its inhabitants. Surely a demented idea: the becoming–Bartleby of New Yorkers. But no matter how demented it could be from the viewpoint of common sense, seen from that far place which is the 'vertigo of spacing', the vertigo of intensities, Bartleby could only be the doctor, never the patient, for he announces the coming, the possibility of arrival of a people yet to come, or of a 'human becoming. A schizophrenic vocation: even in his catatonic or anorexic state, Bartleby is not the patient, but the doctor of a sick America, the *Medicine-Man*' (Deleuze 1997, 90).

TYMPANUM OF THE SECRET

If the conversation Derrida agrees to have with Deleuze were ever to take place, Derrida's first question to Deleuze (a threefold question) would refer to Artaud, the body without organs and the plane of immanence: 'I think my first question would have concerned Artaud, Deleuze's interpretation of the "body

without organs", and the word "immanence", which he always held on to'
(Derrida 2001a, 195). If we are to try to reconstruct this question that was never
asked, if we are to try to mark the points at which Deleuze's thinking of the
plane of immanence is convergent for or divergent with Derrida's acategorial
thinking, then it is not because we are guided by an obtuse idea that differences
between philosophies could or should be reconciled but because we have the
impression that at stake here is a very beautiful philosophical 'dispute', one,
namely, that produces the 'modern' kind of philosophical friendship about
which Deleuze spoke, one that, as Derrida explained, means a 'nearly total
affinity concerning the "theses" . . . across very obvious distances, in what I
would call – lacking any better term – the "gesture", the "strategy", the
"manner" of writing, of speaking, of reading perhaps' (2001a, 192).

This nearly total affinity in the theses Derrida determines as the effort of
thought to think 'an irreducible difference in opposition to dialectical opposition, a difference "more profound" than a contradiction' (2001a, 192–3). In
other words, maybe we could explain this affinity as the fundamental effort of
both philosophies to think (through the same, but different, conceptual persona
of Blanchot) the outside, the plane of immanence or what Derrida calls the
'beyond' that is neither Being nor beings. Needless to say, the path towards
that beyond also leads, for Derrida, through the effort of inventing thought
that would be neither that of the transcendental field nor that of the speculative
motion of the notion: neither hierarchy nor envelopment, neither Ctesibius'
nor Lafaye's tympanum but a different thought (philosophical of course), the
thought that would 'authorize one . . . to be concerned with *passivity*' and to
disqualify naivete, incompetence or misconstrual (Derrida 1982, xix–xxi) – or
to disqualify opinions as Deleuze would put it. Here, where the stakes are
raised in the game of inventing 'new' thinking, one hears a 'total affinity in the
"theses"', listening with a Deleuzean ear to the Derridean words, or reading
with Derridean eyes these Deleuzean words written down by Derrida, one sees
oneself hearing the same Derridean-Deleuzean claim: to address passivity in a
different way, to think passivity differently. To be concerned with passivity.

But what does it mean to be concerned with passivity, what kind of passivity
is at stake here (what does the tympanum of that passivity look like)? Like
Deleuze's passive syntheses conceived of as constituent passivity beyond the
difference between passivity and activity (for they constitute a passivity that
synthesises without belonging to anybody or to anything, without belonging to
an object or to a subject), the passivity with which Derrida is concerned is
beyond the difference between passivity and activity: 'neither simply active nor
simply passive', an operation 'that cannot be conceived either as passion or as
the action of a subject on an object, or on the basis of the categories of agent
or patient' (Derrida 1982, 9), a passion that does not belong to any subject

and a thought that is outside of categories. This is the question of a beyond that is both *neither or* and *between them*; it is the beyond that is between, an active passivity of an interval that divides itself between passivity and activity, neither indetermination nor determination (but a determinable that remains undetermined, Deleuze would say). The beyond that is between is a force with different intensities, with different degrees: 'There would be no force in general without the difference between forces; and here the difference in quantity counts more than the content of the quantity, more than absolute size itself' (Derrida 1982, 17).

This is because the difference in quantity constitutes a difference in intensity that is not necessarily a difference in quality insofar as the difference in quality could produce real difference between qualities but preserve the numerical sameness of what they are the qualities of (it could, therefore, preserve categorial thinking), whereas difference in intensity refers to real difference, one that does not refer to numerical sameness. After introducing the force that is nothing other than the difference between forces and therefore the difference between 'betweens', Derrida quotes Deleuze: 'Quantity itself, therefore, is not separable from the difference of quantity. The difference of quantity is the essence of force, the relation of force to force. The dream of two equal forces, even if they are granted an opposition of meaning, is an approximate and crude dream, a statistical dream, plunged into by the living but dispelled by chemistry' (ibid.). It is a question of a force made of irreducible differences *between* forces, made of the irreducible differences between betweens, made of pure relations of forces that are therefore – for what is between them is irreducibly different from them – in a relation of non-relation (Deleuze would call it disjunctive synthesis). But if force is the difference between betweens, if it is an interval that endlessly divides itself, the unsynthesisable difference of forces, then this force cannot be present to any consciousness (understood here as an activity of unification of differences). That is to say it is not present at all insofar as something can be present only to or for consciousness. By the same token, if it is not present for any consciousness then it is a 'field of forces' without consciousness since 'most often, in the very form of meaning, in all its modifications, consciousness offers itself to thought only as self-presence, as the perception of self in presence. And what holds for consciousness holds here for so-called subjective existence in general' (Derrida 1982, 16).

However, Derrida does not call this impersonal field of forces the plane of immanence but *différance*. And this difference in names (neither of which is a name and still less a category) marks a fundamental distinction between Derrida and Deleuze (thus 'proving' that total affinity, precisely because it is affinity, affirms differences). It is a *différance* that does not manifest itself, which is not present and because it is not present *is not* (it is not either as presence or as absence). To say that *différance* is not means that it is neither 'non-being' nor the being of nothingness but that it is beyond the difference between being and non-being (a difference more profound than a contradiction). Derrida makes clear that by means of this 'determination' of difference he is not repeating the gesture of negative theology insofar as its 'God is not' means that 'God is refused the predicate of existence, only in order to acknowledge his superior, inconceivable and ineffable mode of being. Such a development is not in question here' (Derrida 1982, 6).

If such a development is not in question here it is because by saying that *différance is not* Derrida is not refusing a predicate of a category only in order to re-affirm the category, for *différance* is precisely outside categorial thought, it announces the acategorial. On the other hand, the fact that he takes his distance from negative theology does not mean that he does not 'keep' and radically reformulate equivocity (precisely by removing it from the 'context' of negative theology) in a way similar to the way in which Deleuze reformulates Duns Scotus' univocity. For when Deleuze writes that being is always stated in the same way but that it can only state difference he is, in fact negating Duns Scotus' distinction according to which being is univocal on condition that it is a metaphysical entity (that it is a category), but is analogical on condition that it is physical, which means that it can be said in several ways or senses. By subverting this distinction that sought to preserve categorial thinking, saying simply that being is univocal, Deleuze tried to abandon categorial thought and to introduce 'the thought of the non-specific'. Derrida is also trying to think without the category of being, to which negative theology refers and by which it is conditioned, but by keeping equivocity. This intervention will have radical consequences for the 'determination' of *différance*.

What is *différance* then? *Différance* is the same or, more correctly 'The same precisely is *différance* (with an a) as the displaced and equivocal passage of one different thing to another, from one term of an opposition to the other' (Derrida 1982, 17). What does the 'equivocal passage' mean? If the passage is precisely what is beyond, between or outside ('life without death. The perishable itself . . . The eternally perishable . . . the passage' (Blanchot 1995, 41)), then this (acategorial) equivocity could be translated in the following way: not only that the same is always said about whatever it is said, although in a different way, but that it is always said as unsayable, as difference and deferral – as 'between'. That is why the same unfolds itself as *différance*. The same unfolds itself only as the equivocal passage, only as always different beyond. Always different refers to repetition. Therefore: the same is stated as the always different repetition of the beyond, of the unthinkable.

Instead of Deleuze's same, the one, or the being that 'would be expressed in the same fashion for every difference, but could only express differences' (Foucault 1998, 360), we now have: the same is *différance*, the same is the equivocal passage or the same is the irreducibility of differences and deferrals. That is why the same *is not* or why *différance is not*. It is not to the extent that it is equivocal passage, to the extent that, as difference and deferral of the between which is between betweens, it is unrepresentable and therefore not present. However, *différance is* as something that cannot be exposed and manifested, it is as something that, by the motion of relations which are in non-relation, subverts any determination and its domination thus soliciting any determinate: 'It is the domination of beings that *différance* everywhere comes to solicit, in the sense that *solicitare* in old Latin means to shake as a whole, to make tremble in entirety' (Derrida 1982, 21). It is, therefore, what cannot be exposed but what makes everything and everybody, Being and each being tremble. At stake is a secret.

'A secret always makes you tremble' (Derrida 1995e, 53). But what is trembling? Trembling does not belong to the gaze or to knowledge. Trembling is neither a quiver nor shiver, it is not 'a preliminary and visible agitation'; and it does not belong to knowledge because before knowledge it already took place, it happened before we sensed it. When we feel the trembling we are already trembling, the trembling trembles: 'trembling is something that has already taken place' (ibid.). Trembling, therefore, does not belong to any 'now', in its 'now' it has already passed, it is the always already past past that repeats itself as what never happened, that is to say as the unknown: it has already happened as what will happen like the hour of midnight that strikes only after the dice are thrown, that happens only as a future that will repeat the past that never happened thus tying us to an 'irrefutable past': 'We tremble in that strange repetition that ties an irrefutable past . . . to a future that cannot be anticipated; anticipated but unpredictable; *apprehended*, but, and this is why there is a future, apprehended precisely *as* unforeseeable, unpredictable' (Derrida 1995e, 54).

This strange repetition, therefore, ties what never happened, what is not, to a future, to what never happened, to what is not, to what will be as what is not. 'Repetition: nonreligious repetition, neither mournful nor nostalgic, the undesired return. Repetition: the ultimate over and over, general collapse, destruction of the present' (Blanchot 1995, 42). This is a repetition that destroys the ultimate, the now, the livable life of the now, it is the ultimate destruction of the ultimate, the general collapse of the bearable that always, ultimately, repeats the difference or the impossibility of the ultimate, the unpredictable, thus making of every new instant something that is going to be repeated – the unlivable. 'The new instant of that happening remains untouched, still inaccessible, in fact unlivable' (Derrida 1995e, 54).

Trembling is, therefore, the unlivable that lives the same that is not, it is at the disposal of what always repeats what is not, which repeats precisely the 'meanwhile' or the 'between', the non-relation, the non-present, the hidden or the secret. As repetition of what is not, trembling is an inexperienced experience since it experiences what is not, what never was and what will be as what will remain inaccessible. Or, it is the experience of secrecy, the experience of what is never 'there', never present, the experience of the non-arrival of what arrives, it is the possible experience of the impossible, the horrible experience of the impossible experience of what takes place only as something that is going to take place. It is innocence exposed to the repetition of the unlivable, and it is the non-action of that exposure: '"Innocence alone is nonaction (the absence of operation)"' (Blanchot 1995, 40). The activity of trembling is the passion of the unlivable, the passivity of patience exposed to the unlivable (what would the tympanum of trembling look like?), exposed to life without individuated, determined life (which always needs now and is now), it is the life of the unlivable, living without life or dying without death. It is, therefore, impersonal and neuter: trembling is the life of disaster or it is disaster, it is already outside, the dream of not being born.

The dream of not being born evokes the immemorial past, not in the sense that we could not remember or reconstruct the content of that dream, and not simply in the sense that every dream of which we have any knowledge or remembrance is passed. The dream of not being born belongs to a 'different' past, to a past that always *was*, which could be renewed only in a future that would be the unthinkable. This dream, therefore, inverses the structure of the dream that dreams of being present at one's own birth. To be present at one's own birth always represents the subject's desire to go behind his own back, to catch the moment of his origin: it is a dream of absolute self-appropriation. It is, therefore, the dream of the subject trying to catch himself, to escape the inaccessible, to escape the life of the unlivable and to individuate life in such a paranoid way that the individuated life precedes its own emergence. But to dream of not being born is to dream of being without being. It is not, of course, the dream of the negative, the dream that dreams about non-existence or death; it is, on the contrary, a dream of the non-individuated existence, existence in that something (secret?) in which everything exists neither as articulated nor as unarticulated but as neuter, as pure life or as pure dying: it is the dream of the inexperienced experience of secrecy, it is the dream of the trembling that dreams of the secret.

That is Bartleby's dream: 'In Melville's "Bartleby the Scrivener", the narrator, a lawyer, cites Job ("with kings and counselors"). Beyond what is a tempting and obvious comparison, the figure of Bartleby could be compared to Job – not to him who hoped to join the kings and counselors one day after his death, but to him who dreamed of not being born' (Derrida 1995e, 74). This dream, therefore, is a dream without dreamt reality, or it is a dream of an impossible reality, of a reality that was never represented and that never could be represented, not even in a dream. That is why this dream is not a dream at all but rather a wakefulness and vigilance, almost an absolute insomnia (does Bartleby ever sleep, has anyone seen his bed, is he not the one who is always awake, is he not the embodiment of an insomnia taken to its extreme, an absolute vigilance incapable of sleeping?). It is not an insomnia that doesn't want to miss anything, that wants to appropriate everything, but an insomnia that brings the body to complete impassivity, impassively longing for a change of state. It is an insomnia that can happen only in what Fitzgerald (who had a special gift for it) called the real night, 'the darkest hour', tiredness, horror and waste without the lullaby (Fitzgerald 1993, 66), an insomnia that dreams of complete disappropriation, of the *first day of dying after death*. The one who awakes on that first day after death, the one who awakes in a night that is never nocturnal, which is simply the bright night 'where [there] . . . can be no question of sleeping' (Blanchot 1995, 48), is not an 'I' with its proper name, but something, an 'acute singularity', some-body: 'Something wakes: something keeps watch without lying in wait or spying' (ibid.).

Bartleby the insomniac is neither a spy nor a detective, he does not know of inspection, detection, overseeing or overhearing. His is a neutral insomnia, the insomniac gaze that does not watch: 'Who watches? The question is obviated by the neutrality of the watch: no one watches. Watching is not the power to keep watch – in the first person; it is not a power, but the touch of the powerless infinite, exposure to the other of the night, where thought renounces the vigor of vigilance . . . in order to deliver itself to the limitless deferral of insomnia, the wake that does not waken' (Blanchot 1995, 49). It is the wake that *cannot* awaken anybody, a powerless vigilance that does not belong to anybody, exposure to the limitless deferral of the day or of the night. It is a neutrality of the watch that belongs neither to the day nor to the night, that happens between night and day, beyond the difference of day and night, beyond the difference of whatever takes place during the day or during the night.

This insomnia is, therefore, not the vigilance of the will but the vigilance of an exhausted inclination that inclines towards the unpresent and unpresentable, precisely towards the secret, towards what is neither here nor there, what does not belong either to the subject or to the absolute subject or what, quite simply, does not belong: 'This secret would not even be of the order of absolute subjectivity, in the rather unorthodox sense, with respect to a history of metaphysics that Kierkegaard gave to existence and to all that resists the concept or frustrates the system, especially the Hegelian dialectic . . . This secret . . . would be neither sacred nor profane' (Derrida 1995c, 24–5). The dream that Bartleby dreams is the dream of the insomniac, anorexic, exhausted body that longs for being impassive in order to become neither passive nor active, in order finally to make that step beyond where (to quote Derrida who quotes Deleuze) there happens that 'something *in* what occurs, something to come that conforms to what occurs, in accordance with the laws of an obscure, humorous conformity: the Event' (Derrida 2001a, 192; Deleuze 1990, 149).

The event is the secret that is only possible neither here nor there but 'some-where', somewhere where there are no witnesses but where there is also nothing that could be witnessed, it is the event that is the seal, 'that would have the form of the seal, as if, witness without witness, it were committed to keeping a secret, the event sealed with an indecipherable signature, a set of initials, a line before the letter', or 'the coming of a writing after the other: post-scriptum', but in any event 'wounded writing', *a* wound which can again be called – an event: 'a wound . . . do you know another definition of event?' (Derrida 1995c, 60–1). In his insomniac dream Bartleby is dreaming of an event, of the possibility of an impersonal wound. A 'humorous' wound however, because impersonal.

A life, a dying, an event, a wound, a secret. A secret that precisely because it is a secret, because it does not belong to anyone does not speak to anyone; or simply does not speak, and therefore does not answer, does not respond or correspond. In that sense any human language, any language, even private, of any being whatsoever, is not secret, because as soon as it is pronounced or uttered or said it is already a response. The secret is mute and in that sense no language speaks the secret although there are secret languages, languages that would be the outcome of a trembling dream about a secret, an outcome of that insomniac impassivity that invents a language that has the form of a secret. This means: it is the language that responds (that has to respond insofar as it is a language, insofar as language is always already a response) but responds by not responding. Bartleby's language. 'Bartleby's "I would prefer not to" takes on the responsibility of a response without response. It evokes the future without either predicting or promising; it utters nothing fixed, determinable, positive, or negative. The modality of this repeated utterance that says nothing, promises nothing, neither refuses or accepts anything, the tense of this singularly insignificant statement reminds one of a nonlanguage or a secret language' (Derrida 1995e, 74–5).

Why is it a nonlanguage, therefore? It is a nonlanguage because it *evokes the future without predicting it*. In other words it remembers the unknown without knowing it; or it recollects the unforeseeable without foreseeing it; that is why it is a remembrance which is not, a foreseeing which is not, a language which is not. A secret language. For in what 'tense' could something be expressed to express the past that was never present because it was the always already past future? What Bartleby evokes cannot be expressed by any past, present or future tense for it evokes the hour of midnight, it remembers what escapes remembering, it recalls what never happened, it evokes the inexperienced of experience, it evokes the secret and therefore does not evoke. It is a language without 'tenses' and 'cases', without predicates and without subject. A language without language, an innocent language without performatives (without promises) and without constatives (the repeated utterance that says nothing), a language that does not 'operate', a non-active language of passion, the language of a wound.

Or, to put it differently, this secret language is the language by which the secret mimes itself, revealing itself and at the same time remaining non-revealed, 'neither phenomenal nor noumenal', announcing itself without announcing itself, saying itself within a language by remaining silent. 'It remains silent, not to keep a word in reserve or withdrawn, but because it remains foreign to speech [la parole], without our even being able to say in that distinguished syntagm: "the secret is that in speech which is foreign to speech". It is no more in speech than foreign to speech' (Derrida 1995c, 27). It is a voiceless cry, the scream of muteness, the silence of sounds, the blind gaze of a voice, it is what simply exceeds the play of silence and sound, neither a word nor its absence, neither articulation nor inarticulation, but beyond or between their difference, a difference infinitely differentiating differences, differentiation that exceeds difference, pure excess. Bartleby is the being of excess, the being in excess or the absolute secret insofar as for Derrida the absolute secret 'simply exceeds the play of veiling/unveiling, dissimulation/revelation, night/ day, forgetting/anamnesis, earth/heaven, etc.' (Derrida 1995c, 26); the absolute secret is the excess of a play that plays outside of the play of veiling and unveiling, it is the play of the outside that happens within the outside. Translated into Derrida's idiom, Deleuze's sentence that Bartleby is 'the being as being, and nothing more', would therefore read as follows: 'Bartleby is the absolute secret as absolute secret, and nothing more.'

This is to say that Bartleby is nothing other than pure passion: 'In place of an absolute secret. There would be the passion. There is no passion without secret, this very secret, indeed no secret without the passion' (Derrida 1995c, 28). However, this passion is not a passion for something or somebody and therefore it is not passion for oneself, it is not the passion of a subject that passionately desires or loves the other. If the absolute secret is passion then it is so because passion is the secret, because it is the passion that does 'not answer: either for itself or to anyone else, before anyone or anything whatsoever. Absolute nonresponse' (Derrida 1995c, 27). This non-response is not simply a refusal to respond to the other (and therefore the refusal of the other), it is neither the negation nor the affirmation, it is, again, beyond the difference of affirmation and negation, it is a non-related relation of an absolutely solitary existence, of a *Sein* without *Mitsein*: 'Solitude, the other name of the secret to which the simulacrum still bears witness, is neither of consciousness, nor of the subject, nor of Dasein, nor even of Dasein in its authentic being-able? The secret never allows itself to be captured or covered over by the relation to the other, by being-with or by any form of "social bond"' (Derrida 1995c, 30).

Bartleby is precisely the name for such secret passion that is not for somebody or to somebody, Bartleby is the name for a being that is not being-with, but being without (with), outside of 'social bonds'. Bartleby is a passion of the body that is in abstinence from itself, an absolutely virginal body, 'a sort of innocent and transformed Marius brooding among the ruins of Carthage' (Melville 1990, 17), completely solitary, without any bodily origin, without father or mother, without any bodily connections, without a fiancée, a bachelor who cannot hope for the activity of semen, the eternal bachelor who keeps 'bachelor's hall all by himself', the bachelor of all bachelors: pure passion that 'gives rise to no process'. Pure passion that produces nothing and waits for nothing, the passion of the autochthon, as Deleuze would say (Deleuze 1997, 76), the passion of the autonomous as Derrida would say (Derrida 1995c, 13). The 'pure patient passivity, as Blanchot would say', says Deleuze (1997, 71), or as Derrida says interpreting Blanchot, 'passion' that 'implies a certain passivity in the heteronomic relation to the law and to the other, because it is not simply passive and incompatible with freedom and with autonomy, it is a matter of the passivity of passion before or beyond the opposition between passivity and activity' (Derrida 2000a, 26).

It is a matter of passivity that eternally patiently passes away as what never happened and therefore as what will never disappear, the neutral passion of the neuter, of 'a voice without person' (Derrida 1995c, 26). And precisely because it is a voice without person the response of this voice is a non-response for it does not belong to anybody. That is why Derrida can say that Bartleby's response is a response without response. For it is a response of a neutral passion, of absolute secret: 'it is what does not answer. No *responsiveness*. Shall we call this death? Death dealt? Death dealing? I see no reason not to call that life, existence, trace' (Derrida 1995c, 31). This 'no responsiveness' of the passion of the neuter is therefore life, the absolute secret or, in the Deleuzean version, a life, the plane of immanence.

And this life that is pure trembling of a non-related relation is not simply a life of nobody and still less the life of the subject or an individual; it is (a) life of some-body or some-thing 'who' is 'with', 'within' or 'on' the 'out', some-body without somebody, X without X, life that has freed itself from life:

One might just as well say that life has been relieved of life. A life that simply stops is neither weighty nor light. Nor is it a life that simply continues. Life can only be light from the moment that it stays dead-living while being freed, that is to say, released from itself. A life without life, an experience of lightness, an instance of 'without', a logic of the 'X without X', or of the not or of the 'except', of the 'being without being'. (Derrida 2000a, 89)

This life that has the 'form' of a humorous trembling wound, of a dying, a secret or a plane of immanence is the life lived by the neuter, by an *impersonality*; it is a life of a Bartleby.

As the name of impersonality, Bartleby is the name of namelessness, the other way to write X which is the mark of what is not marked and what frustrates the identity, the narcissism of any identity (say, the attorney's). 'The naïve rendering or common illusion [*fantasme courant*] is that you have given your name to X, thus all that returns to X, in a direct or indirect way, in a straight or oblique line, *returns* to you as a profit for your narcissism? Conversely, suppose that X did not want your name or your title; suppose that, for one reason or another, X broke free from it and chose himself another name' (Derrida 1995c, 12).

Bartleby is that X that has broken free, that has entered the relation of non-relation and that therefore returns nothing. By returning nothing (by responding without response) he breaks free from the play of de-appropriation and appropriation: he is not constituted by others, named by them, produced by them (that is why he has no family, no father and no mother), and he is not the object that, objectivised by the other (by the attorney for example), becomes the subject; he has no genealogy, no static ontological genesis can constitute him, he has no history, he is the secret 'foreign to every history, as much in the sense of *Geschichte* or *res gestae* as of knowledge and of historical narrative (*episteme, historia rerum gestarum*) and outside of all periodization, all epochalization' (Derrida 1995c, 27).

He is a child always already without parents (and therefore without name), the eternal orphan that plays within the outside where 'there is no longer time nor place'. That is to say that he is the problem: 'the child is the problem, always, that is the truth' (Derrida 1995c, 13). This could be read the other way around: the truth is the problem, always, it is always the problematic truth and therefore always the truth without truth. That is the truth. Or, that is the problem.

CHAPTER 9

Beyond Hermeneutics:
Deleuze, Derrida and Contemporary Theory

Jeffrey T. Nealon

An essay on Deleuze and Derrida, and their legacy in the contemporary American academic world, had best begin by confronting a series of paradoxes: first, it's ironic that Deleuze and Derrida so scrupulously avoided writing about each other's work – especially given the fact that both, for example, wrote extensively about contemporaries like Foucault and Lacan; and both Derrida and Deleuze have been cagey in discussing the possible relations between their theoretical projects. Derrida's written work very rarely refers to Deleuze, and Derrida didn't devote a text to analysing or commenting on Deleuze until 'I'm Going to Have to Wander All Alone', the brief eulogy written at Deleuze's death in 1995 (Derrida 1995a; 2001a). And for his part Deleuze, while referring to Derrida's work more often in footnotes, never produced any kind of extended treatment of Derrida's work.

So, the first paradox or difficulty is that there isn't much *within* either thinker's corpus that refers overtly to the other's texts. Though of course a massive amount of indirect reference is easy enough to spot: for example, Derrida's early insistence on *force* seems very much influenced by Deleuze's 1962 Nietzsche book,[1] and Derrida's 1974 *Glas* seems very much influenced by the stylistic ambitions of 1972's *Anti-Oedipus*. On the other side of the coin, 1968's *Difference and Repetition* – 'the first book in which I tried to "do philosophy"' (Deleuze 1994, xv), Deleuze writes – is a keenly Derridean book, written in the orbit of the philosophical agenda set by Derrida's three 1967 books (*Speech and Phenomena*, *Writing and Difference* and *Of Grammatology*).

Second series of paradoxes: at the present historical moment, their respective discourses remain much more influential in the English-speaking world than in their native France, where the philosophical climate has shifted considerably in recent years.[2] So, oddly enough, much in the way of their similarity and difference is being worked out in territories far from those native to Derrida and Deleuze – outside the discipline of philosophy, and outside of France.

Third paradox, one that emerges on the 'personal' register, but I feel compelled to mark it nonetheless: the person who writes this essay is wholly a *product* of the phenomenon that the essay hopes to comment upon, the North-Americanisation of French theory. As an undergraduate in the early 80s, I was taught in an English department by the first generation of Yale School graduates and assorted *boundary 2*-ish Heideggerian-Derrideans; graduate school focused on American readings of continental philosophy; and certainly the hybrid of cultural studies and theory that I find myself aligned with now doesn't really come at this material from a primarily 'European' perspective. I guess I'm trying to mark that fact that I have, from the get-go to the present, been configured as an academic subject wholly *within* the thoroughgoing and sometimes hasty American reception and transformation of European thought over the past 25 years – which I suppose makes me either a privileged subject on this topic, or a particularly blind one.

Of course, there is a typically American pathology of reception, immigration or assimilation: whether it be a theory or a subject, once it gets to North America, it's fair game for appropriation by the myriad forces already on the ground. But just as certainly, there's something about Deleuze's or Derrida's thought that makes them appropriable for a set of North American disciplinary imperatives – there's a series of things 'in' their thought (their concepts, their linkages, their respective tonalities, their speeds and slownesses, their sheer difficulty perhaps) that makes way for the cross-disciplinary response that they have provoked in the North American academy. Such a friendship or alliance with transformation is indeed central to both thinkers' projects – to Derrida's insistence on the ethical necessity of responding to and welcoming the future, and to Deleuze's focus on building concepts and thinking the event.[3]

So, with those as opening caveats, I'd like to focus in this essay on the deployment of Derrida and Deleuze (or Derrida vs Deleuze) that's presently being undertaken in the cross-disciplinary set of terrains that comprise North American 'theory' – a hopelessly complicated terrain, a mongrel hybrid of disciplines and methodologies. To try and give some shape to this hopelessly amorphous mass, I would simply note that there seems to be a general sense that we've passed from the 'age of deconstruction' as the dominant 'theory' discourse in the humanities and social sciences, to a more slippery terrain that sometimes simply goes by the name 'cultural studies'. No matter how sceptical one is of such periodising hypotheses, diagnostically speaking it does seem to be the case that 'theory' in the North American humanities has passed from a phase when it was primarily a tool for producing 'new' readings of texts (remember 'reader-response'?), to a phase where theory takes itself to have a greater purchase on world-historical events. In any case, it is from within this shifting, 'anti-hermeneutic' climate that I'd like to situate the interventions of Deleuze and Derrida.

If theories are like financial instruments (which, of course, they are and they aren't), then Deleuze has been the strongest 'buy' recommendation among the recent theoretical growth stocks on the American Exchange. You see him quoted everywhere these days, and oftentimes in unhelpfully incantatory ways: the internet is a 'rhizome'; cybernetics is a 'line of flight'; Fred Flintstone is the 'body without organs', while Barney Rubble is the 'plane of consistency'. To cut through that kind of sloganeering and put it as straightforwardly as possible, it seems to me that the cash value of Deleuze within recent theoretical discourses rests in his swerve around the despotic nature of signification, 'the unimportance [of the question] of "what does it mean"'? (DG 1984, 180). 'Interpretation is our modern way of believing and being pious' (DG 1984, 171), Deleuze and Guattari write, because signification is consistently territorialised on neo-theological questions about meaning and its absence ('the symbolic lack of the dead father, or the Great Signifier' (1984, 171)). Because every signifier fails adequately to represent its signified (attesting to the *absence* of the signified, not its presence), then every interpretation always already lacks – it inevitably fails to do justice to the text at hand. Such an assured interpretative failure (and its symmetrically inverse flipside, the postmodern infinity of interpretation) inexorably defines meanings and subjects in terms of what they *can't do*: be whole. Such an 'interpretosis' comprises, for Deleuze, the 'despotic' legacy of any discourse whose primary pivot is the signifier.

As Deleuze and Guattari hold in *Anti-Oedipus*, 'there are great differences between . . . a linguistics of flows and a linguistics of the signifier' (1984, 241), insofar as a linguistics of the signifier remains territorialised on tautological questions of representation (on the question, 'what does it mean?'), rather than on axiomatic determinations of force or command (the question 'what does it do?'). For Deleuze and Guattari, 'language no longer signifies something that must be believed; it signals what is going to be done' (1984, 250): 'There is no problem of meaning, but only of usage' (1984, 77–8). As they argue in *A Thousand Plateaus*, 'The elementary unit of language – the statement – is the order-word. Rather than common sense, a faculty for the centralization of information, we must define an abominable faculty consisting in emitting, receiving, and transmitting order-words' (DG 1987, 76). Language, in short, is better treated as a form of interpellation than it is as a form of mediation, communication, information or signification. Language commands and configures–'"I"' is an order-word' (DG 1987, 84) – and hence it is never treated productively as the trace of an absent or future meaning. In short, Deleuze and Guattari teach us that language is not primarily meant for interpretation, but for obedience and resistance: 'Writing has nothing to do with signifying. It has to do with surveying, mapping, even realms that are yet to come' (DG 1987, 5). One might say that the performative in Deleuze doesn't succeed by failing to be a constative; but rather it succeeds the old fashioned way – as a deployment of force, as a provocation.

In terms of its North American reception, then, Deleuze and Guattari's work represents a golden opportunity for theoretical work in the humanities finally to free itself from its long apprenticeship to the paradigms of literary criticism, and simultaneously to free itself from the charge that cultural studies or political theory merely produce more or less 'literary' readings of 'cultural' phenomena – the charge that disciplines produce interpretations of Disney's suburb-cum-theme-park Celebration in much the same way that literary critics might produce interpretations of Harry Crews' novel by the same name. This move – or at least this *claim* to move – 'beyond' signification and interpretation is, I think, the lynchpin of the warm reception that Deleuze has received in North America.[4]

And much of this welcoming of Deleuze has come overtly at the expense of Derrida and deconstruction – indeed, at the seeming expense of the entire 'post-structuralist' second wave of French theory's immigration. As Lawrence Grossberg sums up various recent critiques of deconstruction, 'Derridean practice condemns us to an endless reading, an endless problematizing in which everything is reduced to a trace of *différance*' (Grossberg 1997, 75). This is by now a quite familiar critique of deconstruction: in the end, Derrida supposedly reduces everything to language, which is to say signification, 'meaning' and its absence. I'll talk more about this below, but what particularly interests me here is Grossberg's linkage of the anti-deconstructive critique specifically to Deleuze, under the flag of contemporary cultural studies and its commitment to studying *social production* rather than mere *textual interpretation*. Grossberg continues, 'Derrida's argument, that by seeing the signifier already insinuated into the signified we can escape the transcendental problematic of representation, has been challenged by Deleuze and Guattari. . . . Derrida fails to see discourse as production' (Grossberg 1997, 75–6).

And I suppose we should note here that there is some warrant for seeing Deleuze as a sceptical voice when it comes to deconstruction's thematics of signification and interpretation. In response to a question about Heidegger and deconstruction posed to him at the 1972 Cerisy colloquium on Nietzsche, Deleuze responds:

If I understand you, you say that there is some suspicion on my part of the Heideggerian point of view. I'm delighted. With regard to the method of deconstruction of texts, I see well what it is, I admire it greatly, but I don't see it having anything to do with my own. I never present myself as a commentator on texts. A text, for me, is only a little cog in an extra-textual practice. It is not a question of commenting on the text by a method of deconstruction, or by a method of textual practice, or by any other method; it is a question of seeing what use a text is in the extra-textual practice that prolongs the text. (Boudot et al. 1973, 186–7).

Whatever one might want to say about them, these remarks are interestingly at odds with Derrida's sentiments in his eulogy for Deleuze, 'I'm Going to Have to Wander All Alone'. Derrida reveals that he had always felt quite close to Deleuze personally, and especially close to Deleuze's work. As Derrida puts it, in re-reading Deleuze he feels 'the flustering, really flustering, experience of a closeness or of a nearly total affinity concerning the "theses"' (Derrida 2001a, 192) of his work and Deleuze's. Derrida also remarks on the affinity of their philosophical styles, the similarity of 'the "gesture", the "strategy", the "manner" or writing, of speaking, of reading perhaps' (2001a, 192). Derrida maintains that, in the end, 'Deleuze undoubtedly still remains, despite so many dissimilarities, the one among all those of my "generation" to whom I have always considered myself closest' (2001a, 193) within the French intellectual scene.

Of course, Derrida has a long-standing attraction to the elegiac mode, and to the work of mourning. He has written eloquent essays (collected by Michael Naas and Pascale-Anne Brault under the title *The Work of Mourning*) to commemorate the passing of a who's who of contemporary French thought – Althusser, Barthes, Foucault, Kofman, Marin, Levinas, Lyotard – so it's perhaps not surprising that he would offer some response on the passing of Deleuze in 1995. But at the same time there's something kind of shocking here, very unlike most of his other mourning essays. Derrida's eulogy for Deleuze is riven by a kind of weirdly public confessional tone that laments missed encounters, or specious rivalries. In any case, what Derrida recalls as 'the flustering, really flustering, experience of a closeness or of a nearly total affinity concerning the "theses"' and styles of their work seems a very far cry indeed from Deleuze's remarks on deconstruction: 'I admire it greatly, but I don't see it having anything to do with my own [work]' (Boudot et al. 1973, 186–7).

So, taking Derrida at his word, perhaps we need to ask ourselves, what might comprise this 'nearly total affinity' in their work? If, as Derrida writes about Deleuze, 'I have never felt the slightest "objection" arising in me, not even potentially, against any of his works'(Derrida 2001a, 193), we should at least try to thematise and tease out this common ground. Likewise, I'm hoping to examine what their agreements or disagreements might have to say about the transformation, reception and the future of their thought in contemporary North American theory.

In the interest of time, I'll just blurt out my thesis: if Derrida and Deleuze agree on anything, it's the irreducible role of illocutionary *force* in culture and language – oddly enough, the very thing that supposedly separates them within their current reception and deployment in America. Despite the flood of readings that argue the contrary, Derrida's work is quite simply *not territorialised on the signifier or on interpretation*. As he writes in 'Signature Event Context', 'the word *communication* . . . opens a semantic field which precisely is not limited to semantics, semiotics, and even less to linguistics' (Derrida 1982, 309). He adds, 'meaning, the content of the semantic message, is . . . trans-mitted, *communicated*, by different *means*, by technically more powerful medi-ations' (1982, 311). Meaning or signification, in other words, is always already inscribed within and carried along by a field of *forces* – which Derrida calls, among other things, 'writing'.

Of course these foldings of force apply to any linguistic act, insofar as such an act 'is not exhausted in the present of its inscription', but is rather the bearer of 'a force of breaking with its context', a 'force of breaking [which] is not an accidental predicate, but the very structure of the written' (Derrida 1982, 317). As Derrida makes clear, this force – this rending, gapping or spacing – 'is not the simple negativity of a lack, but the *emergence* of the mark' (ibid.); likewise, this productive emergence has no exclusive (or even primary) relation with the signifier or signification. Force is not a 'signifying' practice, though it makes such practices (im)possible.

Derridean deconstruction, as I've tried to argue numerous times in other venues, *is not a demonstration of lack, negativity or neutralization*.[5] Force in Derrida's linguistics is not primarily the force of *lack* or the demonstration of an inevitable absence, but is rather the positive or affirmative force of context breaking, the necessity of responding to emergence or the event. Derrida, then, is not at all concerned with demonstrating the irreducibility of signification or the open-endedness of interpretations.[6] As Derrida insists, 'Deconstruction does not consist in passing from one concept to another, but in overturning and displacing a conceptual order, as well as the nonconceptual order with which the conceptual order is articulated' (1982, 329): 'it is only on this condition that deconstruction will provide itself the means with which to *intervene* in the field of oppositions that it criticizes, which is also a field of non-discursive forces' (ibid.).

Of course, the work that Derrida's discourse has done in North America – from its reinscription in Yale School literary criticism all the way through the work it does in discourses like Judith Butler's queer theory – is almost completely territorialised on the work of signification, and more specifically on the hermeneutic work of demonstrating meaning's *failure*. But what I learned about language from Derrida can perhaps be best summed up by Deleuze: the meaning effects of language (interpretation, signification, metaphor, etc.) are beholden to a *field of forces* that is, in Deleuze and Guattari's words, 'asyntactic, agrammatical: . . . language is no longer defined by what it says, even less by what makes it a signifying thing, but by what causes it to move, to flow, and to explode' (DG 1984, 133).

By way of a stilted conclusion, then, just a few words on why this genealogy or seeming homology between Derrida and Deleuze might be important for contemporary questions concerning the study of culture – other than to say that Derrida's been misread on these points or too hastily dismissed or whatever. Rather than police that road, I'd like to highlight the fact that recent theoretical work in the humanities very much likes to understand itself in terms of this metaphoristics of force – all use, no interpretation; all power, no signification. But on the whole, this space of forceful provocation where Derrida and Deleuze meet remains more of an invitation or provocation than it does a working hypothesis.

Much cultural studies in North America remains stuck squabbling over what 'authentic' resistance to a kind of omnipresent Capitalism might look like. After Elvis Costello, one might name this the 'I used to be disgusted, now I try to be amused' quandary: Are contemporary consumption practices to be condemned as the inauthentic hijacking of consumer desire by capitalist marketing masters? Or are such practices to be celebrated as forms of subversive agency performed by market-savvy consumers? Are we, following a certain Frankfurt School trajectory of cultural studies, to be 'disgusted' by capitalism – and bravely denounce it? Or are we, following a strain of cultural studies inflected by Michel de Certeau's analysis of everyday subversion, to be 'amused' by the multi-faceted subjectivities that are born in and around contemporary consumption practices – are we to learn to appreciate late, later, or just-in-time capitalism?

If one really wanted to take seriously the Derridean or Deleuzean insistence on force, however, one would have to admit that this is a go-nowhere debate, precisely because of the legacy of *force*: capitalism, like language, works *axiomatically*; one doesn't get to 'decide' to denounce it, judge it or appreciate it. But you most certainly do have to *respond* to it, insofar as capitalism is all about deployments of force – from its significations right through its police patrols. Capital, for example, works through axioms like, 'consume!'; and you really don't get to ignore or refuse that axiomatic pronouncement – it's not up to 'you', whomever 'you' might be. One could certainly learn from Deleuze or

Derrida that the point or upshot of an analysis of force fields is never judgement, condemnation, authenticity or moralism.

However, much theoretical work in the age of cultural studies, despite its protestations, remains territorialised on such ideology critique, and its tools of interpretation and representation. In other words, lots of theoretical work in the humanities is still devoted to producing a hermeneutic 'understanding' of culture – unmasking its operative ideologies – and through such an understanding, crafting a strategy of refusal and resistance. If we really understood or properly represented the work of Disney, or Quentin Tarrantino, or the distribution of recorded music, or racial profiling – then we could properly resist them, prove to others that these things are regressive, so they too could choose to refuse or resist them.

By far and away, 'resistance' remains the humanist concept most consistently affirmed in so-called post- or anti-humanist thought: after all, what is 'humanism' (what is 'freedom') if it's not about resistance to domination? Of course, in the wake of Foucault, post-structuralist theory will trouble this humanist legacy by insisting that there is not a (human) power of resistance that is somehow separate from the power of domination. However, the humanist pathos and desirability surrounding 'resistance' is taken up into contemporary theory almost wholesale – that is, with surprisingly little commentary or hesitation concerning its costs. Political and cultural theorists of all types have, for the past decades, been involved in a thoroughgoing interrogation and deconstruction of humanist notions like the subject, consciousness and the (im)possibility of ethical agency; but nary a peep concerning the status of 'resistance' as a holdover category of humanism. It would seem, then, that in recent theoretical discourse, 'resistance' costs us less than these other humanist notions – or, conversely, perhaps this neglect suggests that it would cost too much to 'give up' the thematics of resistance.

But I want to end this essay by polemically opening the question: is the thematic of 'resistance' an essentially benign or necessary legacy of humanism, one that would be too expensive for any politically engaged theorising to jettison? Resistance to *what*, one might ask? If we learn from Derrida and Deleuze (through Foucault) that force or power produces, we can hardly be 'against' power – especially a globalised capitalism that, by definition, has no 'outside'.

I take as my primary cue in this line of questioning Deleuze's 'Desire and Pleasure' notes on Foucault, where he states polemically: 'I myself don't wonder about the status phenomena of resistance may have, since lines of flight are the first determinations. Since desire assembles the social field, power arrangements are both products of these assemblages and that which stamps them out or seals them up' (Deleuze 2000a, 254). This questioning of resistance is, of course, not merely to say that one assents or agrees to the status quo, but it does name a certain kind of question about how one best *transforms* this status quo. If, as Deleuze holds, there is nothing but desire and the social, if all being is becoming, then there is nothing but the endlessly productive quality of desire. But if power or desire don't work by repression of a preexisting humanist subject, but rather by incessant production of serial subjectivities, then what does it mean to 'resist' power or desire? And doesn't the vocabulary of resistance, however much we nuance it, entice us unconsciously to think that resistance is a relatively stable signifying quality of authentic subjects, rather than a hazardous and uncertain attribute of an a-signifying, social relation of force?

Finally, given the radically non-humanist form of power that we live within, I wonder whether it costs left theorising too much to territorialise itself on the category of resistance, precisely because resistance implies or necessitates a kind of totalised, normative, repressive enemy and/or a kind of authenticity of subversive response? Concretely, I think we can see this 'cost' of resistance being played out in contemporary cultural studies, much of which remains mired in a kind of dead-end bickering over what would constitute 'authentic' resistance to an unhelpfully totalised notion of capitalism, the repressive enemy. Recent theoretical work, in other words, remains hamstrung by the hermeneutic question, 'what does it mean?' Capitalism is changing rapidly all around us, but I often wonder whether our modes of resistance and response remain ineffective because they're stuck in the era of the Cold War.

In the end, perhaps this is merely to suggest that the diagnostic project of 'theory' in the humanities is ongoing, as are the collective processes of constructing ways to hack the contemporary world. At any rate, it seems to me that the discourses of Derrida and Deleuze are two key sites for this continuing working *through*. However, I think we learn from Deleuze and Derrida that, as a conceptual apparatus, 'resistance' to contemporary culture may not be exactly the most productive tack for cultural studies to take, insofar as such 'resistance' can often name a stopping point rather than a rallying cry – a moral condemnation or judgement rather than an ethical provocation or map. Such judgements seem eerily to shadow the unquestioned privilege of the reader/subject in hermeneutics. As Deleuze argues concerning the differing affects and capacities distributed by the social, 'It's not a matter of asking whether the old or new system is harsher or more bearable, because there's a conflict between the ways they free and enslave us. . . . It's not a question of worrying or hoping for the best, but of finding new weapons' (1995b, 178).

In other words, it seems that if one is to take social force seriously, one has to start with the provocation to respond, and one is forced to end with something other than a condemnation or judgement – the tautological conclusion that x or y is 'bad' or 'false'. Let's give credit where credit is due: it's really not a matter of whether anyone *believes* the bullshit served up by her boss or his governor, or whether this bullshit is true or not. Those questions of hermeneutic depth aside, we are nevertheless left with the material fact this bullshit certainly does produce effects: we certainly do have to *respond* – outside the economies of representation, assured failure, moralising judgement, and signification. In short (and in conclusion), it seems that Derrida and Deleuze both present us with a similar provocation: cultural studies, like political and sexual difference, must consistently be reinscribed outside the realm of hermeneutic ideology critique – outside the still-dominant theoretical horizons of interpretation, judgement, normativity and representation.

Notes

1. In 'Différance', for example, Deleuze's *Nietzsche and Philosophy* is cited to make the Nietzschean point that 'force itself is never present; it is only a play of differences and quantities' (Derrida 1982, 17).
2. See Ferry and Renault 1990, and their dismissal of the 'May 68' thinkers, Derrida and Deleuze chief among them.
3. And while we're tarrying with the personal, just a quick parenthesis here to clarify a bit my own position in the debate surrounding the transformations of French philosophy in North America: in my book *Double Reading* (Nealon 1993), dealing with the reception of Derrida and Foucault in North America, I was trying not so much to argue that the Yale School of literary critics had got Derrida wrong or that New Historicism had somehow misread Foucault, but to ask what institutional imperatives are at work in and furthered by such appropriations? I am, then, not interested in trying to defend the purity of Derrida's texts from the transformations they inevitably undergo, but rather trying to ask, 'What does it *cost* to read Derrida in this way, to reduce his concerns to the concerns of literary criticism, or to conflate his work with de Man's? What institutional *effects* does such a reading practice produce?' Then as now, I take my project to be not a pooh-poohing of transformation or nomadic reinscription, but a genealogical attempt to map the consequences – the force – of specific deployments of theory within a particular disciplinary frame.
4. Deleuze himself takes this non-hermeneutic imperative from much the same place that cultural-studies thinkers do: the Marxian insistence on intervening in the world, rather than merely interpreting it. Within contemporary cultural studies, this non-hermeneutic emphasis has been heard and taken up most effectively, and takes myriad forms – emphasising economics, policy studies, pedagogy, the work of institutions, studies of the culture industry and its distribution mechanisms, work on globalisation, migration, immigration, science and disability studies, critical legal theory, etc. Few of these discourses are directly 'Deleuzean' in orientation, but most of them share a fundamental

scepticism toward textual hermeneutics. These aggressively non-hermeneutic discourses, it seems to me, comprise the deterritorialising future of theory in the humanities, and I guess the point I'm trying to make here is simple: both Derrida and Deleuze have a tremendous amount to add to this itinerary.

5. See especially Chapter 2 of Nealon 1993 and Chapter 5 of Nealon 1998.

6. This reading of Derrida rests on the reception and translation of at least two early Derridean catchphrases – 'there is nothing outside the text' and his work on the supposed 'freeplay' of signification. The second is easy enough to dispose of, as 'freeplay' was the translation of '*jeu*' (with no '*liberté*' anywhere nearby in the text) rendered by the early and influential publication of 'Structure, Sign, and Play' in *The Structuralist Controversy* collection (Macksey and Donato 1970). Rendering '*jeu*' as 'freeplay' is more than just a semantic infelicity, as one of the essay's central points is that 'play' – especially the play of signification – is anything but 'free' or unconstrained. On the 'text' and its outsides, see Derrida's re-translation of *il n'y a pas de hors-texte*: 'there is nothing outside context. In this form, which says exactly the same thing, the formula would doubtless have been less shocking' (Derrida 1988b, 136).

CHAPTER 10

Language and Persecution

Alphonso Lingis

There is no purely physical inflection of a voice. Sounds are carriers
of memory and of sensory experience, and sounds are immediate.
My sounds are in you now, my body has become yours. We are
breathing, all enveloped in our human breath. Inhaling and exhal-
ing the air, the subtlety of pheromones, exchanging the denseness
of hormonal rhythms, we are one breath, one body. We cross the
fragmented, the manifest, and the explicit with the inseparable, the
transitory, the implicit. Sounds, like breaths and melodies, are
contingencies of present, past, and future, which my sounds
actively transform. (Joanna Frueh)

'We must, according to this sort of contortion and contention which the
discourse is obliged to undergo, exhaust the resources of the concept of
experience.' 'It must be heard in the openness of an unheard-of question that
opens neither upon knowledge nor upon some nonknowledge which is a
knowledge to come.' 'We don't have time or space here, but we should have
to examine this further.' 'This could be one of our questions, the most obscure
one no doubt.' 'Since this Note and the Note on a note will be part of our
premises . . .' 'His discourse is at times close to Heidegger's very complicated
and equivocal discussion of the Heraclitean *polemos*, closer to it than ever, and,
it seems to me, . . . in spite of one essential difference that can't be elaborated
here.' 'And so on ad infinitum.' 'There are an infinity of questions to be raised
here.' 'Etc.' Such expressions regularly punctuate Jacques Derrida's writing.
There is a sort of ceaseless vigilance against that transcendental illusion
intrinsic not only to the metaphysical language that structures Western science
and discourse, but all language – the illusion that presence has been touched
here. Instead, every term with which you invoke some entity or event refers to
further terms. You are not going to come upon, by reading a text, the
landscapes the author saw, nor even what he really meant. There are an

uncountable number of interpretations possible of his text. Derrida offers this to us as a liberation, every text an open-ended map to immense riches.

But what is more striking is the imperative, the urgency. 'We should . . .' 'We must . . .' Derrida badgers, harasses, the text. We don't feel a twinge of pity for the text, though we may feel harassed ourselves, accused of being cavalier, peremptory, high-handed or heavy-handed.

From the start Derrida dissolved the distinction between speech and writing: there is not a presence in the living voice that writing would signal in its absence. So we have the uneasy feeling that Derrida could attach his deconstruction and infinite interpretations on whatever we say. To open our mouths and say something is to find ourselves caught up in an infinite spiderweb connecting each word with networks of words, and those to further networks.

It is not only our mouth that feels beset upon, forced to utter unending explications of every word, but our bodies. For words energise, prod, badger, poke at, harass, excite, agitate, soothe, hypnotise and stupefy our bodies.

WHEN EXPRESSION INTERVENES

Expressions are gestures, dances, rituals, vocalisations and speech. They can accompany anything our bodies do, anything that happens in our environment. But expressions do not simply correspond to or conform to what our bodies do and to the things and events we perceive. Expressions never simply represent, depict, describe or report on the things we couple up with. They do not simply refer to things, designate and fix referents. Expressions have their own forms, which develop independently of the way things with which we are actively and productively coupled break up, spread out and take form. Italian kinesics before similar situations differs from Brazilian or Mongolian. The grammar of statements does not reproduce the shapes and layout of the things we talk about.

More than simply depicting entities, situations and actions, expressions *intervene*, as Gilles Deleuze and Félix Guattari put it, in the course and rhythm of our movements and interactions with our environment. Expressions antici-pate couplings our bodies will make, go back to couplings our bodies have already made and no longer make, slow down the couplings our bodies are making with things and events or accelerate them, detach them or unite them, map them out or segment them. Our bodies, for their part, with the couplings they make with things, expose themselves in expressions, extend themselves in turn.

DIRECT EXPRESSIONS

Shaking your head forward rapidly can speed up what you (or someone else) are doing. It can launch you, or another, into the next step of an operation: the novice hang-glider now balanced will now run and take off from the cliff. It can affirm what action a leader is launching, confirming your allegiance to him and to the action: 'Right on!' Deleuze and Guattari call this 'presignifying semiotics'; let us call them 'direct expressions'. The expression diagrams the movement of the body, without first designating a meaning.

In Peter Weir's film *The Last Wave*, the lawyer who is defending some urban aborigines who have killed another aborigine for, they say, having violated tribal law, goes to search out an old man who seems to have a hold on them. The old man is seated on the floor of an empty room. 'Who are you?' the lawyer demands. The old man answers: 'Who are you?' Repeating the question in diminuendo: who are you? . . . who are you? . . . who are you? . . . his voice finally shifting into humming. The humming begins to evoke the song lines with which aboriginal Australia is mapped out since the dreamtime. Instead of responding with words the lawyer could interpret and understand, the old man summons the dreamtime map of aboriginal Australia about this white lawyer, leaving him with a question for which there is no answer in meaningful English.

There are things we cannot say with words, but we express with a tender or incredulous or awestruck gaze – or a hand that reaches out to stroke the arm of the dying person. There are things we cannot express with gestures, but we do with our body rhythms or movements or dance. There are things we cannot express with words or gestures, but we do with rituals.

An unknown person left a gym bag in a pub in Soho; after he left, a home-made nail bomb in it exploded, killing three people, and tearing wounds through flesh and eyes of a hundred others. The next day at the police barricade people placed flowers. All day and all evening people were coming to visit the site, contemplating the growing pile of bouquets. They are not asking: what did this killing mean? What do these flowers mean? Or, what do I mean in coming here? Yet the ritual does intervene in human intercourse; in London it launches a movement of solidarity with gay people and other marginals. It links arms momentarily against intolerance and bigotry. The ritual expression breaks off; it does not propel an unending sequence of expressions, connect up with a total, complete, meaning-system. They walk away silent. There is nothing to say.

Direct expressions form segments, bound to a specific territory. Ron Zera was pursuing graduate work in philosophy at the university; his wife Carol took a job teaching first graders at a local school. At Easter her pupils gave her a baby rabbit. An expressive gesture, surely, but it did not simply signify the notion of affection; the baby rabbit nestling in her hand extended the warmth and pleasure the pupils enjoyed in their contact with Carol. She had to take the baby rabbit home, and extend to him the care and attentive concern she has devoted to her first graders. But her house is a different kind of territory from the classroom. The lease specifies no pets. The landlord, an elderly Chinese man, did courteously phone first whenever he had the occasion to check on something in the house, so Carol could put the rabbit in a dark closet to keep quiet. But the inevitable day came when the landlord arrived unannounced. Ron and Carol tried to keep him on the porch, but he did have to check on some utility meter inside. Just as he looked to step inside the rabbit came hopping across the front room door. 'Oh!' he said, 'you have a rabbit!' Then instinctively looking upward and searching anxiously the sky, he said: 'You have to watch out for the eagles!' Suddenly the scene had shifted, the old man was no longer a landlord on the porch of a house he owned in an American town; he was a boy caring for a rabbit in the vast open plains of central China. The concept 'affection' can be a universal, remaining the same whenever, wherever it is invoked with a verbal sign; but the direct expression is bound to its territory, becoming different expressions in the schoolroom, the teacher's home, the landlord's homeland.

But the use of direct expressions of any given form does come to an end. We do not generalise the ritual of piling flowers at the site of street aggressions. Her pupils will not give Carol another rabbit next Easter. When someone dies, Australian aborigines cease pronouncing his name for a given number of years, and if he had done paintings, his name will be effaced from them. Museum curators of collections of aboriginal art will have to remove his paintings from public display. It is as though there is an obscure awareness of a danger in the abstraction that makes expressions repeatable, a danger in linking them in ever wider systems of contrast, in ever wider contexts, where interpretation begins and will be required.

So many facial expressions and body kinesics are direct expressions. To respond to someone's accusations of your actions as unjustified with an abrupt show of the upturned third finger does not *mean* 'fuck you'. It is equivalent to saying 'fuck you', but it does not mean 'I want to fuck you' or 'I hope somebody fucks you', which after all the accuser might find pleasurable. The gesture or the words instead directly break off the demand for an explanation and a justification. A smile, a shout, laughter, a handshake, an embrace are direct expressions – as are words of greeting: 'Hello!', 'Hi!', 'Hey man!', words whose meanings have completely vanished. Fights too are expressive.

An argument gets *settled* with a fight. Especially an argument about your courage, your honour, your loyalty, or the sincerity and strength of your conviction.

Much street talk is fragmentary because the expressions are direct rather than conceptual statements. Street talk does not theorise: All the capitalists are exploiters of workers, but: The owner of that gas station has shit for brains. When people drift from New York to Miami or Los Angeles, what they say about New Yorkers no longer applies to Angelinos. Words and turns of phrase are short-lived and die without leaving a trace.

MEANINGFUL LANGUAGE

Language can be soothing, rumbling, annoying, explosive. It can also be meaningful. In meaningful words and phrases we distinguish the signifiers from the signified meanings. For a sound to count as a signifier, abstraction is made of its material qualities – the tone and pitch of voice, the pacing, the resonance, the timbre with which it is uttered, as from vertical or Palmer-slanted when it is written and from the Courier 10 or 12 typeface when it is recorded on a computer screen. It is as a repeatable form that a sound or visual pattern can function as a word. It can then be taken to signify a meaning which is taken to be the same whenever, wherever it is invoked by that signifier.

Thus there really is no first occurrence of a word in a language: from the first it was formed as repeatable. And a word does not really die out; its use becomes obsolete, it can always be understood by scholars and can be revived by writers who put it back into use.

Each statement survives its object: nothing changes in the meaning or the truth of the statement 'Elsbeth went to Reno and got a face-lift' after Elsbeth returns to the Hamptons, or after she dies. Every name survives its owner: Elsbeth's husband Julius Benway is dead, but his name is still there, intact, functioning as it did when he was alive.

We cannot teach the meaning of the signifier 'divan' all by itself – say to an infant or to an immigrant who knows not a word of English; to really know what 'divan' designates you have to know the system of contrasts between 'sofa', 'couch' and 'davenport'. Simple pointing, in the furniture store, to an example of a 'divan' will overcome ambiguity only if you point out the significant details contrasting 'divans' from 'sofas', 'couches' and 'davenports'. Meaningful language, in infants as at some stage of the evolution of the human species, was not constructed piecemeal. All at once the child got the idea, began to have the signifier-signified system.

There was then a time when nothing was meaningful. There were to be sure signals, directly coupled on to what they signalled. The infant reached out to make contact with what was being offered him or what he saw at a distance, reached out to kiss his mother or suckle her breast; he covered his face, pushed his hand back from something being offered him. Now he uses sounds to refer to things, first to joyously acknowledge, or to demand, their being given or to joyously acknowledge, or to demand, their being gone, then to acknowledge or demand individuals and details. The sounds designate meanings detached from things, in the absence of things. This at first global, and then increasingly articulated, system of signs and their meanings extends a sort of layer between the subject and the whole of his environment.

Jacques Lacan identified the moment when the child got the idea in the 'Fort-Da' game Sigmund Freud recounted. Baby-sitting for his grandson, Freud picked up a toy the child had thrown out of his crib. The child greeted the return of the toy with a cry of pleasure, but then threw it out again. Repeat. Freud noticed the child has two different cries for the toy being there, and then it being gone. Freud recognised that the child's cries meant '*Fort!*' '*Da!*' – 'Gone!' 'Here!': 'Absent!' 'Present!'. 'Absent!' and 'Present!' were two contrasting terms attached to the same toy; but they were already universal categories, as Freud verified when the child greeted the return of his mother with the 'Da!' cry. It was already the basic system of language: sounds that designate referents by way of meaning, and that do so by contrast with one another. The whole subsequent development of language will be inserted into this system, making ever more detailed contrasts.

Every language can say everything. All languages are equal in power. Every language has terms capable of designating 'present', 'absent', and has floating signifiers ('*chose*', 'thingamajig') capable of designating what it does not yet have specific words for ('*cette chose-là*', 'that thingamajig over there'). Yoruba, Lani and Ifugao have means within the system to generate words to discriminate the parts of computers and satellites.

Knowledge consists, to be sure, of discovering more entities, events, situations, details in the environment, but also of retaining them and communicating them in the meaningful system of a language. It then consists in articulating the system, in discovering new resources in the system, making coherent distinctions and relationships between signs, and fitting these distinctions more and more suitably with the discriminations in the environment that are observed.

'The universe took on meaning long before we began to know what it meant; that is no doubt obvious', Claude Lévi-Strauss wrote. 'But from the previous analysis, it also follows that it meant, from the beginning, the totality of what humanity can expect to know' (Lévi-Strauss 1987, 61). Deleuze and

Guattari write: 'The world begins to signify before anyone knows *what* it signifies; the signified is given without being known' (DG 1987, 112).

The realm of meaning haunts us; it is endless, circular, none of its elements ever die. Whenever we speak, we get caught up in it. Deleuze and Guattari speak of entering the labyrinth of signs, and finding that the circles intersect with still more circles.

August Strindberg's *Inferno* invokes an individual haunted by the oppressive spectre of meaning which is everywhere, equivocal and indecipherable. The existence of this floating, unfixable, realm of meaning obsesses him, persecutes him. In Witold Gombrowitz's *Furdydurke,* the narrator comes home to find a cat hung by the neck in his garden. Somebody did this. What does it mean? Then he notices a paper on the floor he is pretty sure he did not leave there. Before long he sees or thinks he sees signs everywhere. Is he being spied on? Followed? With what intent?

In another land, you have a conversation with someone and then a dinner together and find yourself turned on by her or him. In the anonymity of the night, in this place where no one knows you, you end up abandoning yourself to the longings and pleasures of the flesh, losing yourself in the swoon and release of orgasm. It happens again the next night, and the night after that. Then you begin to ask what it means. Is she really drawn to me? Is she playing some sort of game with me? Is she faking orgasm? Does she expect presents, money, does she want to tie me to her so that I will bring her to America? Does she want to trap me by getting pregnant? As soon as the question 'what does this mean?' arises, everything she does becomes a sign to be interpreted – every phrase, every sigh or gasp in lovemaking, whether she comes early or comes late, whether she dresses up carefully or dresses down. Then you find yourself shifting into another cycle of questions: Is she aiming for some kind of triumph in seducing a white man, one of the colonial race? Is it because the GIs were here during the Vietnam war that the local morality broke down and women started going to bed with foreign strangers? Then: what do her parents think of her and me, what does her society think? Are they simply Buddhists free from Judeo-Christian hangups about sex, is it the breakdown of their society under the pressure of Western world-market consumerism that makes her willing to go to bed with me – something that women back home do not. Another circle. And what about me? Is this a serious affair, which I will have to explain to my wife when I get back? Or is it a secret affair, which means something only to me? Another circle. What does it mean in my life that I am having an affair, far from my wife? How does this affect my whole conception of myself, of my status as a married man? Another circle. What will it mean when I go back to post as a university professor – will I miss this detour into exoticism? What will it mean when I teach ethics to young people, I who am harbouring this secret double life? Another circle. There is no end. This is how you construct a paranoia for yourself.

Then there is a second level, where meaning gets doubled up over itself. The way you respond to the question, 'What does it mean?' is to say: the fact that she is late means that I am not the centre of her life; she has a double life. The fact that I am having an affair means that I am being unfaithful to my wife and children. The interpretation opens up the possibility, and necessity, of another level of interpretation, in which you ask what a double life means, what infidelity means. You enter a realm in which there are no facts, only interpretations of interpretations. Infidelity means violating my marriage vows to my wife. But what does marriage really mean? And what does having a wife, what does 'my wife' mean? My wife – my house, my car: am I unfaithful to my house if I stay half the time in hotels? Unfaithful to my car if I buy a motorcycle too? 'In truth, significance and interpretosis are the two diseases of the earth or the skin, in other words, humankind's fundamental neurosis', Deleuze and Guattari write (1987, 114). That will certainly be the opinion of the woman who comes each night into my bed if she never asks herself the question, 'What does it mean – what am I doing?', if she just slips off her clothes and entangles herself in me.

This thin, invisible layer of meaning between oneself and things, this labyrinth of meanings, these circles upon circles, is anchored somewhere. It is anchored, Deleuze and Guattari say, on a face. The blank wall of a face pulled over the substance of the head originally issues the demand, the *mot d'ordre*: 'What does it mean?' The questions: 'What does she mean?' 'Does she want to get something from me, does she expect presents, money, does she want to tie me to her so that I will bring her to America?' anticipate a moment when she will stand before you and face you and ask you to take her to America with you. The question: 'Is it because the GIs were here during the Vietnam war that the local morality broke down and women starting going to bed with foreign strangers?' anticipates the time when someone back home with political and ethical convictions will call you to an accounting of what you were doing with that woman in a backward country. The question: 'What does it mean in my life that I am having an affair, far from my wife?' anticipates some friend back home, or some marriage counsellor or pastor, some Judge Starr who will demand an accounting of you.

It was not all by yourself that you started asking 'What does it mean?' and entered into these labyrinths and circles upon circles of interpretation. After all, you do not ask yourself what does it mean that you eat breakfast, that you eat oatmeal with strawberries for breakfast, that you sink into a hot tub for half an hour when you get back from work; you do not ask yourself what does it mean that humans eat breakfast, that humans eat, that humans immerse themselves in warm water – not unless, of course, the psychoanalyst faces you to ask: 'What does that say about you?' As a little child you were allowed to suck on your thumb, play for hours with your toys, run again and again through piles of autumn leaves, without having to worry about what it all meant.

But then they started. They faced you, and demanded you give an account of your behaviour. Now the social worker turns up, and asks what it means that there is a new big-screen television in your house, although you are on welfare? You have to give an explanation, one in conformity with welfare-recipient expectations: you say your uncle died and left it to you. The social worker has questions about that, and she will return with more questions. Her supervisor will have questions. Every time we turn on the television there are those faces: pundits and senators demanding what it means that we do not vote, experts demanding what it means that we parents are not disciplining our children, preachers demanding what it means that we don't seem to care that no real meaning can be assigned to our lives, to human life on earth. Week after week *Time* and *Newsweek* ask what it means that high-school kids are shooting down their comrades in school, that people are buying more and more cellular phones, that the most successful film of the year is *Fight Club*. These feature articles are always prominently signed; they show photos of the authors' faces.

A face is not only where the questions come from; it is also where the interpretation will be fixed, where it will be judged, approved or disapproved in the black holes of his eyes where subjectivity turns. A face gives the signs uniform meaning, uniform referents. You try to line up the equivocal directions of what you are doing in an interpretation you address to that face that decrees Yes, No. You look into the black holes of his eyes to see if he sanctions or stigmatises, if those eyes are pleased or displeased.

Over against the despotic, accusatory, judgemental face there is the body of the excluded. Somebody is identified as a locus of resistance to all signs, a locus of refusal of the (over)coding; he is invested with all that is unacceptable, intolerable. Somebody has lost his face and has become an animal, a body to be manipulated and disposed of, scum, black or white trash. 'Look at you! What kind of high school student are you? What kind of athlete are you? You're a disgrace to the team, to the school, to your family, to the community!' 'Drug addicts, perverts, thieves – lock them up and throw away the key!' All that is threatening the system is localised in the body of some individual, and he is driven out.

The scapegoat was an institution of the Bible. The ancient Israelites would once a year select one of their numbers, charge him with all the sins of the community, and then drive him out into the desert. 'The goat's anus stands opposite the face of the despot or god' (DG 1987, 116). Under the Roman Empire, the Jews selected one of their kind, Jesus of Nazareth, and dragged him to the court of Pontius Pilate to accuse him of all the insubordination and rebellion in Palestine that pre-occupied the Roman authorities, delivered him to be their scapegoat. The complete system, Deleuze and Guattari write, thus comprises: the paranoid face or body of the despot or God as the signifying centre of the temple; the priest-interpreters in the temple who continually invest signs with meaning; the hysterical crowd outside being shifted from circle to circle of meaning; the faceless scapegoat being driven out into the desert. This system is found not only in every despotic imperial regime, but in political parties, literary movements, psychoanalytic associations, families. In the university too: there in his ivory tower sits the University President, who periodically comes out to show his face and utter watchwords: banish sexual harassment, do more research, improve teaching, stop binge drinking. There are the experts, who determine what is serious philosophy, what canonical authors are to be mastered, interpreted, and what prominent interpretations of Aristotle, of Kant, of Heidegger, are to be interpreted in turn; experts then who determine what vocabulary is to be used, what the leading journals are in which to publish – faces, blank walls that issue verdicts, with the black holes of their eyes that sanction and judge, and who regularly select professors responsible for all that escapes the system to fire, as professors select students representative of all that escapes the system to drive into the outer deserts of menial employment.

BREAKOUT

Then there are those moments, when the face is effaced, and the sensitive and sensual animate, animal head shows through. 'We have entered another regime, other zones infinitely muter and more imperceptible where subterranean becomings-animal occur, becomings-molecular, nocturnal deterritorializations overspilling the limits of the signifying system' (DG 1987, 115).

How she hated him! How he wronged her! He took her and made love to her without a condom. When she got pregnant, he demanded that she have an abortion. He did not go to the clinic with her; much later she found out that that very night he picked up a woman in a bar and spent the day with her. Then he made her pregnant again. She was determined to keep the baby. She didn't see him for days. Then he would come in the middle of the night, stoned and horny. Finally she pushed him off; he came the next morning and said he loved her, could not live without her, would agree to anything, would marry her. But after marriage again he would disappear for days, and come back stoned on cocaine or heroin. He lost his job; she had to go to look for work, leaving the baby with her mother. Then he took off with her car, vanished. Weeks later he was arrested in another state, having crashed the car and badly injured the woman who was with him; he tested positive for heroin. He was sentenced to thirty years in prison. She came with her lawyer, to make him sign divorce papers. He is brought in by two guards in prison garb, his thick wavy copper hair cut to the skull, his eyes dull. At the sight of him, she falters. She says nothing, she impulsively advances toward him, suddenly throws her arms around him, weeps on his shoulder, then pushes back his head and gazes at his scarred and swollen face, her gaze softens into tenderness and tact, touching, caressing that broad forehead, those long black eyelashes, that strong chin, those soft broad lips. He looks shyly at her, sees all the accusation has vanished from her face, all the judgement, she has nothing to say. Under the obsessed caresses of his hands, she is these eyes rolling in their wet sockets, this freckled skin, this mass of dull hair, he presses his face against the shell of her ear, pushes his tongue like a mollusk around its coils, presses his face against her neck, his eyes lose all perspective, sees the strange organic matter of which it is made, sees the pulsing of blood through the skin of her neck. He starts to murmur, 'I'm so sorry . . .', but she violently stops him, shutting his mouth with hers. For an hour their eyes caress at random inches of one another's body, they sigh, they push their tongues everywhere, no words come. The hour comes to an end, the guards come and separate them, her eyes glued to his strong animal back being led back to his cage.

BREAKOUT

One escape from the labyrinth of meaning is, then, direct expression. Another is subjectification. The subject is constituted in a relationship between two 'subjects', the subject of a statement: 'I am an American philosophy student', 'I am in pain', 'I am the owner of this car', and the subject who is making a statement: 'I am telling you . . .', 'I think that . . .', 'I hope that . . .'. In the 'as for me' a bundle of signs is detached from the ever widening circle of signs. A line opens out of the circles of signs relaying one another. It betrays the hierarchical and closed field of signs; the subject is, Deleuze and Guattari say, constituted as a traitor (DG 1987, 123–6).

A first form of subjectification is the constitution of a subject as a self-conscious consciousness. To call somebody an adult, an American, a consciousness, a mind, a spirit, a member of the human species – all that is to fit him into a network of meanings, which open into circles of further meanings.

But the suject that arises and says 'I' – 'for my part, I wonder . . .', 'I doubt . . .', 'On the contrary, I feel . . .' – is removing himself from any concept with which he gets included in the system. Who or what am 'I'? 'I' don't know. 'I' am this gap in the web of meanings.

The 'I' has been defined negatively: the transcendental ego in Kant as in Husserl is a pure identity-pole, to which intentions, volitions, memories and expectations are ascribed. In Hegel, Kojève, Sartre and Lacan, the ego is an insubstantial point from which issue needs and desires. For Deleuze and Guattari, the subject is positive, a machine producing excess energies which betray meanings, which have no meaningful purpose. There is no concept of the 'I' that is self-conscious, not because it has no positive existence, but rather because it is radically innocent, no concept can capture it, it is a break in the circular relay of concept to concept. It generates energies outside the semiotic circles.

A second form of subjectification is the constitution of a subject of passionate love. Here you exist as a subject in the ecstatic absorption in someone else. You exist as a statement in another's mouth. And the other exists as a subject making a statement in your mouth. This relationship tends to union – but the union is betrayed: the man remains a man, the woman a woman (DG 1987, 131).

The subject breaks out of the circles of meaning: I am an adult American, a professional, I have my place and function in the meaningful field of the economy, I work; I perform a meaningful activity; it makes sense to others and to myself, my work has a future and I have a future. But now I have lost my head over this illiterate woman in an underdeveloped country. I keep it a secret as long as I can, for it makes no sense. I am no longer behaving like a professional with professional responsibilities, I am no longer acting like an adult, I no longer know what to make of this passion, I no longer know what is good for me, I no longer know what I want or even what I feel – love, infatuation, self-deception; I no longer know who or what I am.

Such passionate attachment could be made with all sorts of things: the anorexic is attached to food, but not food as it is meaningful within the despotic semiotic system; she or he undermines the received meaning of food, finding food disgusting, seeing it swarming with microbes, germs, maggots. The fetishist is attached to a dress, lingerie, a shoe, taken outside their meanings in common discourse. Education imposes on individuals a succession of ideals – team player, valedictorian, law student, professional; you can become passionately attached to them in ways that subvert their meaning: obsessed with cheerleaders, seeking public office in order to avenge yourself for racial or childhood slights. The subject can be a group or collective subject: a group can betray the current semiotic system, and constitute itself as an ethnic or religious minority, a street gang, an insurrectional guerrilla. Jean Genet isolates himself utterly from humanity, and proceeds to put on himself the statements that anyone can put on him when they say 'he': he's a thief, a queer, a pervert, a hustler, a deserter, a convict. But Genet makes each of these statements into glorious attributes of his subjectivity, and blazes for himself a route into the wastelands, the urban underground, the sexual underground, the refugee camps of the Palestinians, outside of the meaningful political, social, ethical discourse of his society.

Just as direct expressions and states of self-consciousness and of passionate attachment can be subjected to interpretation, all kinds of expressions can get transformed into self-consciousness or into passionate attachment. While dancing in the disco, you begin to say to yourself: 'Why am I here?', 'Why am I spending the night doing this?' While watching a Balinese shadow play, trying to follow the plot, you find yourself entranced by it. While giving a public address full of political argument you become aware of how you look, how smooth your delivery is. While seated in a slum home of someone on welfare, you begin to gaze passionately at her wistful and elegant face. While marching in a squadron off to the battlefront, you ask yourself if you will survive, if this is how your life will end – and then you gaze at your buddies, feeling you have never cared more about anyone.

The face that commands meaning, requires meaningful responses, sanctions or blames, can itself be transformed: the workers see the boss as a snarling pit bulldog or a yelping hyena or a fat pig. Balinese or Papuans, ordered to perform a ritual dance before the masters, the tourists or the visiting governing dignitary, come stoned, get caught up in their own trance, and break out of all control, such that they no longer even see the scowling face of the Mayor or the tour guide. It can happen that the student, soldier, factory worker takes the orders of the teacher, lieutenant or boss as the very voice of conscience in himself. It can happen that he or she may fall in love with the teacher, lieutenant or boss and seduce him.

It could also happen that you see the despotic face when it is in fact effaced: someone meets you, his eyes light up, blood begins to circulate more intensely, there was the simple pleasure of seeing a beautiful person that radiates warmth over his own eyes and lips and warmed his body and his loins. There was no question put, no demand made, no order-word issued. But you set out to interpret, interpret every look, every word, every gesture that he made.

The self-conscious consciousness, as well as the passionate subject, betrays the signs put on them, and blazes a line of escape from the circle of signs. But these lines of escape are finite, they are segments; they do not, like the lines of meaning, extend indefinitely and close in on themselves. 'Every consciousness pursues its own death', Deleuze and Guattari write, 'every love-passion its own end' (DG 1987, 133). Self-consciousness ends when passionate love begins; passionate love ends when self-consciousness begins.

BREAKOUT

It would be possible to shift the subject entirely out of its position of self-conscious consciousness where it is a pure ego-pole, and out of its position of passionate love where it is a subject subjected to another, into the consistency of the substantial, closed body without organs. This would happen when self-consciousness becomes wholly an experimenting with life, an experimenting life. Instead of identifying itself with the sign for a subject, it would become a consistent force of life, pulsating and without needs or lacks. It would become an animal life. Instead of identifying itself with another subject who speaks, it would become a pure field of intense forces. The man would no longer answer to the woman, but find himself becoming female in the embrace with her. You would use self-conscious consciousness and passionate love to abolish all subjectification, all subjection.

Love

John Protevi

Once one of the most important philosophical concepts (it is impossible to think of Plato without *erôs*, or Aristotle without *philia*), love isn't a central focus for post-structuralism's greatest thinkers, Jacques Derrida and Gilles Deleuze. Or so it seems. But couldn't one just as well say that Derrida and Deleuze think about nothing but love? What have they written that isn't linked rather directly to desire, to alterity, to getting outside oneself, even if 'love' isn't among their most widely recognised concepts? In this essay I take up their scattered references to love as a way to foreground the differences between their basic philosophical orientations: for Derrida, post-phenomenology; for Deleuze (at least in his collaboration with Guattari), historical-libidinal materialism.[1]

There are three keys to understanding the different notions of love for our thinkers. The first is a note on terminology. While the French noun *amour* corresponds well to the English 'love', the verb *aimer* can also mean 'to like' as well as 'to love'. The ambiguity of *aimer* is noted by Derrida, who coins the term '*aimance*' for that which is 'beyond love and friendship following their determined figures' (Derrida 1994a, 88; 1997a, 69). We will follow Derrida's lead and talk of 'love' without reference to the difference between the Romantic/erotic and friendly/philic registers.

The second key rests on the ambiguity of the French term *expérience*. For the post-phenomenologist Derrida, the sense of the *expérience* of love is the English 'experience' and the German *Erlebnis*: that which one undergoes, what one lives through. (Derrida will of course change the sense of 'living through': love is precisely that which forces us to recognise that the living present has always already been disrupted, so that the experience of love is living through what can't be experienced, if experience is restricted to an event recorded in a supposedly self-present living present.) For the historical-libidinal materialist Deleuze, on the other hand, the sense of the *expérience* of love is the English 'experiment': that which one does in order to provoke a novel occurrence, to elicit a new event, to produce a new body.[2]

The third key is the status of 'memory' in the *expérience* of love. For Derrida, the memory of love is not the recall of time gone by, what we once experienced in the living present of our consciousness, but is an originary difference, the possibility of mourning that inaugurates friendship in an absolute past that vitiates the living present. For Deleuze, the memory of love is the rumble of Body without Organs, the roads not taken in the virtual that echo in the actual, the memory of the body they stole from us. Love is the call to enter that virtual and open up the actual, to instal inclusive disjunctions so that the roads not taken are still accessible, so that we might experiment and produce new bodies.

DERRIDA

Since Gasché's work in *The Tain of the Mirror* (1986), we've become accustomed to reading Derrida's first 25 years of work as the working out of a network of concepts or quasi-concepts, each of them displaying a family resemblance, each of them expressing from a different angle 'the same thing': the breakdown of the living present. In this network *différance* is only the most famous of a long list of post-phenomenological and (hence, since phenomenology is the capstone of metaphysics) marginally metaphysical terms, including *pharmakon*, *hama*, trace, supplement. . . . Since the late 1980s or early 1990s however, Derrida has shifted the register of his thought from what had become for many a relatively familiar strategy of discovering or inventing[3] quasi-concepts that perform a deconstructive 'solicitation' (shaking) at the margins of metaphysics to a stance which highlights the experience of 'aporia'.

We must not exaggerate the import of this shift, however, and think Derrida has left behind his post-phenomenological orientation – nor indeed, that there are not aporetic moments in his early work. The shift from deconstructive quasi-concept to experience of aporia maintains a continuity of concerns with his earlier work, even if there is a sort of figure-ground inversion. Thus in 'Finis', the first essay in *Aporias* (Derrida 1993a), he goes all the way back to 'Ousia and Grammè' (in Derrida 1972b) to pick up his 'analysis of the Aristotelian-Hegelian aporetic of time, carried out with Heidegger' (Derrida 1993a, 15). He then mentions 'the interminable list of all the so-called undecidable quasi-concepts' in order to place them under the rubric of 'aporia', calling them 'so many aporetic places or dislocations'; in this catalogue he specifically mentions concepts we'll need to investigate to articulate the aporia of love: 'the work of impossible mourning' and 'the gift as the impossible' (1993a, 15–16). After a brief recall of his analysis of decision and of duty, Derrida then firmly knits together these early and late approaches, deconstructive and aporetic, in commenting on his work on the unity of Europe: 'This formulation of the paradox and of the impossible therefore calls upon a figure that resembles a structure of temporality, an instantaneous dissociation from the present, a *différance* in being-with-itself of the present' (1993a, 17).

After showing how 'aporia' is now his favoured way of expressing the breakdown of the living present – in other words, that 'aporia' remains a post-phenomenological strategy – it remains for Derrida to show that aporia isn't simple, that there is a 'plural logic' (1993a, 20) at play here. He mentions three figures that do not oppose each other, but are instead 'hauntings' of each other. The first case of aporia as non-passage is that of impermeability, 'the opaque existence of an uncrossable border'; the second is non-passage due to the absence of limit; the third that of 'the impossible, the antinomy, or the contradiction [which] is a non-passage because its elementary milieu does not allow for something that could be called passage, step, walk, gait, displacement, or replacement, kinesis in general. There is no more path (*odos*, *methodos*, *Weg*, or *Holzweg*)' (1993a, 20–1).

To focus now on Derrida's explicit treatments of love, let us note that in his early work the key to love is the acceptance of the necessary possibility of mourning the other. In *Memoires: for Paul de Man* (1989a) Derrida writes some of his most moving passages about love, talking precisely about one he loved:[4] 'We know, we knew, *we remember* – before the death of the loved one – that being-in-me or being-in-us is constituted out of the possibility of mourning' (1989a, 34). The very constitution of subjectivity, and *a fortiori* of friendly or loving subjectivity, passes not only through the other, but through the other as mortal: 'It suffices that I know him to be mortal, that he knows me to be mortal – there is no friendship without this knowledge of finitude. And everything that we inscribe in the living present of our relation to others already carries, always, the signature of *memoirs-from-beyond-the-grave*' (1993a, 29).

This focus on love as accepting the necessary possibility of mourning is intensely conveyed in 'Aphorism Countertime', Derrida's reading of *Romeo and Juliet*: 'To no matter whom, I must be able to say: since we are two, we know in an absolutely ineluctable way that one of us will die before the other. One of us will see the other die, one of us will live on, even if only for an instant. One of us, only one of us, will carry the death of the other–and the mourning' (1987b, 524; 1992a, 422).

In the experience of love the living present, the very seat of experience, is rent by finitude and by the necessity of possible mourning (here we clearly see an aporia: the mourning that is necessarily always possible is itself an impossible tension between introjection and incorporation); returning to *Memoires* we clearly see in this theme Derrida's debt to Levinas, his friendship or love of Levinas: 'This finitude can only take that form through the trace of the other in us, the other's irreducible precedence; in other words, simply the trace which is always the trace of the other, the finitude of memory, and thus the approach or remembrance of the future' (1989a, 29). Love marks the necessity of reading the constitution of subjectivity as passage through the finitude of the other. Since it's impossible to experience in the living present the love of the other, because it's precisely the other that rends the living present, then the self-presence of the living present itself must be a fiction, it must have always already been rent asunder by an originary alterity. Hence we need to redefine subjectivity in order to save the experience of love.

It is within this very work of mourning for a loved one, within *Memoires: for Paul de Man*, that Derrida begins to discuss love, the deconstructive breakdown of the living present, in the terms of the experience of aporia. Indeed, Derrida reports, the thought of aporia is a gift from a loved one, for when the necessary possibility of mourning Paul de Man becomes an actual duty, the working through of his mourning brushes up against 'aporia', first the word, then the experience: 'The word "aporia" recurs often in Paul de Man's last texts . . . the experience of the aporia, such as de Man deciphers it, gives or promises the thinking of the path, provides the thinking of the very possibility of what still remains unthinkable or unthought, indeed impossible' (1989a, 132). *Memoires*, the work of mourning dedicated to the memory of Paul de Man, then is the path *to* aporia, the path to the thinking and the experience of the non-path, and hence to the later Derrida: 'No path is possible without the aporia of the gift, which does not occur without the aporia of the promise. I have tried to show elsewhere, in a seminar on the gift (given at Yale on Paul de Man's invitation), that there is no gift except on the aporetic condition that nothing is given that is present and that presents itself as such. The gift is only a promise and a promised memory' (1989a, 147).

Now that we have learned to express the breakdown of phenomenological accounts in terms of the experience of aporia, now that we have entered the current register of Derrida's thought, we need to see what difference this makes to Derrida's treatment of love. Here we move from love as the acceptance of the necessary possibility of mourning the other to love as the experience of the impossibility of a pure relation to the other, to love as endurance of aporia. Although to my knowledge Derrida does not articulate an 'aporia of love' in just those terms, we can try to work out the structure of such an aporia, following the third sense of aporia noted above, that of 'the impossible, the antinomy, or the contradiction'.

First, let us use the aporia of the gift as our model, following the analyses in *Politics of Friendship*. Pure love is impossible, it cannot be experienced or be present, for any love that is acknowledged or recognised by lover or beloved would fall into an economy, a reciprocity of mutual benefit and hence cease to be love and become a mere 'friendship of utility', as Aristotle might say. That is, such a friendship is not really a loving friendship, an *aimance*, since it reduces the alterity of the 'friend' to a mere element in a calculus of utility. Yet for the relation to the other to be a relation, there must be a moment of re-appropriation that reaches through a certain self-image, through a certain narcissism (Derrida 1995d, 199). But then we are back at the beginning once again: any relation to the other that passes through a living present is an appropriation, a domestication, that destroys alterity. But yet again, it must be my love, I must be the one committed to the other, the one who gives my love, for what is a love that is not my commitment?

Another way to articulate the aporia of love would be to use the model of the aporia of decision: pure love is impossible because it can not follow a programme of previous love without the risk that the partners are simply 'in love with love' and not with each other; but on the other hand, not just any relation deserves the name of love, and so it cannot not have a relation to past loves.

In either register, early or late, deconstructive or aporetic, we see Derrida describing the experience of love though a series of linked terms: alterity, trace, intersubjectivity, mourning, mortality, finitude, law, tragedy, desire. In the early Derrida, our subjectivity is redefined as a passage through the other by the experience of accepting the necessary possibility of mourning; this redefinition is needed in order to save the experience of love as originary relation to alterity. But in later Derrida, love is the very experience of aporia or nonpassage, the passion or endurance of the impossibility of an experience of pure love, the impossibility of a pure relation to alterity. In the early work, love is the passage through the other that disrupts presence, that redefines experience in terms of alterity rather than identity; in the later work love is the nonpassage through the other that reinforces the experience of the impossibility of identity or present-based 'experience'.

Let's recap our philosophical passage in terms of love: Derrida's first (philosophical) love was for Husserl, and love for Levinas' love of the other and for Heidegger's love of difference led him to deconstruct Husserl's love of presence. His love for Paul de Man brought him to think of the gift, and mourning de Man's death brought him to think of de Man's love of aporia, to which his thought passes. Paul de Man's gift of love then for Derrida is the thought of aporia.[5]

DELEUZE (AND GUATTARI)

For Deleuze and Guattari love is a form of desire, the process of material nature. In *Anti-Oedipus* love is anti-Oedipality itself: 'sexuality and love do not live in the bedroom of Oedipus, they dream instead of wide-open spaces, and cause strange flows to circulate' (DG 1972, 138; 1984, 116). In *A Thousand Plateaus* it is life itself, the very process of creating novel uses for available materials: 'Why not walk on your head, sing with your sinuses, see through your skin, breathe with your belly: the simple Thing, the Entity, the full Body, the stationary Voyage, Anorexia, cutaneous Vision, Yoga, Krishna, Love [in English in the original], Experimentation' (DG 1980, 187; 1987, 151).

In *Anti-Oedipus*, love has two valences, Oedipal/paranoid and revolutionary/ schizophrenising. (It's important, of course, to emphasise Deleuze and Guattari's focus on the process of schizophreni*sing*; they don't valorise the schizophrenic as entity, which is precisely the failure of the process.) When desire is captured in capitalist axiomatics, it takes the Oedipal form. Analysed by the five paralogisms, Oedipal love is personal, exclusively differentiated, fixed in meaning, guilty and familial. This is what they will call 'sick desire': 'a desire to be loved, and worse, a sniveling desire to have been loved' (1972, 399; 1984, 334). Oedipus is the name of a sick desire, a desire hardly worthy of the name; but Oedipal love is not the only kind; there is also what we can call schizo love: love that is material (not representational), social (not familial) and multiple (not personal). Revolutionary desire as sketched out in *Anti-Oedipus* is a desire for higher intensity in an encounter of multiple flows on a body without organs. Schizo love is only unleashed at the level of multiple flows unhooked from a statistically dominant pattern. This is made clear in *A Thousand Plateaus*, to which we now turn.

In the second volume of *Capitalism and Schizophrenia*, love is the release of multiplicities from their servitude[6] as predicates of a subject. 'What does it mean to love somebody? It is always to seize that person in a mass, extract him or her from a group, however small, in which he or she participates, whether it be through the family only or through something else; then to find that person's own packs, the multiplicities he or she encloses within himself or herself which may be of an entirely different nature' (DG 1980, 49; 1987, 35). A pack or multiplicity is a set of gestures, of part objects, or organs (an 'emission of particles') analysed in itself, not as predicates of a subject. A multiplicity is the multiple treated as a substantive, so that it 'ceases to have any relation to the One as subject or object' (1980, 14; 1987, 8). A multiplicity thus has 'only determinations, magnitudes, and dimensions that cannot increase in number without the multiplicity changing in nature' (ibid.). Love then is exactly this creative novelty of connection, this joining of multiplicities: 'To join them to mine, to make them penetrate mine, and for me to penetrate the other person's. Heavenly nuptials, multiplicities of multiplicities' (1980, 49; 1987, 35).

But it's not easy to join multiplicities. They must be freed from bondage to the organism and to the person: 'Every love is an exercise in depersonalization on a body without organs yet to be formed, and it is at the highest point of this depersonalization that someone can be named, receives his or her family name or first name, acquires the most intense discernibility in the instantaneous apprehension of the multiplicities belonging to him or her, and to which he or she belongs' (ibid.). Only haecceities are named: that is, multiplicities of flows and gestures, freed from organism and subject respectively and set loose on a Body without Organs, a body freed for novel, creative interactions. Haecceity is a body defined in terms of its flows and affects, its speeds and slownesses and what it can do, its 'longitude' and 'latitude'. A haecceity thus occupies a position on the Body without Organs of the Earth and thus also receives one of 'all the names of history'.

Treating a body as a multiplicity, respecting the uniqueness of its assemblage, is thus different from treating it as an organism: an organism is 'a phenomenon of accumulation, coagulation, and sedimentation that, in order to extract useful labor from the BwO, imposes upon it forms, functions, bonds, dominant and hierarchized organizations, organized transcendences' (DG 1980, 197; 1987, 159). Our 'body' (that is, our Body without Organs, our ability to form new connections with others, new patterns and triggers arranged in inclusive disjunction – these connections, and those, and why not those others too?) is 'stolen' and replaced with an 'organism', the stereotyped pattern of material flows we call Oedipus: what we're allowed to be turned on by, what organs and bodies (somatic and social at once) we're able to hook up with, arranged in exclusive disjunctions: these connections and only these – never those, no, never!

All love then must be a material dismantling of the organism and the subject to reach the 'body', that is, a reshuffling of the stereotyped patterns and triggers of Oedipal living: 'Make the body without organs of consciousness and love. Use love and consciousness to abolish subjectification' (1980, 167; 1987, 134). And this dismantling of the organism to regain the body, must, notoriously, and certainly not unproblematically,[7] pass through 'becoming-woman': 'The question [of becoming-woman] is not, or not only, that of the organism, history, and subject of enunciation that oppose masculine to feminine in the great dualism machines. The question is fundamentally that of the body – the body they *steal* from us in order to fabricate opposable organisms' (1980, 338; 1987, 276).

Here Deleuze and Guattari recreate the story of Oedipalisation: 'This body is stolen first from the girl [*la fille*]: Stop behaving like that, you're not a little girl [*une petite fille*] anymore, you're not a tomboy [*un garçon manqué*], etc. The girl's [*la fille*] becoming is stolen first, in order to impose a history, or prehistory, upon her' (1980, 339; 1987, 276). The history of femininity is imposed on her; a stereotyped set of triggers and patterns. A feminine organism is produced by contraction of the body's affects to a small set, the feminine set.[8] Or indeed it is the prehistory of femininity that is imposed: the essence of woman, that which has never changed. Masculinity is then produced in relation to an imposed essentialised femininity: 'The boy's [*garçon*] turn comes next, but it is by using the girl [*la fille*] as an example, by pointing to the girl [*la fille*] as the object of his desire, that an opposed organism, a dominant history is fabricated for him too. The girl [*la fille*] is the first victim, but she must also serve as an example and a trap' (ibid.).

To avoid Oedipality, the fate of being an organism and a subject, to avoid being a good little boy in relation to a nice young lady, to avoid being the nice young lady who must wait to be pursued but whom the good little boy can never imitate, all of us, regardless of which gendered organism has been imposed on us,[9] must 'become-woman'. 'That is why, conversely, the reconstruction of the body as a Body without Organs, the anorganism of the body, is inseparable from a becoming-woman, or the production of a molecular woman . . . becoming-woman or the molecular woman is the girl [*la jeune fille*] herself' (ibid.).[10]

Once the restricted body of the Oedipal boy/man is constructed in relation to the 'young lady' (the girl whose body was stolen and who was then used as example and trap, the anti-model), it can then be used to shame the young lady. To use an American discourse: 'see, you're not brave and tough like the boys, so don't even bother trying to play football: everyone knows football is a boy's sport', and so on. And it's true; young ladies can't play football, and neither can sissies. But girls can! The 'girl' is the name for the body as multiplicity, as BwO: 'The girl is certainly not defined by virginity; she is defined by a relation of movement and rest, speed and slowness, by a combination of atoms, an emission of particles: haecceity. She never ceases to roam upon a body without organs. She is an abstract line, or a line of flight' (DG 1980, 339; 1987, 276–7).

The mention of 'speed and slowness' reminds us that the discussion of 'becoming-woman' belongs to a section entitled 'memories of a molecule', in which Deleuze and Guattari spell out their appropriation of Spinoza and ethology. The body is here shown to be susceptible to definition not only by subject and predicate (and hence by genus and species), but also by 'longitude and latitude'. Longitude measures the body in terms of the speed and slowness of its material flows, while latitude measures the body by its affects: what the body can do. The 'girl' is chosen as the name for this treatment of the body in terms of flow and affect because 'she' lives a body that avoids capture by the developmental line that leads from little girl to nice young lady. Because the 'girl' avoids this line, 'she' is not a tomboy either when acting against gender stereotype and experimenting with the capabilities of the body (how fast can I run? how tough can I be?). But by avoiding the Oedipal organism, the option of 'girl', if it can be accessed, can also include experimentation with patterns stereotyped as 'feminine' (how pretty AND tough can I be?). Accessing the 'girl' in all of us is a question of constructing political and social frameworks: Deleuze and Guattari are never 'lifestyle' mavens, never 'individualists', as the collective sense of the French word *corps* (as in *corps sans organes* = Body without Organs) shows: Deleuze and Guattari urge us all to become a Corps of Engineers, cautious yet daring experimentalists who construct bodies politic, somatic and civic at once.[11]

Whatever the anthropological accuracy of these statements taken as observations of contemporary bourgeois child rearing, in France in the 1970s or the New World Order in the 2000s, whatever their worth as guides for practical experimentation by people whose bodies were stolen and who had gendered organisms given them in their stead, the historical-libidinal materialist rather than purely psychoanalytic context of Deleuze and Guattari's notion of the 'girl' should be clear. The 'girl' is not the name for a particular stage of development, but is the name for the experimenting body: 'Thus girls do not belong to an age group, sex, order or kingdom: they slip in everywhere, between orders, acts, ages, sexes; they produce n molecular sexes on the line of flight in relation to the dualism machines they cross right through' (DG 1980, 339; 1987, 277).

How then does love enter the picture at this point? What is love, if not 'girling', experimentation with the organism they gave you to find the body you might make with others? 'Knowing how to love [*Savoir aimer*] does not mean remaining a man or a woman; it means extracting from one's sex the particles, the speeds and slownesses, the flows, the n sexes that constitute the girl of *that* sexuality' (1980, 340; 1987, 277). Love is freeing bodies from the organism and subject, allowing their triggers and patterns to interact and form new maps (new longitudes and latitudes) that allow new types of flows and hence new affects. When bodies join in the mutual experimental deterritorialisation that is love, we find Deleuze and Guattari's most adventurous concept: the living, changing, multiplying virtual, the unfolding of the plane of consistency. Love is complexity producing novelty, the very process of life.[12]

In other words, love is a war machine: '[Sexuality] is badly explained by the binary organization of the sexes, and just as badly by a bisexual organization within each sex. Sexuality brings into play too great a diversity of conjugated becomings; these are like n sexes, an entire war machine through which love passes' (1980, 341; 1987, 278). 'War machine' of course is another name for creativity. Only the failure of the war machine leads to war, as they stress again and again (1980, 283; 1987, 231).[13] 'This is not to return to those appalling metaphors of love and war . . . it is only after love is done and sexuality has dried up that things appear this way. What counts is that love itself is a war machine endowed with strange and somewhat terrifying powers. Sexuality is the production of a thousand sexes, which are so many uncontrollable becomings' (1980, 341; 1987, 278).

CONCLUSION

We have considered the different treatments of love in Derrida and Deleuze, the different ways difference pulls us outside our allegedly secure and self-identical subjectivity (Derrida's post-phenomenology) or outside both our subjectivity and our organism (Deleuze's historical-libidinal materialism).

While we have emphasised their differences in this paper, perhaps we can fit Derrida and Deleuze together by treating deconstruction as a propaedeutic which disabuses one of metaphysical illusions in order to free one for material experimentation.[14] The danger of deconstruction, however, is getting stuck by focusing exclusively on the awareness of the breakdown of consciousness as experience of aporia, and not shifting registers to material experimentation. Another formulation of this danger might put it this way: while Deleuze and Guattari often note that their *de jure* distinctions are always *de facto* mixes, Derrida will maintain that a supposedly *de jure* distinction can always be shown to result in a *de jure* mixture. In other words, Derrida never seems to leave the realm of law, even if his law (of contamination) forbids what metaphysical laws (of purity) aimed to enforce.

This is not to say Derrida is 'theoretical' and Deleuze 'practical'. On the contrary, both Derridean deconstruction and Deleuzean pragmatics are practical, both are intimately concerned with *expérience*, both urge us to do this, to try that. Derrida tells us: here's a new interpretation of love. Try this way of thinking and see whether it doesn't illuminate your experience of love. Deleuze and Guattari tell us: love is not interpretation of experience, but material experimentation. Here are some hints and guidelines for experimentation; try them out, see what happens!

Notes

1. The relation of the works Deleuze signed alone to those he wrote with Guattari is too complex and important to be treated in a note. Nonetheless, let me cite some words of Deleuze from 'Letter to a Harsh Critic' that are relevant to the topic of this essay: 'I know very well that they're [*Difference and Repetition*

and *The Logic of Sense*] still full of academic elements, they're heavy going. . . . And then there was my meeting with Félix Guattari, the way we understood and complemented, depersonalized and singularized – in short, loved – one another [*on s'aimait*]' (Deleuze 1995b, 7).

2. In one interview, Derrida explicates his sense of 'experience' as 'traversal, voyage, ordeal' (Derrida 1995d, 362). Note that the connotation of 'experiment' is left off the list.

3. Just what it is exactly that deconstruction 'does' is of course an issue to which Derrida devoted many complex pages. See for example, 'Psyché: Invention de l'autre' in Derrida 1987b.

4. Recall the shift in tone in the *Symposium*, famously noted by Martha Nussbaum (1986), from abstract discussion to Alcibiades' impassioned discourse about his concrete love for Socrates.

5. In a longer work, one might try to insert Deleuze into the history of Derrida's philosophical friendships. As he writes in his eulogy for Deleuze: 'Deleuze undoubtably still remains, despite so many dissimilarities, the one among all those of my "generation" to whom I have always considered myself closest. . . . I only know that these differences never left room for anything between us but friendship. There was never any shadow, any sign, as far as I know, that might indicate the contrary' (Derrida 2001a, 193).

6. The 'body politic' implicit here has a long heritage. The body as tool of a soul (as *organon*) is enslaved, as Aristotle tells us. Under the rule of the soul, the body becomes unified, a single organ, *panta yar ta physika sômata tês psychês organa* (*De Anima* 2.4.415b18). Any formation of a unity is always that of ruler/ruled, and the unification of the animal body under the rule of the soul is masterly rather than political (*Politics* 1.5.1254a30). Thus psychic organisation entails somatic enslavement. I have worked out this connection in Protevi 2001a and 2001b.

7. The notion of 'becoming-woman' continues to attract attention from feminist philosophers. See, *inter alia*, Braidotti 2002, Buchanan and Colebrook 2000, Lorraine 1999 and Olkowski 1999. I will restrict myself to what I hope is a careful and clear exposition of Deleuze and Guattari's writings on the connection of 'becoming-woman', the 'girl', and love, and forego a direct confrontation with the many different feminist treatments of these issues.

8. Iris Marion Young's famous essay 'Throwing Like a Girl' (1990) maintains all its relevance here, as it details the small set of constricting affects to which the feminine body is restricted. But perhaps Deleuze and Guattari would want to amend to the title to 'Throwing Like a Young Lady'.

9. Anne Fausto-Sterling's *Sexing the Body* (2000) details the literal meaning of 'imposition' by describing the surgical and hormonal interventions that produce gendered organisms out of the bodies of intersexual babies.

10. Massumi elides the difference between *la fille* and *la jeune fille*, using only 'girl' in his translation. Why is this an excellent move on his part? Although the consecrated French phrase for 'nice young lady' is *la jeune fille*, Deleuze and Guattari move without comment from *la fille* to *la jeune fille* as the name for 'Body without Organs'. Now it would have been more elegant if Deleuze and Guattari had left *la fille* as the name for the BwO, for one could easily see *la fille* as the escape from the developmental line that steals the body and imposes

a gendered organism (that restricts the body's affects to those approved as feminine), that leads from *la petite fille* to *la jeune fille* by avoiding *le garçon manqué*, that is, that leads from 'little girl' to 'nice young lady' by avoiding the 'tomboy'. Unfortunately, in the latter part of the passage they insert *la jeune fille* as the name for BwO; the only way I can see to avoid charging them with a confusing terminological choice is to propose we read *la jeune fille* as 'une fille qui est jeune', as 'a girl who is young', rather than 'nice young lady'. In that way we refer to Deleuze and Guattari's treatment of youth in the passage under consideration as the maintenance of a relation to flexible body patterning, as a contemporary 'block of becoming', rather than as regression or nostalgia. All in all, Massumi's choice of 'girl' to cover both *la fille* and *la jeune fille* helps us by omission; you could say it helps Anglophone readers *use A Thousand Plateaus* more effectively, even if by standards of translation drawn from a signifier-signified model of language it is deficient, it drops some meaning. But after all, it's Deleuze and Guattari who remind us to 'never interpret' and who criticise the assumption that meaning is primary in language.

11. Two recent works influenced by Deleuze and Guattari attest to the political nature of love. See Hardt and Negri: 'Militancy today is a positive, constructive, and innovative activity. . . . This militancy makes resistance into counterpower and makes rebellion into a project of love' (2000, 413). See also Sandoval 2000, Part IV: 'Love in the Postmodern World'.

12. Ansell-Pearson 1999 opens the field for investigating Deleuze and biology.

13. I have produced a detailed treatment of the war machine in Protevi 2000.

14. Foucault writes in *Discipline and Punish* that 'the soul is the prison of the body' (1977, 30).

Bibliography

Agamben, Giorgio. 1999. *Potentialities: Collected Essays in Philosophy*. Trans. Daniel Heller-Roazen. Stanford: Stanford University Press.

Ansell-Pearson, Keith, ed. 1997. *Deleuze and Philosophy*. London: Routledge.

Ansell-Pearson, Keith. 1999. *Germinal Life*. London: Routledge.

Badiou, Alain. 2001. *Ethics: An Essay on the Understanding of Evil*. Trans. Peter Hallward. London: Verso.

Bearn, Gordon C.F. 2000. Differentiating Derrida and Deleuze. *Continental Philosophy Review* 33:441–65.

Beckett, Samuel. 1997. *Trilogy*. New York: Knopf.

Blanchot, Maurice. 1989. *The Space of Literature*. Trans. Ann Smock. Lincoln: University of Nebraska Press.

Blanchot, Maurice. 1993. *The Infinite Conversation*. Trans. Susan Hanson. Minneapolis and London: University of Minnesota Press.

Blanchot, Maurice. 1995. *The Writing of the Disaster*. Trans. Ann Smock. Lincoln: University of Nebraska Press.

Boudot, Pierre, et al. 1973. *Nietzsche aujourd'hui? Exposés*. Paris: Union générale d'éditions.

Boundas, Constantin, and Dorothea Olkowski, eds. 1994. *Gilles Deleuze and the Theater of Philosophy*. London: Routledge.

Braidotti, Rosi. 2002. *Metamorphoses: Towards a Materialist Theory of Becoming*. Cambridge: Polity.

Bréhier, Emile. 1928. *La Théorie des incorporels dans l'ancien stoïcisme*. Paris: Vrin.

Brisson, L. 1987. *Platon. Lettres*. Paris: Flammarion.

Buchanan, Ian. 2000. *Deleuzism: A Metacommentary*. Durham, NC: Duke University Press.

Buchanan, Ian, and Claire Colebrook, eds. 2000. *Deleuze and Feminist Theory*. Edinburgh: Edinburgh University Press.

Buydens, Mireille. 1990. *Sahara. L'Esthétique de Gilles Deleuze*. Paris: Vrin.

Caputo, John. 1997. *Deconstruction in a Nutshell*. New York: Fordham University Press.

Cassin, Barbara, ed. 1992. *Nos Grecs et leurs modernes*. Paris: Seuil.

Coward, Harold and Toby Foshay, eds. 1992. *Derrida and Negative Theology*. Albany: SUNY Press.

Critchley, Simon. 1999. *Ethics-Politics-Subjectivity*. London: Verso.

Deleuze, Gilles. 1962. *Nietzsche et la philosophie*. Paris: PUF.

Deleuze, Gilles. 1966. *Bergsonisme*. Paris: PUF.

Deleuze, Gilles. 1968. *Différence et Répétition*. Paris: PUF.

Deleuze, Gilles. 1969. *Logique du sens*. Paris: Minuit.

Deleuze, Gilles. 1983. *Nietzsche and Philosophy*. Trans. Hugh Tomlinson. New York: Columbia University Press.

Deleuze, Gilles. 1986. *Foucault*. Paris: Minuit.

Deleuze, Gilles. 1988a. *Le Pli*. Paris: Minuit.

Deleuze, Gilles. 1988b. *Foucault*. Trans. Séan Hand. Minneapolis: University of Minnesota Press.

Deleuze, Gilles. 1989. *Masochism: Coldness and Cruelty & Venus in Furs*. Trans. Jean McNeil. New York: Zone Books.

Deleuze, Gilles, 1990. *The Logic of Sense*. Trans. Mark Lester with Charles Stivale. New York: Columbia University Press.

Deleuze, Gilles. 1991a. *Bergsonism*. Trans. Hugh Tomlinson and Barbara Habberjam. New York: Zone Books.

Deleuze, Gilles. 1991b. *Empiricism and Subjectivity*. Trans. Constantin Boundas. New York: Columbia University Press.

Deleuze, Gilles. 1992. *Expressionism in Philosophy: Spinoza*. Trans. Martin Joughin. New York: Zone Books.

Deleuze, Gilles. 1993. *The Fold: Leibniz and the Baroque*. Trans. Tom Conley. Minneapolis: University of Minnesota Press.

Deleuze, Gilles. 1994. *Difference and Repetition*. Trans. Paul Patton. New York: Columbia University Press.

Deleuze, Gilles. 1995a. *Cinema 2: The Time Image*. Trans. Hugh Tomlinson and Robert Galeta. London: Athlone.

Deleuze, Gilles. 1995b. *Negotiations*. Trans. Martin Joughin. New York: Columbia University Press.

Deleuze, Gilles. 1995c. L'Immanence: une vie. . . . *Philosophie* 47: 3–7.

Deleuze, Gilles. 1997. *Essays Critical and Clinical*. Trans. Daniel W. Smith and Michael A. Greco. Minneapolis: University of Minnesota Press.

Deleuze, Gilles. 2000a. Desire and Pleasure. Trans. Lysa Hochroth. In *More and Less*, ed. Sylvère Lotringer. Brooklyn: Semiotexte.

Deleuze, Gilles. 2000b. *Proust and Signs*. Trans. Richard Howard. London: Athlone.

Deleuze, Gilles. 2001. *Pure Immanence: Essays on A Life*. Trans. Anne Boyman. New York: Zone Books.

Deleuze, Gilles. 2002. *L'Ile déserte et autres textes: Textes et entretiens 1953–1974*. Ed. David Lapoujade. Paris. Minuit.

Deleuze, Gilles, and Félix Guattari. 1972. *L'Anti-Œdipe*. Paris: Minuit.

Deleuze, Gilles, and Félix Guattari. 1980. *Mille Plateaux*. Paris: Minuit.

Deleuze, Gilles, and Félix Guattari. 1984. *Anti-Oedipus*. Trans. Robert Hurley, Mark Seem and Helen R. Lane. London: Athlone Press.

Deleuze, Gilles, and Félix Guattari. 1987. *A Thousand Plateaus*. Trans. Brian Massumi. London: Athlone Press.

Deleuze, Gilles, and Félix Guattari. 1994a. *Kafka: Toward a Minor Literature*. Trans. Dana Polan. Minneapolis: University of Minnesota Press.

Deleuze, Gilles, and Félix Guattari. 1994b. *What is Philosophy?* Trans. Hugh Tomlinson and Graham Burchell. New York: Columbia University Press.

Deleuze, Gilles and Claire Parnet. 1977. *Dialogues*. Paris: Flammarion.

Deleuze, Gilles and Claire Parnet. 1987. *Dialogues*. Trans. Hugh Tomlinson and Barbara Habberjam. New York: Columbia University Press.

Derrida, Jacques. 1962. *L'Origine de la géometrie de Edmund Husserl: traduction et introduction*. Paris: PUF.

Derrida, Jacques. 1967a. *De la Grammatologie*. Paris: Minuit.

Derrida, Jacques. 1967b. *La Voix et le phénomène*. Paris: PUF

Derrida, Jacques. 1967c. *L'Ecriture et la Différence*. Paris: Seuil.

Derrida, Jacques. 1972a. *La Dissémination*. Paris: Seuil.

Derrida, Jacques. 1972b. *Marges: de la philosophie*. Paris: Minuit

Derrida, Jacques. 1972c. *Positions*. Paris: Minuit.

Derrida, Jacques. 1973. *Speech and Phenomena*. Trans. David Allison. Evanston: Northwestern University Press.

Derrida, Jacques. 1974. *Of Grammatology*. Trans. Gayatri Spivak. New York: Columbia University Press.

Derrida, Jacques. 1977. *Edmund Husserl's 'Origin of Geometry': An Introduction*. Trans. John Leavey. New York: Nicholas Hays.

Derrida, Jacques. 1978. *Writing and Difference*. Trans. Alan Bass. Chicago: University of Chicago Press.

Derrida, Jacques. 1979a. Living On: Borderlines. Trans. James Hulbert. In *Deconstruction and Criticism*. Boston: Seabury Press.

Derrida, Jacques. 1979b. *Spurs: Nietzsche's Styles*. Trans. Barbara Harlow. Chicago: University of Chicago Press.

Derrida, Jacques. 1981a. *Dissemination*. Trans. Barbara Johnson. Chicago: University of Chicago Press.

Derrida, Jacques. 1981b. *Positions*. Trans. Alan Bass. Chicago: University of Chicago Press.

Derrida, Jacques. 1982. *Margins of Philosophy*. Trans. Alan Bass. Chicago: University of Chicago Press.

Derrida, Jacques. 1984a. My Chances/Mes Chances: A Rendezvous with some Epicurean Stereophonies. Trans. Irene Harvey and Avital Ronell. In *Taking Chances: Derrida, Psychoanalysis and Literature*, eds. Joseph H. Smith and William Kerrigan. Baltimore: Johns Hopkins University Press.

Derrida, Jacques. 1984b. Two Words for Joyce. Trans. Geoff Bennington. In *Post-Structuralist Joyce: Essays from the French*. Ed. Derek Attridge and Daniel Ferrer. Cambridge: Cambridge University Press.

Derrida, Jacques. 1986. *Parages*. Paris: Galilée.

Derrida, Jacques. 1987a. *De l'Esprit*. Paris: Galilée.

Derrida, Jacques. 1987b. *Psyché: Inventions de l'autre*. Paris: Galilée.

Derrida, Jacques. 1987c. *The Postcard: From Socrates to Freud and beyond*. Trans. Alan Bass. Chicago: University of Chicago Press.

Derrida, Jacques. 1987d. *Ulysse gramophone. Deux Mots pour Joyce*. Paris: Galilée.

Derrida, Jacques. 1988a. Letter to a Japanese Friend. In *Derrida and Difference*, eds. David Wood and Robert Bernasconi. Evanston: Northwestern University Press.

Derrida, Jacques. 1988b. *Limited Inc*. Trans. Samuel Weber. Evanston: Northwestern University Press.

Derrida, Jacques. 1988c. Mes chances, Au rendez-vous de quelques stéréophonies épicuriennes. *Cahiers confrontation.* 19:19–45.

Derrida, Jacques. 1989a. *Memoires: for Paul de Man.* Rev. edn. Trans. Cecile Lindsay, Jonathan Culler, Eduardo Cadava and Peggy Kamuf. New York: Columbia University Press.

Derrida, Jacques. 1989b. *Of Spirit.* Trans. Geoffrey Bennington and Rachel Bowlby. Chicago: University of Chicago Press.

Derrida, Jacques. 1990a. Donner la mort. In *L'Ethique du don, Jacques Derrida et la pensée du don.* Paris: Transition.

Derrida, Jacques. 1990b. Epreuves d'écriture. *Revue philosophique de la France et de l'étranger.* 115.2: 269–84.

Derrida, Jacques. 1990c. *Le problème de la genèse dans la philosophie de Husserl.* Paris: PUF.

Derrida, Jacques. 1990d. Sendoffs. Trans. Thomas Pepper. *Yale French Studies* 77: 7–43.

Derrida, Jacques. 1992a. *Acts of Literature,* ed. Derek Attridge. London: Routledge.

Derrida, Jacques. 1992b. Force of Law. In *Deconstruction and the Possibility of Justice,* ed. Drucilla Cornell. London: Routledge.

Derrida, Jacques. 1992c. *Given Time I: Counterfeit Money.* Trans. Peggy Kamuf. Chicago: University of Chicago Press.

Derrida, Jacques. 1992d. Nous autres Grecs. In Cassin 1992.

Derrida, Jacques. 1992e. How to Avoid Speaking: Denials. In *Derrida and Negative Theology,* eds. Harold Coward and Toby Foshay. Albany: SUNY Press.

Derrida, Jacques. 1993a. *Aporias.* Trans. Thomas Dutoit. Stanford: Stanford University Press.

Derrida, Jacques. 1993b. *Khôra.* Paris: Galilée.

Derrida, Jacques. 1993c. On a Newly Arisen Apocalyptic Tone in Philosophy. In *Raising the Tone of Philosophy,* ed. Peter Fenves. Baltimore: Johns Hopkins University Press.

Derrida, Jacques. 1993d. *Spectres de Marx.* Paris: Galilée.

Derrida, Jacques. 1994a. *Politiques de l'amitié.* Paris: Galilée.

Derrida, Jacques. 1994b. *Specters of Marx.* Trans. Peggy Kamuf. London: Routledge.

Derrida, Jacques. 1995a. Il me faudra errer tout seul. *Libération.* November 7, 1995.

Derrida, Jacques. 1995b. *Mal d'Archive: une impression freudienne.* Paris: Galilée.

Derrida, Jacques. 1995c. *On the Name.* Trans. David Wood, J. P. Leavey, Jr, and Ian McLeod. Stanford: Stanford University Press.

Derrida, Jacques. 1995d. *Points: Interviews 1974–1994.* Trans. Peggy Kamuf. Stanford: Stanford University Press.

Derrida, Jacques. 1995e. *The Gift of Death.* Trans. David Wills. Chicago: University of Chicago Press.

Derrida, Jacques. 1995f. The Time Out of Joint. In *Deconstruction Is/in America: A New Sense of the Political,* ed. Anselm Haverkamp. New York: NYU Press.

Derrida, Jacques. 1997a. *Politics of Friendship.* Trans. George Collins. London: Verso.

Derrida, Jacques. 1997b. The Villanova Roundtable: A Conversation with Jacques

Derrida. In *Deconstruction in a Nutshell*, ed. John Caputo. New York: Fordham University Press.

Derrida, Jacques. 1998. *Resistances of Psychoanalysis*. Trans. Peggy Kamuf et al. Stanford: Stanford University Press.

Derrida, Jacques. 2000a. *Demeure: Fiction and Testimony*. Trans. Elizabeth Rottenberg. Stanford: Stanford University Press.

Derrida, Jacques. 2000b. *Of Hospitality: Anne Dufourmantelle Invites Jacques Derrida to Respond*. Stanford: Stanford University Press.

Derrida, Jacques. 2001a. I'm Going to Have to Wander All Alone. Trans. Leonard Lawlor. In *The Work of Mourning*. Trans. and eds. Pascale-Anne Brault and Michael Naas. Chicago: University of Chicago Press. 192–5

Derrida, Jacques. 2001b. *On Cosmopolitanism and Forgiveness*. Trans. Mark Dooley and Michael Hughes. London: Routledge.

Derrida, Jacques. 2001c. *Jacques Derrida: Deconstruction Engaged*. Eds. Paul Patton and Terry Smith. Sydney: Power Publications.

Derrida, Jacques. 2002a. Politics and Friendship. In *Negotiations: Interventions and Interviews 1971–2001*. Trans. and ed. Elizabeth Rottenberg. Stanford: Stanford University Press.

Derrida, Jacques. 2002b. *Who's Afraid of Philosophy?* Trans. Jan Plug. Stanford: Stanford University Press.

Descombes, Vincent. 1971. *Le Platonisme*. Paris, PUF.

Descombes, Vincent. 1980. *Modern French Philosophy*. New York: Cambridge University Press.

Fausto-Sterling, Anne. 2000. *Sexing the Body*. New York: Basic Books.

Ferry, Luc, and Alain Renault. 1990. *French Philosophy of the Sixties: An Essay on Antihumanism*. Trans. Mary H. S. Cattani. Amherst: University of Massachusetts Press.

Fitzgerald, F. Scott. 1993. *The Crack-Up*. New York: New Directions.

Foucault, Michel. 1966. La Pensée du dehors. In *Dits et écrits*, eds. Daniel Defert and François Ewald. Vol. 1, 1954–1975. Quarto edition (2001): 546–67. Paris: Gallimard.

Foucault, Michel. 1970a. *The Order of Things*. New York: Random House.

Foucault, Michel. 1970b. Theatrum Philosophicum. In *Dits et écrits*, eds. Daniel Defert and François Ewald. Vol. 1, 1954–1975. Quarto edition (2001): 943–67. Paris: Gallimard.

Foucault, Michel. 1971. Nietzsche, la généalogie, l'histoire. In *Dits et écrits*, eds. Daniel Defert and François Ewald. Vol. 1, 1954–1975. Quarto edition (2001): 1004–24. Paris: Gallimard.

Foucault, Michel. 1972. Mon corps, ce papier, ce feu. In *Dits et écrits*, eds. Daniel Defert and François Ewald. Vol. 1, 1954–1975. Quarto edition (2001): 1113–16. Paris: Gallimard.

Foucault, Michel. 1977. *Discipline and Punish*. Trans. Alan Sheridan. New York: Random House.

Foucault, Michel. 1988. *Madness and Civilization*. Trans. Richard Howard. New York: Vintage Books.

Foucault, Michel. 1997. *Ethics*. Essential Works of Foucault, vol. 1. Ed. Paul Rabinow. New York: The New Press.

Foucault, Michel 1998. *Aesthetics, Method, and Epistemology.* Essential Works of Foucault, ed. James D. Faubion, Vol. 2. New York: The New Press.

Frueh, Joanna. 1996. *Erotic Faculties.* Berkeley: University of California Press.

Gasché, Rodolphe. 1986. *The Tain of the Mirror.* Cambridge: Harvard University Press.

Goldschmidt, V. 1947. *Le Paradigme dans la dialectique platonicienne.* Paris: PUF.

Goodchild, Philip. 1996. *Deleuze and Guattari: An Introduction to the Politics of Desire.* London: Sage.

Grossberg, Lawrence. 1997. *Bringing it all Back Home: Essays on Cultural Studies.* Durham NC: Duke University Press.

Hardt, Michael. 1993. *Gilles Deleuze: An Apprenticeship in Philosophy.* Minneapolis: University of Minnesota Press.

Hardt, Michael and Antonio Negri. 2000. *Empire.* Cambridge, MA: Harvard University Press.

Harvey, Irene. 1986. *Derrida and the Economy of Différance.* Bloomington: Indiana University Press.

Hayden, Patrick. 1998. *Multiplicity and Becoming: The pluralist empiricism of Gilles Deleuze.* Peter Lang: New York.

Heidegger, Martin. 1982. *Nietzsche. Vol. 4: Nihilism.* Trans. Frank A. Capuzzi. San Francisco: Harper & Row.

Holland, Eugene. 1999. *Deleuze and Guattari's* Anti-Oedipus: *Introduction to Schizoanalysis.* London: Routledge.

Husserl, Edmund, 1954. *Cartesian Meditations.* The Hague: M. Nijhoff.

Husserl, Edmund, 1969. *Ideas: General introduction to pure phenomenology.* London: Allen and Unwin.

Kant, Immanuel. 1929. *Critique of Pure Reason.* Trans. Norman Kemp Smith. London: Macmillan.

Kierkegaard, Søren. 1985. *Fear and Trembling.* New York: Penguin Books.

Lawlor, Leonard. 2000a. Phenomenology and Bergsonism: The Beginnings of Post-Modernism. In *Confluences: Phenomenology and Postmodernity, Environment, Race, Gender.* The Seventeenth Annual Symposium of the Simon Silverman Phenomenology Center, Duquesne University.

Lawlor, Leonard. 2000b. A Nearly Total Affinity: The Deleuzian Virtual Image versus the Derridean Trace. *Angelaki,* 5.2 (August 2000): 59–72.

Lawlor, Leonard. 2002. *Derrida and Husserl: The Basic Problem of Phenomenology.* Bloomington: Indiana University Press.

Lawlor, Leonard. 2003. *The Being of the Questions: Investigations of the Great French Philosophy of the Sixties.* Bloomington: Indiana University Press.

Lévinas, Emmanuel. 1969. *Totality and Infinity.* Trans. Alphonso Lingis. Pittsburg, PA: Duquesne University Press.

Lévi-Strauss, Claude. 1987. *Introduction to the Work of Marcel Mauss.* Trans. Felicity Baker. London: Routledge.

Llewelyn, John. 1986. *Derrida on the Threshold of Sense.* New York: St Martin's.

Lorraine, Tamsin. 1999. *Irigaray and Deleuze: Experiments in Visceral Philosophy.* Ithaca, NY: Cornell University Press.

Lyotard, Jean-François. 1985a. Les Immatériaux. *Art and Text* [Australia], 17:8–10, 47–57.

Lyotard, Jean-François. 1985b. *Les Immateriaux. Vol. 1: Album. Inventaire.* Paris: Centre Georges Pompidou.

Lyotard, Jean-François. 1987. Rewriting Modernity. *Substance*, 54:3–9.

Lyotard, Jean-François. 1988. *Réécrire la modernité.* Lille: Les Cahiers de Philosophie.

Lyotard, Jean-François. 1989. Argumentation et présentation: la crise des fondements. In *Encyclopédie philosophie universalis, Volume I: L'Univers Philosophique*, ed. André Jacob. Paris: PUF, 738–750.

Macksey, Richard, and Eugenio Donato, eds. 1972. *The Structuralist Controversy: The Languages of Criticism and the Sciences of Man.* Baltimore, MD: Johns Hopkins University Press.

Man, Paul de. 1996. *Aesthetic Ideology.* Minneapolis: University of Minnesota Press.

Marks, John. 1998. *Gilles Deleuze: Vitalism and Multiplicity.* Pluto Press: London.

Massumi, Brian. 1992. *A User's Guide to Capitalism and Schizophrenia: Deviations from Deleuze and Guattari.* Cambridge, MA: MIT Press.

Melville, Herman. 1990. *Bartleby and Benito Cereno.* New York: Dover Publications.

Nancy, Jean-Luc. 1996. The Deleuzian Fold of Thought. In Patton ed. 1996.

Nealon, Jeffrey T. 1993. *Double Reading: Postmodernism After Deconstruction.* Ithaca, NY: Cornell University Press.

Nealon, Jeffrey T. 1998. *Alterity Politics: Ethics and Performative Subjectivity.* Durham, NC: Duke University Press.

Nietzsche, Friedrich. 1990. *Beyond Good and Evil.* Trans. R. J. Hollingdale. London: Penguin.

Nussbaum, Martha. 1986. *The Fragility of Goodness.* Cambridge: Cambridge University Press.

Olkowski, Dorothea. 1999. *Gilles Deleuze and the Ruin of Representation.* Berkeley: University of California Press.

Patton, Paul, ed. 1996. *Deleuze: A Critical Reader.* Oxford: Blackwell.

Patton, Paul. 1997. Strange Proximity: Deleuze et Derrida dans les parages du concept. *Oxford Literary Review*, 18:117–33.

Patton, Paul. 2000. *Deleuze and the Political.* London: Routledge.

Plato. 1961. *The Collected Dialogues, including The Letters.* Eds. Edith Hamilton and Huntington Cairns. Princeton: Princeton University Press.

Plotnitsky, Arkady. 1993. *In the Shadow of Hegel: Complementarity, History, and the Unconscious.* Gainesville: University Presses of Florida.

Plotnitsky, Arkady. 2000. Algebra and Allegory: Nonclassical Epistemology, Quantum Theory, and the Work of Paul de Man. In *Material Events: Paul de Man and the Afterlife of Theory*, ed. Barbara Cohen. Minneapolis: University of Minnesota Press.

Plotnitsky, Arkady. 2002. *The Knowable and the Unknowable: Modern Science, Nonclassical Thought, and the 'Two Cultures'.* Ann Arbor: University of Michigan Press.

Protevi, John. 2000. A Problem of Pure Matter. In *Nihilism Now!: 'Monsters of Energy'*, eds. Keith Ansell-Pearson and Diane Morgan. London: Macmillan.

Protevi, John. 2001a. The Organism as Judgment of God. In *Deleuze and Religion*, ed. Mary Bryden. London: Routledge.

Protevi, John. 2001b. *Political Physics: Deleuze, Derrida and the Body Politic.* London: Athlone.

Rajchman, John. 2000. *The Deleuze Connections.* Cambridge, MA: MIT Press.

Rey, Jean-Michel. 1971. *Lecture de Nietzsche: L'Enjeu des signes.* Paris: Seuil.

Rosset, Clément. 1972. Sécheresse de Deleuze. *L'Arc* 49: 89–93.

Sallis, John. 1990. Doublures [Stand-ins]. *Revue philosophique de la France et de l'étranger.* 115.2: 349–60.

Sandoval, Chela. 2000. *Methodology of the Oppressed.* Minneapolis: University of Minnesota Press

Sartre, Jean-Paul, 1972. *The Transcendence of the Ego: An Existentialist Theory of Consciousness.* New York: Octagon Books.

Schürmann, Reiner. 1978. *Meister Eckhart: Mystic and Philosopher.* Bloomington: Indiana University Press.

Simondon, Gilbert. 1964. *L'Individu et sa genèse physicobiologique.* Paris: PUF.

Stivale, Charles. 1998. *The Two-Fold Thought of Deleuze and Guattari.* New York: Guilford.

Villani, Arnaud. 1999. *La Guêpe et l'orchidée: Essai sur Gilles Deleuze.* Paris: Belin.

Williams, Charles. 1994. *The Figure of Beatrice: A Study in Dante.* New York: Boydell and Brewer.

Wolff, Francis. 1992. Trios: Deleuze, Derrida, Foucault, historiens du platonisme. In Cassin 1992.

Wyschogrod, Edith. 1990. *Saints and Postmodernism: Revisioning Moral Philosophy.* Chicago: University of Chicago Press.

Young, Iris Marion. 1990. *Throwing Like a Girl.* Bloomington: Indiana University Press.

Index